Student FAITH Advanced:
Making Connections through FAITH

I COMMIT MYSELF to continue
Student FAITH Sunday School evangelism training
in my church.

I recognize FAITH training
as a way to help my church and Sunday School,
to continue to grow as a Christian,
to be obedient to God's command to be an active witness,
and to equip others to share their faith.

_____
(SIGNATURE)

Address: _____

Phone Number: _____

My Role in Student FAITH:

❑ Learner ❑ Assistant Team Leader ❑ Other_____

Dates of My Student FAITH Advanced Training: _____

ISBN: 0-6330-0377-8

This book is a resource in the Leadership and Skill Development Category of the Christian Growth
Study Plan for course numbers
LS-0037, LS-0050, and LS-0054 (Sunday School).

Dewey Decimal Classification: 269.2
Subject Heading: EVANGELISTIC WORK IN THE SUNDAY SCHOOL

Printed in the United States of America

Youth Ministry Services Section
Youth Sunday School Ministry Department
LifeWay Christian Resources of the Southern Baptist Convention
127 Ninth Avenue, North
Nashville, Tennessee 37234

Acknowledgements:
Scripture quotations marked NIV are from the Holy Bible, *New International Version* © copyright
1973, 1978, 1984 by International Bible Society.

The *New King James Version* is the text for Scripture memory in the FAITH
gospel presentation. Scripture quotations marked NKJV are from *New King James Version,* © 1979,
1980, 1982, Thomas Nelson, Inc. Publishers. Used by permission.

Contents

What's Ahead
in Student FAITH Advanced

Date, _____   **Session 1: Making Connections—Getting Started**

Purposes/outcomes: To overview goals and content for the next 16 weeks; to equip Team Leaders to lead their Teams in Student FAITH; to emphasize the Sunday School as a visible, vital bridge between saved/unsaved people and the church

Date, _____   **Session 2: Strengthening Your Commitment**

Purposes/outcomes: To review growth commitments a new believer might make during a FAITH visit and the Team's use of *A Step of Faith (Student Edition)*; to reinforce the responsibility of the FAITH Team to follow up; to emphasize the Sunday School's role in making connections between the new believer and the church

Date, _____   **Session 3: Making A Baptism Visit**

Purposes/outcomes: To enable Team members to participate effectively in a FAITH follow-up visit for baptism and to use the leaflet *Student Baptism* as a tool for encouraging a new believer to take that step of obedience

Date, _____   **Session 4: Making A Follow-up Visit**

Purposes/outcomes: To review principles and processes for making other kinds of follow-up visits

Date, _____   **Session 5: Using the Opinion Poll**

Purposes/outcomes: To enable Team members to use the Opinion Poll as a tool to discover prospects, to engage in nonthreatening conversation with the unchurched/unsaved, and to share the gospel as opportunities allow

Date, _____   **Session 6: Reviewing the FAITH Visit Outline: FORGIVENESS and AVAILABLE**

Purposes/outcomes: To review FORGIVENESS and AVAILABLE in the FAITH Visit Outline, adding some verses and illustrations to increase understanding

Date, _____   **Session 7: Reviewing the FAITH Visit Outline: IMPOSSIBLE and TURN**

Purposes/outcomes: To review IMPOSSIBLE and TURN in the FAITH Visit Outline, adding some verses and illustrations to increase understanding

Date, _____ **Session 8: Reviewing the FAITH Visit Outline: HEAVEN and the Invitation**

Purposes/outcomes: To review the letter H and the Invitation; to equip Team Leaders to lead their Teams effectively through these points in a visit

Date, _____ **Session 9: Connecting to Students Through the Sunday School**

Purposes/outcomes: To reinforce the importance of the various kinds of Sunday School ministry visits; to explain the Sunday School's role in assimilating new believers; to suggest ways classes/departments might be more effective in assimilation actions

Date, _____ **Session 10: Connecting to the Entire Family**

Purposes/outcomes: To remind participants to consider the potential of reaching an entire family for Christ, especially after one member has made a decision; to point out approaches for follow-up, cultivation, or conversation according to the age group being addressed; to emphasize Sunday School enrollment

Date, _____ **Session 11: Recognizing A Divine Appointment**

Purposes/outcomes: To remind participants how God works ahead of them to prepare hearts for the gospel; to encourage dependence on the Holy Spirit

Date, _____ **Session 12: Making Connections Through Practice**

Purposes/outcomes: To devote time to practice by Teams

Date, _____ **Session 13: Making Connections in Daily Life**

Purposes/outcomes: To remind participants to be sensitive to daily-life witnessing opportunities and to be intentional in sharing FAITH in such settings

Date, _____ **Session 14: Dealing with Difficult Visits**

Purposes/outcomes: To provide Student FAITH participants with specific approaches for handling situations they may encounter

Date, _____ **Session 15: Strengthening the FAITH Strategy**

Purposes/outcomes: To emphasize the importance of continuing in FAITH; to connect with potential Learners, encouraging them to be part of Student FAITH

Date, _____ **Session 16: Celebrating Student FAITH**

Purposes/outcomes: To assess, through a written review, how much participants have learned during Student FAITH; to provide a time of celebration and recognition (if a FAITH Festival is not scheduled later)

A Look at Your Resources

Student FAITH Advanced: Making Connections Through FAITH will enhance and reinforce earlier FAITH training experiences. There is no new memory work; you already have learned the FAITH Visit Outline. You will continue using it in visits and will learn to share it with greater confidence.

Student FAITH Advanced can help you continue to grow as a Christian. During the next 16 weeks, expect God to work in your life, in your Sunday School/church, in the lives of people you meet, and in your Team.

As was true in Student FAITH Basic, you have a Journal as your main resource. You can expect similar training times each week—Team Time (15 min.), in which you debrief and work together as a Team; Teaching Time (45 min.), in which you and Learners go separate directions for a focused time to learn appropriate new information; Visitation Time (110+ min. depending on your church's schedule), that vital time when, as a Team, you put feet to prayers and training; and Celebration Time (30 min.), a time to report Team and FAITH strategy victories.

Each week commit to be on time; to listen attentively during Teaching Time; and to ask questions. After you have filled in the blanks for each session, it can be helpful during home study to re-read that session for the big picture.

If you are a Team Leader, the "Team Time" suggestions each week will help you debrief, practice, and review with your Team.

Home Study Assignments continue to be important. They provide ways for you to reflect on your growth as a Christian and tools to help you do your work if a Team Leader (for example, "The Weekly Sunday School Leadership Meeting" and "For the Team Leader").

"The Daily Journey" is designed to teach and encourage students to make their relationship with God intimate, honest, consistent and applicable. Daily Journey Quiet Times are prepared to reinforce the truths of the material being learned each week in the FAITH classes. Each day, students should spend time praying, reading, reflecting and journaling. During the "Check It" time, the FAITH Team should hold each other accountable for having completed their Daily Journey times each day.

In addition, you will learn to use a new leaflet: The *Student Baptism* tract. This resource may be used in follow-up visits when baptism is discussed.

Your Facilitator will also use video and cels or PowerPoint® to help you fill in the blanks and understand that session's teaching.

Your Sunday School class is one of your "main resources." It is the unique dynamic of FAITH. Your class or department can be where names become faces, needs become visible, and *assimilation* becomes more than a term. Attending the weekly Sunday School leadership meeting can make this connection.

Prayer is your most important and most powerful resource. The Lord has promised to hear us when we call on Him. Call on Him throughout FAITH.

FAITH PARTICIPATION CARD

Name _____ Semester Dates _____

Address _____ Phone _____

Sunday School Dept. _____Teacher _____

Other Team Members: _____

Circle One: FAITH Learner   Assistant Team Leader

	1	2	3	4	5	6	7	8	9	10	11	12	13	14	15	16	Totals
CLASS PARTICIPATION *Place a check to indicate completion for appropriate session.*																	
Present																	
Home study done																	
Outline recited																	
VISITATION *Indicate a number for following areas.*																	
No. of Tries																	
No. Visits																	
No. People Talked with																	
TYPE OF VISIT (Assignments)																	
Evangelistic																	
Ministry																	
Follow-up																	
Opinion Poll																	
GOSPEL PRESENTED																	
Profession																	
Assurance																	
No Decision																	
For Practice																	
GOSPEL NOT PRESENTED																	
Already Christian																	
No Admission																	
SS ENROLLMENT																	
Attempted																	
Enrolled																	
LIFE WITNESS																	
Profession																	
Assurance																	
No Decision																	

Making Connections—
Getting Started

LIBBA GILLUM

AS KERI ARRIVED FOR THE FIRST SESSION of Student
FAITH Advanced, she overheard Bethany and Hallie (who were just beginning
basic Student FAITH) discussing their fears about sharing with others. Bethany is
a new Christian and anxious to share with her friends. Hallie grew up in church,
but has never taken her responsibility to share with others seriously. *I can't believe
how scared our new recruits are!* Keri thought as she listened to them carry on.

As Keri made her way to the meeting room, she ran into Jeff and commented,
"Bethany and Hallie are so scared about telling others about Jesus. I don't
understand what they are so uptight about. They are so silly."

"Ummm, Keri, if I remember, it wasn't too long ago that someone who looks a lot
like you was saying the same thing," commented Jeff.

"Well that was different," replied Keri. "I was young and immature then."

Jeff, with a big smile, reminded her of their conversation as they arrived for their
first session of FAITH training. Keri remembered the fears she had and how those
fears were slowly removed as she gained confidence through the FAITH semester.

Keri paused and said a quick prayer. "Lord, help Bethany and Hallie overcome
their fears. Help them share their faith in Jesus. Help us to find ways to encourage
them over the next weeks. Amen."

Jeff opened the door for Keri as he exclaimed, "We'd better hurry and get our
pizza. Remember, last time all we got was that veggie stuff!"

Continuing Your Journey

Welcome to the second course in FAITH training, *Student FAITH Advanced: Making Connections through FAITH*. Your journey in faith indeed will continue as you participate in this vital second part of FAITH training.

If you are like most FAITH participants, you can recall some wonderful spiritual experiences and insights from Student FAITH (basic)—and some challenges! Know that God will keep on honoring your commitment and desire to grow as a Christian. Know also that you are helping your church and Sunday School in many ways.

Everyone receiving this training has learned the FAITH Visit Outline; you have participated as a FAITH Team Learner. You will be assisting individuals who are learning to share their faith; you will be encouraging them as, through FAITH training, they take steps of obedience to God.

Although there is no additional memory work in Student FAITH Advanced, this course will help you focus on being a student God uses to bring others to Him. You will continue to gain confidence as you have opportunities to share your faith.

God Uses Christians to Make Connections

Do you remember Blake from the video in Student FAITH? Blake was visited by a FAITH Team, and he gave his life to Christ. During the weeks that followed, the FAITH Team made connections to Blake and his family. Blake was welcomed by his new Sunday School class; he also accepted the opportunity to receive training in FAITH so he could share with others.

The Blakes you encounter in FAITH will motivate you to continue and to train others, as Christ commanded (Matt. 28:19-20). And don't forget that the people on his FAITH Team—Lizzie, Guy, and Terry—were changed, too!

FAITH: Making the Connection

By virtue of having completed the first semester of training, you have experienced all of the basic ingredients of the FAITH Sunday School Evangelism Strategy. This course will help you refine what you have learned and become more confident in sharing your faith. This advanced study will enable you to increase your skills, knowledge, and participation in FAITH.

This study emphasizes opportunities for establishing vital relationships and connections, between yourself and (___ _ _ ____ __) for the first time. Since evangelistic prospect visits will continue to be a major focus, you will learn to connect your FAITH Team and (____ _ __ _____) in a visit.

You will learn how to make connections between your church and (____ _____), often to students who have never heard about Jesus. You will receive help in handling new and sometimes difficult situations.

You will learn to involve students your FAITH Team visits in your (_____ _____ _____ __ _____) as we continue to make Sunday School ministry visits. You can see how to include your faith in the different settings of your (____ ____).

During this study you will discover how to:
- Better understand your role in encouraging others in FAITH
- Strengthen ministry visit opportunities
- Learn how to use the Opinion Poll and the Student Opinion Poll
- Strengthen opportunities for follow-up, for example helping someone who trusts Christ to follow Him in baptism
- Effectively deal with difficulties that may arise when a FAITH Team makes evangelistic and ministry visits.

(Although there is no new memory work, you will learn supportive material such as illustrations and other verses to give you more confidence at any point in sharing the FAITH Visit Outline. As a result you will be better able to answer a question or challenge posed in a visit.)

Know Your Role

Student FAITH Advanced training is intentionally designed for the student who already has learned the FAITH Visit Outline. Everything is planned to encourage individuals who are learning the FAITH Visit Outline for the first time. Although not every participant is a Team Leader, the importance of this role will be evident in this course.

If you are in this training as an Assistant Team Leader, you will be learning specific ways to help your Team through training. If you are participating in some other way, you still will be focusing on actions you can take to enhance your skills in leading students to faith in Christ.

God may be preparing you for the time when you will lead a Team of Learners through FAITH.

First and foremost, you are a (____ ____).

You already have memorized the FAITH Visit Outline and have shared it during visits. Now you are being looked to as one who will demonstrate how to (____ _ ____ ____). Your Team members will be watching you. They will be learning from you what to say.

It is very important that you follow the FAITH Visit Outline in leading a visit. You will be showing others what to do and what to say in a visit. This modeling role is significant.

You know from experience the importance of FAITH leaders being a positive role model in (____ ____). By example, you model:
- being on time for Team Time;
- learning and demonstrating what you have learned in FAITH Basic and Advanced;
- keeping up with all Home Study Assignments; and
- participating in Celebration Time.

You know the importance of FAITH leaders being positive role models in (____ ____). You know by now that FAITH cannot be separated from effective Sunday School work. Many who are participating in FAITH training are declaring that FAITH teaches us how to do Sunday School as it was intended to be.

Students will look to you to be a positive example of—
—taking leadership roles in Youth Sunday School;
—participating in weekly Sunday School leadership meetings; and
—involving people, especially new members, in Sunday School.
Your example may be more important to Team members than the training sessions themselves. Team members will be looking to you to set a good example.

You are needed as an (_____ ___ _____), one who recognizes and responds to Learner needs.
 Do you remember times of discouragement while in FAITH training? Did you ever consider dropping out? Just as you may have needed encouragement when you began FAITH training, so do your Team members need you to be an encourager and motivator. You can be an encourager by:
• recognizing Learner needs;
• helping class and department members know about and want to be part of the FAITH strategy;
• letting Learners know you are praying for them;
• getting to know Learners and helping them feel comfortable with you during training sessions and throughout the week;
• assisting Learners as they memorize various parts of the FAITH Visit Outline during the week;
• encouraging Team members in things they are doing well leading up to, during, and after visits;
• helping Learners during Team Time to recite memory work and to share experiences from home study;
• modeling the outline in visits;
• using the Opinion Poll correctly in visits;
• celebrating what Learners have memorized and completed by signing off on their assignments during Team Time; and
• (at the appropriate times and with sensitivity) gently persuading Learners to take the lead in specific parts of the visit for which they have received training.

Because you have been where Learners now are, you can respond appropriately to their needs. Someone learning the FAITH Visit Outline for the first time needs a Team Leader who will work with him or her during training sessions and during the week; one who will gently correct in words and model appropriately in visits; one who knows how to make adjustments and then explains why changes were made.
 Learners need to be a part of actual visits. They need to experience the satisfaction of finishing the course. As you are aware of these and other uniquely personal needs, you become an encourager and a motivator.

Be aware that Learners will face "(_____ _____)" at specific times throughout training. Be sensitive as Learners are called on to:
• write and share their evangelistic testimonies (Sessions 4 and 5)
• (at the Team Leader's cue and with his or her help) present appropriate parts of Preparation and the gospel presentation in an actual visit (Session 6);
• memorize and recite the FAITH Visit Outline (Session 10);
• take the leadership of an entire visit (after Session 11); and
• complete a final written review (Session 16).

For some Learners, such pressures can result in drop-out if care is not taken. So, be especially sensitive to (_____ _____). Some symptoms include:
- failure to attend a session without alerting the Team Leader;
- getting behind in memory assignments;
- resistance to reciting the FAITH Visit Outline;
- arriving too late to participate in Team Time or any part of Teaching Time;
- not having a prayer partner within the Sunday School class or department;
- experiencing learning difficulties or challenges;
- disinterest in regularly attending Celebration Time; and
- expressing fear about the final written review.

You are expected to be one who is (_____ __ ____ _____).
FAITH training brings together many ingredients that help a Christian grow in maturity. Other experiences also help us grow as Christians. It will become obvious if you are studying and applying God's Word. Making yourself available to be used of God is essential.
FAITH participants, as well as other church members, will be watching to see ways you are being challenged and blessed through FAITH training experiences. They will be particularly interested to see how you grow through the challenges and valleys of life. "The Daily Journey" journaling pages are designed to help you focus on ways God is helping you grow throughout your training experiences.

Making Connections with the FAITH Visit Outline
God is using the FAITH Visit Outline in significant ways. For example, in the FAITH video visit, did you observe—
- the Team connecting to Blake in various ways (Sunday School testimony, Key Question, and so forth)?
- some initial relationships established that made follow-up easy?
- Blake being enrolled in Sunday School?
- discussion about family members?
These will be important points of emphasis—points of connection—in your Student FAITH Advanced training.

Overview What Happens During Team Time
Team Time is a very important time for FAITH Learners. This is when they recite the portion of the FAITH Visit Outline they have been assigned to learn up to that point. You recall how important it is that all Team members know the entire outline. Team Time becomes an important time of accountability.
If You're a Team Leader or Assistant Team Leader:
Your job is to help Learners rehearse the outline so they feel more comfortable and natural in making a visit. Although Team Time is only 15 minutes during most sessions, Learners will increasingly see it as a much appreciated check-up and practice time.
This resource provides some help each session in getting ready for and leading Team Time. Although Team Leaders are responsible for conducting Team Time each week, everyone who has completed FAITH Basic will have an important role. Let's review what is to take place during Team Time.

Team Time begins with the first 15 minutes of Session 2. Since good use of time is extremely important throughout training, it is vital that you model by beginning and concluding on time each week. (Session 12 is an extended Team Time, in which Learners spend the entire session practicing material they have learned.)

Each week, ask Learners to (_____) the assigned portion of the FAITH Visit Outline as designated in the Team Time portion of the *Student FAITH Advanced: Journal*. Take the Learner's FAITH Journal and follow the outline as each student recites it.

Notice that these same assignments are capsuled in your resource in the section, "Team Time," which begins each session. This feature will help you be aware of what Learners are expected to know. Your copy of the FAITH Visit Outline is on pages vi-vii of this resource.

During the first few sessions, you likely will have adequate time for both Team members to recite. Be aware that the longer the recitation, the greater the likelihood that only one student will be able to complete the outline during the 15 minutes before the session. Some of this work can continue in the car, as the Team goes to and from visits.

In early sessions, ask the student who feels most comfortable reciting to share first. Try not to put a Team member on the spot.

As a general rule—and especially in later sessions—try to call on the student who most needs practice to share first. Do so with sensitivity and gentleness.

As a Team member correctly recites each line or phrase of the outline, place a (____ ____) in the box beside the phrase. If the Learner has difficulty or does not recite it appropriately or overlooks any portions, write notes in his or her copy of the FAITH Journal for review. Be prepared to answer any questions the Learner might have regarding the outline, and suggest ways to strengthen sharing the outline. When a Team member has successfully recited the assigned portion of the outline, sign off by writing your name or initials in the space provided.

Overview the Learner's (____ ____ _____) from the previous week. Feel free to raise questions and to discuss any aspect of the assignments. Doing so can help reinforce many of the important concepts taught through these assignments— concepts that only may have been introduced during the session. Once again, sign off in the Learner's Journal any assignments that have been completed and that call for your approval.

As you debrief assignments or answer questions related to the previous session, highlight ones that will appear on the final written review. On a weekly basis, help Learners reduce their anxiety about the final review.

Although you will not be reading the Learner's "The Daily Journal" pages, it will be significant to check to see that the Learner is keeping a (_____ _____) of his experiences throughout FAITH.

Journaling brings an enriching dimension to FAITH training. Suggest that Team members record their experiences and reflections on the Bible study. Encourage Learners to read back through previous journaling pages, particularly during times of discouragement. At the end of this semester, both you and your Learners will be asked to write testimonies of what FAITH has meant personally, so your Journal is a wonderful record.

If You're Not a Team Leader:
You still need to participate in Team Time by being prepared to recite the

FAITH Visit Outline, review the Home Study Assignments, and discuss ways to strengthen a visit. You may be asked to (_____) the Team Leader by working with a Team member who needs help and encouragement in learning and reciting the FAITH Visit Outline.

Remember, as Team members ride together to and from the visits, Learners can continue to practice sharing the outline and discuss ways to strengthen a visit.

Review Ingredients of FAITH Training

While you are meeting, Team Learners are assembled for their orientation to Student FAITH. They are overviewing many of the important ingredients of FAITH. They will learn to depend on you to interpret and reinforce many of the things they are discovering for the first time.

(_____ _____)

Three people are on every FAITH Team. In addition to the Team Leader who has been trained in the FAITH strategy, two Team Learners have been enlisted to be trained and to visit together. Each Team represents a designated Sunday School division, department, or class.

Write the names of your Team members in the space provided. If a Team member already has received training but is not participating as a Team Leader, write that member's name and role on the Team (Assistant Team Leader, for example).

_____

_____

_____
Team Leader

(_____ _____ ____)

One of the first things Team members are doing is preparing their FAITH Participation Cards. You will remember that this card is used each week as a name placard and to record numbers and types of visits attempted and made by the Team. If you have not already completed the top portion of your Participation Card, do so now. Make sure your name is printed in large letters on the reverse side for your name placard.

Take a few minutes to review the categories of the Participation Card. You will be responsible for helping your Team members understand the categories identified on the card. You also will be responsible for helping them complete their cards following visits (beginning with Session 2).

The Participation Card is the basis for information on the FAITH Report Board. Remember that reports from the visits are summarized here. Continue to be familiar with the categories and with recording responses on the board. Your job is to orient your Team members to this process so they can eventually report during Celebration Time.

(_____ __ _____)

Each Team will be prepared to make several types of visits. In all visits you should be ready to share the message of the gospel, and invite unsaved students to saving faith in Christ. You will look for opportunities to represent

Christ by ministering to individuals in need, by enrolling some people in Bible study, and by helping others grow in their journey of faith.

Teams will make visits to Sunday School prospects, some of whom have had contact with your church as visitors to Sunday School, worship, or a special event. Some have been referred by a member, and others were discovered through a People Search opportunity. Generally, prospects are those who are open to a contact from or a relationship with your church.

Teams also will be prepared to make ministry visits to Sunday School members. Teams will learn to make visits using the Opinion Poll. Additionally, Teams will be equipped to make follow-up visits to persons who have made a significant decision (to trust Christ, join the church, enroll in Sunday School).

Although you will discover many new experiences when you make visits, Learners will be interested in knowing about each of these types of visits when they receive their assignments. Your experience, as well as what is taught during Teaching Time, will be particularly helpful as Learners determine ways to participate in each type of visit.

(_____ _____)

Each Team will have a visitation folder that has been prepared for that week's visits. Be prepared to explain the significance and use of each item before, during, and after visits.

Contents of the visitation folder may include these and other items designated by the church:

- Visitation assignment forms—Each week you should have several forms. Some assignments will be to a specific person or family indicated to be a prospect. Other forms might be for visits to members. Some forms will indicate the assignment as a follow-up visit. Each form should indicate the general nature of the assigned visit.

  If the card does not indicate that the person is enrolled in Sunday School, then assume you are visiting to cultivate a relationship on behalf of the church and Sunday School. Approach the visit assuming you may have an opportunity to share the gospel.

  Lead your Team to make as many visits as are feasible during the designated time. If you are unable to make assigned visits and/or have extra time, use the Opinion Poll to identify opportunities for evangelism and ministry.

- Information about your church and Sunday School ministry.—A diagram, list, or information sheet can help family members identify with and know where Sunday School classes and departments meet.

- A Step of Faith (Student Edition)—Use this leaflet when sharing the gospel with a person and issuing an Invitation. Also use it to enroll a person in Sunday School and to record decisions made during a visit.

- Student Baptism tract—In Session 3 you will receive detailed help in using this leaflet to help a new believer take a next step of obedience, through believer's baptism.

- Student Opinion Poll/Opinion Poll cards—Use these forms to ask questions and to record responses when making Opinion Poll visits.

- Bible study material used by your class—Give a copy of current material to new enrollees and to nonattending members during a visit.

- Church and department promotional information about upcoming special events and activities for students.

You will be responsible for demonstrating how to use each item in the visitation folder. Until Learners overview how to use these items and complete the forms, you will be responsible for training them. Briefly review what is expected in completing the visitation forms.

No matter what type of record form is used by the church, you need to take the following actions:

1. (____ __ ____) appropriate blank in which information is requested.
2. If an assigned person is not at home or is not willing to respond to selected questions for information, (_____) the card or blanks left incomplete, and indicate the (____) of the attempted visit and the reason information was not recorded.
3. (____) information legibly.
4. Write information discovered from the visit that will help in making any (_____ _____).
5. Record information about all other (_____) discovered in the home.
6. Turn in the detachable (_____ ____) portion of *A Step of Faith* (_____ _____).

(_____ ___ _____)

As there are a sufficient number of Teams participating in FAITH visits, one group of Teams will be assigned to Prayer and Practice each week. These Teams remain in the Teaching Time room while other Teams make visits. This process will begin no earlier than Session 3. Assignments for Prayer and Practice are made on a rotating basis and are noted in your weekly newsletter or visitation folder.

As soon as visiting Teams depart to make visits, the assigned Group Leader should assemble his or her Teams for prayer. Teams may pray throughout Visitation Time specifically for the Team members visiting and for the individuals to be visited and pray for divine appointments. The Group Leader might call the names of people visiting and being visited.

During Prayer and Practice, the Group Leader also can lead Teams to practice reciting the FAITH Visit Outline with each other. Team members also can spend time writing notes to prospects and members. When Prayer and Practice is over, the Group Leader can lead participants to complete their session Participation and Evaluation Cards.

The Student FAITH Advanced Journal

As a review, your Journal is designed to help you—
- lead Team Time activities (CHECK IT, "Team Time");
- participate in Teaching Time content: Each week's Teaching Time includes an accountability check of the previous week's session, new content and important fill-in-the-blank concepts, video viewing (if applicable), a brief time of practice with a partner, and an overview of Home Study Assignments. Try to preview the session each week, rereading it after fill-ins have been added.
- make visits (DO IT through Visitation Time) and reports (SHARE IT during Celebration Time).

Home Study Assignments facilitate journaling, recording of prayer concerns/answers, additional readings, reporting in weekly Sunday School leadership team meetings, and (for the Team Leader) relating to the FAITH Team during the week.

Your Responsibilities During Celebration Time

During each week's Celebration Time, you are responsible for leading your Team to report about visits attempted and visits made. This can become a very meaningful and motivational time. In addition to helping Team members update and submit their Participation Cards, Evaluation Cards, and visitation assignment cards, help them know how to complete the Report Board.

Particularly during the first few weeks of training, Team members will be looking to you to share verbal reports during the report time. Even if a Team seemingly has not had a productive visit, Team members share in the ministry's victories during this time segment. Keep these guidelines in mind as you lead and help your Team members to verbally report.

1. Be brief. The amount of time needed will be determined by the number of Teams reporting.
2. Be precise. Don't give unnecessary details.
3. Be positive. Discuss problems or negatives in another setting, such as with your Group Leader.
4. Be enthusiastic. Remember, you and your Team have the greatest opportunity in the world!
5. Be accurate. Don't embellish what really happened.
6. Be careful. Don't report anything of a confidential nature that was shared with your Team. Use first names only of the people you visited.
7. Be thankful. Even if no decision was made or no one allowed you to share, be grateful for the opportunity to dialogue.
8. Be affirming. If Joe shared a Sunday School testimony for the first time in a visit and did a great job, tell the entire group. You not only encourage Joe, you motivate other Teams, too!

Ask God to Use You

Think back on your own journey in faith. Reflect on how one or more people connected with you. Who was most influential in leading you to Christ? Thank God for saving you, and thank Him for using these people to reach out to you.

Were specific individuals influential in your growth as a Christian? In your ministry and life calling? In reaching family members for Christ?

Pray that God will use you in significant ways throughout Student FAITH Advanced to establish connections of faith and hope.

The Daily Journey

The Daily Journey section is designed to teach and encourage students to make their relationship with God intimate, honest, consistent and applicable. Daily Journey Quiet Times are prepared to reinforce the truths of the material being learned each week in the Student FAITH classes. Each day, students should spend time praying, reading, reflecting, and journaling. During the "Check It" time, the FAITH Team members should hold each other accountable for having completed their Daily Journey times each day.

Day One:
Read 1 Peter 1:1-12

To be a Good Parent, You Must be a Good Baby

Almost everyone is nervous about going to visit someone in the hospital, unless they are there to see a new baby. There is something about seeing a new baby that fills you with joy, wonder, and excitement, though all babies basically look alike. New Christians are like new babies, they have been given "new birth" through an incredible salvation. Their lives are changed and they are ready to grow, but often they do not know how.

You may have seen someone accept Christ last semester in Student FAITH; that person is a new baby in Christ. He or she needs help learning how to grow in Christ and how to follow Him. The way this new Christian learns is by plugging into Bible study and watching you—how Jesus has changed your life. No matter what the trials and obstacles, has Jesus made a difference?

What does "new birth" mean in your life? What has changed so much in your life that it is obvious that you are not the same person since you accepted Christ?

Spend time praying for the unity of your new FAITH Team.

Day Two:
Read 1 Peter 1:13-25

Disconnected from God?

"Be holy." This passage is full of commands, but the biggest one is "be holy." It is a call to live a life of morality that is connected to the only One who is holy, God. You cannot just decide one day to clean up your life so much that you will be pure. Some Christians think that it is no big deal to live one way at school, another way at church, and another way around their parents. They are wrong—the clear command of God is to walk in relationship with Him all day, every day. Is there a part of your day that is disconnected from God? Are you willing to allow God to have every part of the next 24 hours?

Read 1 Peter 1:13-25 again. Write down any four of the commands of God for your life on the lines below.

_____

_____

Pray that this week you and your FAITH Team will live lives that please God.

Day Three:
Read 1 Peter 2:1-12

How a House Shows God

You have not always been this way. There was a time when you were not a Christian, right? You have not always been headed for heaven and interested in fully following Jesus. But now, you are a new person with a new mission, right? According to 1 Peter 2:9-12 you were separated from God before you became a Christian—but now verse 12 makes our call clear: live so that the people around you will know that you are a royal priest, holy, God's own, in His light, covered by His mercy, and a stranger in this world. Some of the people around you in the next 24 hours will be people who need to hear from you about how they can have a relationship with God. Will they see God in you?

What is one of the "sinful desires" that "wars against your soul"? How can you allow Jesus to take control of that desire in the next 24 hours? According to 1 Peter 2:5, you and your FAITH Team are like a spiritual house being built for God's use.

Pray that you and your FAITH Team would be useful to God this week in your life and lifestyles.

Day Four:
Read 1 Peter 2:13-25

Submit? No Way!

"I don't like my parents, my teachers, my boss, or the policeman who harasses me all the time—just because I'm a teenager!" Sound familiar? If it does, you may have a real problem with submitting to the authorities that God has placed in your life. You will never be able to submit to God if you cannot learn to submit to the authorities that God has placed in your life. God said that we are like sheep in a field, wandering around not following anyone until we give our lives to God. When we become Christians we gladly give our messed up lives to God and submit to His leadership as
our Shepherd.

Is there anyone in your life who is hard to obey? Write their name or title here.

_____

Make a commitment today to submit to the authorities in your life. Ask God for the strength to do what is right as you honor Him, your Christian friends, and the people God has placed in authority over you.

Pray that this week you and your FAITH Team would be great examples to the lost world by honoring authority.

Day Five:
Read 1 Peter 3

Be Ready

At lunch one day, Hannah was with a group of friends who really liked each other (most of the time). When they were not griping, complaining, and picking on each other, they really got along. Hannah worked hard to encourage everyone and not say things that were malicious. She assumed no one noticed, but right in the middle of lunch—in front of everyone—Jon asked Hannah, "Why are you always so nice to everybody?" Hannah knew several people around the lunch table were not Christians, including Jon. Scared to death she answered, "Because several years ago I had a life-changing experience; it changed the way I talk and respond to people. Can I tell you about it?"

First Peter 3:15 sounds easy, until real life comes. FAITH is not about sharing Christ one day a week. FAITH is about equipping you to walk in a lifelong relationship with God and be willing and able to share Jesus with anyone, anywhere. Are you willing to live intimately with God and be ready to share Jesus with anyone, anywhere? Circle one: YES   NO   UNSURE

If you circled *no* or *unsure*, spend time in prayer asking God what is holding you back from being consistent in your walk and faithful in your talk. When God identifies the issue that is holding you back, release it to Him. Pray also that your FAITH Team would be faithful to share Jesus in their everyday lives this week.

Day Six:
Read 1 Peter 4
Give in or Give it Over?
Tony was over the edge when he said, "Let me be real honest with you, I am sick of being the outsider and not going and doing all the stuff everyone else does. I go to school and then sit at home. It seems like a bunch of the people that go to church party with everyone else at school and they get away with it; why can't I? I get harassed and they get by with it. I am sick of it!"

Tony felt the pain of verse 4, haven't you? No doubt Christians are misunderstood in this society. Christians even face some discrimination and pain. But, we do not lose heart and give in to the world's system just because it is hard. Read verse 19 again and think about how much pain you
are willing to take before you walk away from Jesus. Some Christians are willing to follow Christ as long as they can still drink, or smoke, or date how they want, or talk how they want, or do what they want. If Jesus gets in the way, they walk away. How about you? How much of you are you willing to risk to follow Jesus? Write down the greatest area of struggle or pain that you have faced as a Christian._____
Spend some time praying right now that you will not give in to the world because of your struggle.

Pray for a Christian in your youth group who may have walked away from his or her faith in the past year. Pray that you and your FAITH Team will not give up boldly sharing Christ at your school just because it becomes difficult.

Day Seven:
Read 1 Peter 5
But I AM Good!
Humility? You've memorized the FAITH outline and you are one of the leaders of your youth group. You probably know more about the Bible than many adults in your church, and even with all your faults you are still pretty good. Right? Take a deep breath and read verses 5-7 again. God's will for you is to be gentle and humble with other people. If you become self-sufficient and

think that your knowledge, ability, good looks, friends, or grades will get you by in life you will have missed God's will for you.

God desires for you to humbly serve people and throw your needs on Him so that He can show His power in your life. It is not to the proud that God gives His grace, it is the humble. What is your humility level? What truth did you get out of 1 Peter 5 that will apply to your life today?

At some point you become confident that you know the FAITH outline and the right thing to say on each visit—God is the one who saves a person, not the FAITH outline. Pray that you and your FAITH Team will not trust in your ability this week more than you trust in God's power.

The Weekly Sunday School Leadership Team Meeting

Use this space to record ways your FAITH Team impacts the work of your Sunday School department or class. Use the information to report during weekly Sunday School leadership team meetings. Identify actions that need to be taken through Sunday School as a result of prayer concerns, needs identified, visits made by the Team, and decisions made by the persons being visited.

Highlight needs or reports affecting your class, department, or age group.

_____

_____

Pray now for this important meeting.

How does preparation for Sunday need to consider needs of individuals or families visited through FAITH?

_____

_____

How will Team members receiving training be recognized and prayed for?

_____

_____

Indicate ways your Sunday School leaders can help you and Team members in FAITH.

_____

_____

For Further Reading

Read pages 120-26 of *Evangelism Through the Sunday School: A Journey of FAITH* by Bobby Welch.

For the Team Leader

This weekly feature suggests actions the Team Leader can take to support Team members, prepare for Team Time, and consider ways to improve visits. This work becomes part of the Team Leader's Home Study Assignments. Add any actions suggested by your church's FAITH strategy.

The Team Leader is the most vital link in FAITH training. God bless you as you faithfully discharge your responsibilities as a FAITH Team Leader.

SUPPORT TEAM MEMBERS

❏ Contact Team members during the week. Remind them you are praying for them. Discuss their orientation to FAITH. Remind each person of the importance of being present and on time for Team Time. Briefly remind members of their role during Team Time.

❏ As you talk with Learners this week—
  • find out if they understood their Home Study Assignments, especially that of writing their Sunday School testimonies.
  • ask if they have a prayer partner from their class.
  • suggest they preview a FAITH Tip for Session 2, "Helpful Visitation Tips."

❏ Remind members to bring a small Bible with them to take along on visits. Teams will make visits after Session 2 and return for Celebration Time.

❏ Record specific needs and concerns of Team members in the margin to the left.

PREPARE TO LEAD TEAM TIME

❏ Review Home Study Assignments of Team members.

❏ Review Lead Team Time for Session 2.

PREPARE TO LEAD VISITS

❏ Review the FAITH Visit Outline.

❏ Be prepared to explain the contents of the visitation folder.

❏ Be ready to model a visit in which Team members are asked to share their Sunday School testimonies.

❏ Be prepared to lead the Team to participate during Celebration Time.

CONNECT WITH SUNDAY SCHOOL

❏ Participate in your weekly Sunday School leadership meeting. Share pertinent information and FAITH visit results.

Strengthening Your Commitment

LIBBA GILLUM

SHELBY, JOY, AND JOSHUA HAD JUST COMPLETED
a FAITH visit to one of their school friends. During the visit, Amy prayed the
salvation prayer, and it was the first time someone they visited had actually
prayed to accept Christ. They could hardly wait to get back to church and tell
everyone at the Celebration Time. They quickly congratulated Amy and headed
for the door. As Shelby settled into the back seat of the car, she began to replay
the visit. Suddenly something dawned on Shelby and she blurted out, "We forgot
to tell Amy about making her decision public! We didn't finish what we started."
 "Should we go back and tell Amy what she should do next?" asked Joshua.
 Looking at the clock in the car, they realized it was too late for them to turn
around and go back to Amy's. They looked at each other with a sense of defeat,
and not a word was said as they made their way back to the church.
 During the Celebration Time, Shelby shared what happened—including not
completing the presentation. When the celebration time was over, Joy, the Team
Leader, suggested, "Let's call Amy and ask if we can visit again next week and tell
her more. We can also encourage her to be thinking about ways she can share her
decision with others."
 The teens headed for a telephone to call Amy and set up a time for the next
week's visit.

TEAM TIME

The team leader leads this time. Learners are primarily responsible for reciting the assigned portion of the FAITH Visit Outline and for discussing any Home Study Assignments.

Keep in mind how Learners also look to leaders as role models, motivators, mentors, and friends. Team Time activities can continue in the car, as the Team travels to and from visits.

Check It

Since this is the first time for Team Time activities, provide any additional explanation that is needed. Make good use of the 15 minutes that begin each session.

FAITH Visit Outline
❑ Team members should be ready to recite all aspects of Preparation up to INQUIRY and the key words in *Presentation* (*Forgiveness, Available, Impossible, Turn, Heaven*) and *Invitation* (*Inquire, Invite, Insure*).
❑ Indicate your approval by signing or initialing Journals. Encourage Learners.

Sunday School Testimonies Due
❑ Ask Team members for their written Sunday School testimonies, due this session. Help evaluate each testimony to make sure it includes one or two of the following aspects: friendship/support received; assistance received during some crisis; personal benefits of Bible study through the class; or ways they have grown as a Christian through experiences in or through the Sunday School class. Discuss how benefits can and do change, reflecting different experiences.

If the student's written testimony is acceptable, make sure each Team member understands the importance of learning to share it naturally, in his or her own words. Ask for permission to print the testimony in any church materials that publicize FAITH or encourage students to share a testimony.

Session 1 Debriefing (Orientation To FAITH Training)
❑ Make sure major concepts from Session 1 are understood.

Help for Strengthening A Visit
❑ This is the first session in which Teams will make home visits. Encourage students and try to answer any concerns. Explain that the Team Leader will take the lead in the *Introduction* portion of the visit(s) following this session.
❑ Identify a Team member(s) who would be prepared to share a Sunday School testimony during a visit. Be sensitive to persons who are ready to share.

Notes

_____

_____

_____

_____

Actions I Need to Take with Learners During the Week

_____

_____

_____

_____

A Quick Review

If you listed the different types of relationships you have with friends and family each day or week, you would probably be surprised at the variety of people you come in contact with! Student FAITH Advanced will help you become aware of these and other opportunities as a means of connecting to other students through your Sunday School.

This second course (Student FAITH Advanced), which brings your foundational FAITH training to completion, provides additional opportunities for visitation. For an unsaved student, you and your Team may be that individual's first contact with someone who tells them about God. Your Team may help an inactive Sunday School family become involved in church again. You can help new believers begin their journey of faith in an easy and natural way. The visitation assignments each week indicate the nature of the visit and previous contacts that have been made.

As you grow in your commitment as a Christian, you will find yourself becoming a person God can use in great and mighty ways.

Lead Your Team to Growth

One of the greatest joys a Christian can have is to share the gospel with another individual and to lead that person to a saving relationship with Jesus Christ. Your FAITH Team will be making visits to several students who are assigned to your Sunday School class or department and whom you discover to be unsaved.

The next three sessions will help you focus on ways to make follow-up visits to students who make a commitment, particularly to accept Jesus as Savior, during a visit. You will review some ways to use *A Step of Faith (Student Edition)* to begin the follow-up process. You also will be introduced to other resources designed to help you follow up with students who make decisions of commitment.

As your Team reports during Celebration Time, be certain to identify specific opportunities for follow-up. You can help suggest ways your Team and others from your church can be involved in connecting to and helping the student follow up on any decision that was made.

It is possible that your FAITH Team will visit someone after this session who hears the gospel and (_____ _____) as his or her Savior. Your Team might be involved in leading a person to decide to (_____) in Sunday School. Your Team likely could identify specific (_____ __ _____ _____) that need attention during the upcoming days.

It's important to be ready, from the very beginning, to help your Team identify ways to follow up. You have some resources to help.

Tools for Effective Follow-up

• *A Step of Faith (Student Edition)*
You were introduced to this useful leaflet during basic Student FAITH. The picture of young people looking at the cross calls up many emotions, and this picture has been used by God with the result of decisions of commitment. It will always be helpful to refer to *A Step of Faith (Student Edition)* when you follow up with someone who has made a decision.

"(_ __ __ _____)" is a theme that runs throughout this leaflet; as such, it can help you in follow-up discussions. You remind yourself, as well as the student who made the decision, that Jesus was not ashamed to die for you. You also remind yourself and the other person(s) that further steps of faith come because we are not ashamed to follow Him.

The Commitment panel of the leaflet reminds the student of the decision(s) made during a previous visit with the FAITH Team. By showing or referring to this panel, you remind him or her of the exciting and important decisions already made and identify the next steps to be taken.

Highlighting the "Come Grow with Us!" panel (6) gives you opportunity to reintroduce, in a follow-up visit, the importance of (____ _____ _____ __ _____) through the ministry of a Sunday School class and the church.

Finally, the "What about baptism?" panel (7) gives you opportunity to talk with someone about the opportunity and questions they may have about baptism. It also sets the stage for sharing, as needed, the presentation of the *Student Baptism* tract.

• *Student Baptism* tract
The entire third session of Student FAITH Advanced will help you focus on using this new resource to interpret and emphasize the importance of (_____) for a new believer. One of the important connections your Team is to make is between the student who is a new believer and the church.

Since many students your Team will visit may have never been to church, you can understand the apprehension and anxiety they might feel when asked to go somewhere new or to do something new. Your Team has a wonderful and important opportunity to be among those who explain the importance of baptism in a believer's life. Team members can dialogue about what a person should expect during a worship experience that includes baptism.

It's important to remember that your Team now has the responsibility to lead in making a connection so a new believer will follow up his or her commitment to Christ by being baptized.

• *Other visitation assignment follow-up information*
Any contact other than that made by the FAITH Team is indicated on your visitation assignment card. Since the follow-up visit should promptly follow

the person's initial decision, your FAITH Team may have much of the available information.

However, in some cases, there may also have been a staff contact, a contact to reach out to other members of the family, or some other initiative. Much of that information should be summarized for you, so your Team can make an effective follow-up visit. Bible study material or other items provided from the church also may be in your folder for such a visit.

Some Information to Share

You have heard throughout FAITH the importance of the Sunday School in ministering to and teaching believers as well as nonbelievers. One of the vital responsibilities of the FAITH Team is to help build relationships between a student and a caring group of Sunday School members. This is one reason FAITH Teams are all from the same department or class and are assigned to visit students of the same age who would be assigned to that department or class. It is important that the student being visited already knows at least one person who would be in the class he or she would be attending.

Your Team can take several actions during a follow-up visit to connect new members to the Sunday School:

• Share a (_____ _____ _____). One of the first things learned during FAITH training is to share a testimony that identifies examples of support and friendship, assistance received during crisis, benefits of Bible study through the class, and/or examples of ways a person has grown through the Sunday School.

A Sunday School testimony is usually shared during the first part of the initial visit. However, it is important to be prepared to share additional testimony about the Sunday School class during a follow-up visit.

• Share information about the Sunday School. Often, during the first visit with a student, your Team provides basic information about his or her class or the Sunday School. Often, the initial FAITH visit may be the first time the student has heard about the ministry opportunities through that class.

During a follow-up visit, be prepared to share (_____ _____) about the class. This might include (but is not limited to) such things as providing a calendar of upcoming fellowship events, trips, and student activities.

Also appropriate in a follow-up visit is to invite the student to meet at a specified place to sit with you during Sunday School and worship.

• Take specific (_____) to build relationships and ministry opportunities with the student. FAITH Team members should identify specific follow-up actions they can take to build a relationship with a student they have visited. Team members do not have to wait until another visit to initiate actions such as:

• sharing about their personal journeys of faith and experiences in the church;
• making a phone call to respond to ministry needs;
• meeting the student for a meal, at a recreation site, ball game, or some other place;

Remember: It's important to build relationships to students at every opportunity!

• Use other members of the Sunday School in making connections. The FAITH Team is very important in initiating relationships with many unrelated persons. In many instances, the FAITH Team will be the first persons from your class who make contact and share about the Sunday School and/or the gospel.

However, there probably will be several other class members who will share a common interest or will be able to identify with the student.

• (_____) class members who will take such actions as:
– praying for the student who received a visit;
– writing a card, letter, or sending an email message;
– making a phone call;

• Involve professional (_____ _____) in responding to specific needs or concerns. There will be times when the pastor or other staff member may be the best person to be involved in relating to a student who makes a decision during a FAITH visit. Make sure you are sensitive to the person(s) God would involve.

The primary objective of follow-up visits is to build relationships between the student and the church so the student can take the actions needed to grow in his or her new faith. Even though the FAITH Team becomes "the first line of offense" in making contact with a student who makes a decision during a FAITH visit, your job is to begin identifying those who can strengthen possibilities for relationship.

Disciplines Are Brand New

A new Christian likely will have questions about his or her new daily walk. A new member class, plus the Sunday School, can help answer those questions.

POSSIBLE QUESTIONS FROM A NEW BELIEVER

Why is the Bible important?	Share reasons/help to be gained; role of Sunday School; suggest writing down questions and talking with other Christians about them
Why should I pray?	Suggest words to use; a specific time/place to pray can help; talk to God, but listen as well; prayer can occur anytime
Can't I worship God when I am alone?	Describe reasons that fellowship/worship with other Christians is important; share plans for student activities; explain meaning of different parts of the worship service;

Visitation Time

DO IT

As you go . . .

Keep in mind—
- the Team Leader guides preparation for all visits;
- a "game plan" should be in place before visits. This means alerting Team members in advance if they are to do Sunday School/evangelistic testimonies;
- the Team Leader always has the option to change the game plan but the responsibility to say why changes were made;
- the visitation tips from page 26 of the *Student FAITH Journal*. Highlight any you feel are especially helpful or needed.

Most of all, encourage Team members as they make their first home visits. Be prepared to take the lead in all visits. Model a visit and debrief what happened so Team members can learn.

Celebration Time

SHARE IT

As you return to share . . .

Encourage Team members to listen carefully as reports are shared, especially about decisions made in visits; the information can be helpful in follow-up. Take the lead in sharing reports. Help Learners complete the necessary forms.
- Reports and testimonies
- Session 2 Evaluation Card
- Participation Card
- Visitation forms updated with results of visits

THE DAILY JOURNEY

Day One:
Read Luke 19:1-10

Learning from the Wee Little Man

Zacchaeus was a man looking for answers and a different way of life, and he found it in a sycamore-fig tree. When he heard Jesus was walking by he wanted to see this man who had changed so many lives. But Jesus surprised Zacchaeus; He not only noticed him, Jesus spent time with him. The result was a changed life—and another person who was lost was found.

In verse 10 Jesus gives a short mission statement that every Christian should memorize and put into practice. Is this verse the reason you are in Student FAITH? If you started getting involved in FAITH because of friendships, pressure from a leader, or even boredom, now is the time to evaluate why you have stayed with it all these weeks. God has a plan to use you to fulfill His purpose among your friends and peers, to seek and save what was lost.

Two questions for you today: (1) Are you sharing FAITH at school, work, and play just like you share when your FAITH team goes visiting? Jesus was just passing through Jericho when he found Zacchaeus. Are you willing to share Jesus in your everyday life this week? (2) Jesus was willing to spend time with Zacchaeus to encourage him not only to believe, but to also be a disciple. Are you willing to go back to people who have given their life to Christ to encourage them to follow through on their commitment?

Spend a few minutes praying for the other members of your Faith team and the people you visited last week. List the names of the people you visited last week

_____.

Pray also for at least one person whom you know needs to know Christ, but with whom you have not shared about Him. Write their name(s) here _____

_____.

Memorize Luke 19:10 today.

Day Two:
Read 2 Timothy 1
OK, This is Work!

You go to church and just sit down; someone else sets up the chairs, cleans up, and does all the work. You can just go, worship, and have fellowship. Until now. Since you enrolled in FAITH you may be challenged to get up and go to work for the gospel. Challenged to share in the ministry of telling everyone in your community about the incredible message that Jesus really does change people for eternity. Verses 8-10 are Paul's challenge to Timothy to come work and suffer with him for the sake of the gospel. Paul's commitment to share Christ extended beyond the "normal" times of talking about God. Paul was sharing Christ even when he was in prison. Think through your day today—are you or were you willing to share Christ, even if it meant some suffering? Are you or were you willing to live as a holy person today because Jesus has changed you so dramatically?

Write 2 Timothy 1:12 in this space. You may copy it exactly from your Bible or you may write it in your own words. _____

_____

Spend a few minutes praying for your other FAITH Team members and the people you visited last week. Also pray for the people you know who need to know Christ.

Review from memory Luke 19:10.

Day Three:
Read 2 Timothy 2
The Old Stuff

"How do you get away from the old stuff?" Not antiques, the old sin nature. Every person who accepts Christ is turning from sin and self to Christ. Sometimes we make that event sound so easy that it is a shock to read 2 Timothy 2:20-21 where Paul tells Timothy to continue to cleanse himself from the old lifestyle, flee the evil desires, and follow God. Timothy was Paul's disciple and friend, and Paul was wise enough not to share Christ with Timothy and then forget about him. Paul continued to encourage Timothy to know and follow Christ. How do you get away from the old stuff?

Flee from the old desires and pursue God with those who are also pursuing God. Be a disciple and encourage others to follow God with you.

Spend a few minutes praying for your other Faith team members and the people you visited last week. Pray about your role in discipling some of the students whom your Team has led to Christ. Write the name of a person whom you could encourage in the faith. _____ Also, pray for anyone you know who needs to know Christ.

Day Four:
Read 2 Timothy 3
Get Ready, It's Coming!
If you have not already faced some difficulty, trial, or struggle simply because you are a Christian and you follow a different moral code than others at school, get ready—you will. When people pick on you and try to distract you from following God, should you be surprised? Only if you have never read 2 Timothy 3:12. Everyone who wants to live a godly life will face some persecution and pressure. People who do not know Christ will never fully understand those who do follow Christ. This is also true of those who have recently committed their lives to Christ. They cannot understand everything yet. But, God has given us the Bible to equip us for ministry and for life.

According to verses 16 and 17, the more we read and study God's Word, the more we will be able to encourage others to follow God and the more we will be equipped to follow God ourselves. You may be persecuted, but God will get you ready and equipped if you will stay in His Word.

What are some ways you have faced persecution for your faith?_____
_____

Spend a few minutes praying for your other FAITH Team members and the people you visited last week. Pray that you and the new Christians around you will not walk away from God during persecution.

Review from memory Luke 19:10.

Day Five:
Read 2 Timothy 4
Finishing Well
Which quarter of a football game is the most important quarter to be ahead? The fourth quarter, of course. Why? It doesn't matter how far ahead you are at the start of a game or a race if you do not finish well at the end. At the end of his life, Paul could confidently write, "I am finishing well" (v. 7). Many people follow God for a short time, but few finish well. Some of the older adults in your church may have walked with God 50 years or more. They probably know many of their peers who attended church for a few years and were committed for a while, but now are no longer following God.

What will you be like in a few years? Will you still be following God as faithfully as you are now or will you walk away? How about the other members of your FAITH Team and the people you have led to Christ over the past year?

What do you desire for your life spiritually by the time you are 35 years old?_____

What spiritual goals would you have for age 65?_____

Spend a few minutes praying for your other Faith team members and the people you visited last week. Pray that you, your team members, and the people you have shared Christ with will finish well in the Christian life. Pray for people in your Sunday School class who have not attended in a long time. Pray that they would return to a committed walk with Christ. Also pray for the people you know who need to know Christ.

Day Six:
Read Titus 3:1-8
Obedience—Big Deal

Respect, obedience, and honor don't get much air time on TV or the radio, but these characteristics exemplify a Christian. We follow the authorities in our life because God put them there; we are to obey them as if we are following Christ. You get to decide how much you will honor God by honoring the persons in authority that He has placed over you—teachers, administrators, parents, bosses, coaches, police, and so on.

Immediately after you are saved, you also choose how obedient you will be to Christ in the area of baptism. Christ commanded us to be baptized, not for salvation, but as a testimony to the world of how your life has changed. Some persons want to accept Christ but they reject following Him in baptism. Baptism is not an optional activity. Baptism is an initial statement of obedience and submission to the Lordship of Jesus in your life.

Write a brief description of the day you were baptized._____
_____
_____

Spend a few minutes praying for your other FAITH Team members and the people you visited last week. Pray that those who have accepted Christ will be faithful to obey Him in baptism. Also pray for the people you know who need to know Christ.

Review from memory Luke 19:10.

Day Seven:
Read Matthew 3
Church Was Different That Day

John the Baptizer was one strange man! He wore camels' hair clothes, ate bugs, and told anyone who would listen that they should repent and follow God. (I guess the last characteristic is really not all that strange to a person who is committed to FAITH.) The number one characteristic of John the Baptist was *commitment*. He did not water down his words or his commitment when the crowd around him changed, no matter who showed up. When John baptized Jesus, it was not for repentance since Jesus had never sinned. Jesus was baptized as a sign of obedience to his Heavenly Father. His baptism was a distinct starting point to his public ministry. In a similar way we are baptized in obedience to Jesus' command and as a distinct starting point to our public confession of Christ as our Savior and Lord. List one area where you struggle with commitment in your daily walk with Jesus.

_____

Spend a few minutes praying for your other FAITH Team members and the people you visited last week. Pray that you would have the boldness of John this week as you share with everyone you meet at school, work, church, and play how they can know Christ and follow Him just like you follow Him. Also pray for the people you know who need to know Christ.

The Weekly Sunday School Leadership Team Meeting

Use this space to record ways your FAITH Team impacts the work of your Sunday School class. Use the information to report during weekly Sunday School leadership team meetings. Identify actions that need to be taken through Sunday School as a result of prayer concerns, needs identified, visits made by the Team, and decisions made by the students being visited.

Highlight needs and reports affecting your class or department.

_____

_____

Pray now for teachers and department directors.

How does preparation for Sunday need to consider needs of individuals or families visited through FAITH?

_____

_____

How can Sunday School leaders and members pray for and encourage Team members?

_____

_____

What are ways the Sunday School can be prepared to include students being discovered and reached through visits made by FAITH Teams?

_____

_____

For Further Reading

Read pages 113-14—"Visitation: the Way It Usually Is" and "Visitation: the Way It Could Be"—in *Evangelism Through the Sunday School: A Journey of FAITH* by Bobby Welch. Begin your FAITH visits expecting God to make visitation all that it can be for your church!

For the Team Leader

This weekly feature suggests actions the Team Leader can take to support Team members, prepare for Team Time, and consider ways to improve visits. This work becomes part of the Team Leader's Home Study Assignments. Add any actions suggested by your church's FAITH strategy.

Support Team Members

❑ Call Team members and encourage them regarding their participation during the first home visits.

Prepare to Lead Team Time

❑ Overview "Team Time" at the beginning of Session 3.

Prepare to Lead Visits

❑ Review the FAITH Visit Outline to be able to model the entire process for Team members.

❑ Be prepared to explain the procedures in the car, going to and from the church, as well as the role of the Team Leader in making visits.

❑ Be prepared to model a visit in which Team member(s) are asked to lead in sharing a Sunday School testimony.

❑ Be prepared to model the use of the Opinion Poll in making visits.

❑ Be prepared to lead the Team to participate during Celebration Time.

Connecting to Sunday School

❑ Participate in your weekly Sunday School Leadership meeting. Share pertinent information in this meeting using FAITH visit results.

❑ Describe responses to your FAITH Team's first home visits.

Making A Baptism Visit

LIBBA GILLUM

The previous month, Jacqui's FAITH team had made a ministry visit to Cindy Woods' home. Mr. and Mrs. Woods had been members of Jacqui's church for a long time, but since their divorce a few years earlier, none of the family had been to church. Mrs. Woods had recently had surgery and Cindy and her younger brother were keeping house, cooking, and so on. The FAITH team (Jacqui, Jon, and Mr. Lawrence) had visited the family to take a lasagna casserole and invite the two students to come to Sunday School.

As a result of that ministry visit, Cindy and David had accepted Christ and now the team was returning to the Woods' to talk to the teens about getting baptized. As Jacqui sat on the couch with David, she opened the leaflet *Student Baptism* and began to share with him that since he had prayed the salvation prayer, the next step he should take would be to go before the church and request baptism.

After only a sentence or two, David interrupted Jacqui. "I've been thinking about baptism. Dad and our stepmom have a new baby and we went to her baptism a few months ago. Can't I get water sprinkled on me? I'm kind of afraid of the pastor pushing me under the water."

TEAM TIME

The team leader leads this time. Learners are primarily responsible for reciting the assigned portion of the FAITH Visit Outline and for discussing any Home Study Assignments.

Keep in mind how Learners also look to leaders as role models, motivators, mentors, and friends. Team Time activities can continue in the car, as the Team travels to and from visits.

Check It

FAITH VISIT OUTLINE

❑ Be prepared to check off each Learner's memorization of all of *Preparation* (through the Transition Statement) and the key words in *Presentation* and *Invitation*. Approve by signing or initialing each Learner's Journal. Encourage Learners as you do, and indicate any notes you have jotted down that might be helpful.

Session 2 Debriefing (Strengthening Your Commitment)

❑ Answer any questions that remain from Session 2. Emphasize the importance of a good beginning in building trust that ultimately can result in the gospel being shared. Highlight ways the Sunday School testimony helps make connections to students.

❑ Review Learners' written Sunday School testimonies.

Help for Strengthening A Visit

❑ Answer any questions that emerged from home visits following Session 2.

❑ Review ways to begin a visit.

❑ Identify actions Team members took during last week's visits that were particularly good and others that might need to be changed.

❑ Suggest ways Team members can improve sharing their Sunday School testimonies.

❑ Call attention to the evangelistic testimony you shared during last week's visit(s); mention that Team Learners will be introduced during this session to ways to share their testimony during a visit.

Notes

_____

_____

_____

_____

Actions I Need to Take with Learners During the Week

_____

_____

_____

_____

A Quick Review

A FAITH visit in which a student makes a profession of faith is only the beginning. The FAITH Team also is privileged to be a part of follow-up to this new believer. With an official visit assignment in their visitation folders, the FAITH Team should return within two weeks to talk more with the student. This is a time to answer any questions the student may have about his or her decision, to discuss baptism, and to talk about opportunities for growth through involvement in a Sunday School class and in the church.

Additional information can be shared about the class and department at this time. Other students can become involved in reaching out to and involving the new believer in Bible study. Opportunities to reach out to the entire family may become most apparent during times of follow-up. In some instances, a staff member may make a specific follow-up contact.

Transformation Begins at Conversion

The decision to accept Jesus Christ as Savior is unquestionably the most significant action a person can ever take. You know as a believer that the Holy Spirit enters the life of a person at the moment of salvation. Eternal life begins at that moment for the believer—this is truly a time of celebration and life transformation!

You know that a new believer needs to take the next steps designed to help him or her grow as a Christian. Baptism is one of those extremely important next steps. For many new believers, the longer they wait to be baptized, the more difficult it will be to do. This session will help you focus on how to use another simple leaflet, the *Student Baptism* tract.

Many people with a church background have been taught that a person is baptized into the church as an infant; that the person has no decision to make but is "born" into the church. Others, like David in the case study at the beginning of this session, have seen baptism in a form other than immersion. It is important to help a new Christian understand and follow his or her commitment to Christ with believer's baptism.

Your FAITH Team will be assigned to make a follow-up visit to people who commit their lives to Christ. Since this is such a significant opportunity for your Team, let's look at some ways to help someone take the next step of faith.

Baptism—
A Next Step of Obedience

After your Team has become reacquainted with the student you visited previously, there are several steps to take in dealing with baptism. If, by the time you visit again, he or she has not followed up his commitment to Christ by being baptized, then take time to explain each of the following steps. If the person has been baptized since his or her recent commitment, take time to discuss the significance of the issues reflected in the following steps.

1. Remind the student of his or her (_____) to trust Christ. Use appropriate panels of *A Step of Faith (Student Edition)* to recall and celebrate the decision(s) made during the previous visit to follow Christ. Help the new believer recall how Jesus was not ashamed to die for him or her.

Panel 5 of the leaflet, where the person checked his decisions and commitments, is a good one to highlight. Call attention to panel 7—baptism. Ask whether he or she has had a chance to read that information.

2. Call attention to the importance of (_____) as a next step in being obedient to Christ after salvation. Share a brief testimony about the significance of baptism.

Such a testimony could have three short parts. Perhaps you can remember the parts with these words: (_____ _____ _____). The following example uses this format:

AFTER I prayed and trusted Jesus as my Savior, I was so thankful that He was not ashamed of me and had died for me. I was not ashamed to obey and follow Jesus in scriptural baptism.

NEXT, I was baptized by the pastor.

ALTHOUGH I knew baptism did not save me, I understood that it showed a symbol of what had happened to me—dying to my sins, burying my former rebellious life, and being raised to a new life in following Jesus.

You might choose to give a personal illustration to validate how baptism strengthens and encourages you as a believer. For example, one Team member might recall, "I knew I was being obedient to Jesus. I also knew baptism was a great way for me to share with my friends and family what Jesus had done for me." Continue by saying something like: "I'd like to explain the next step to take as you begin to follow Jesus."

3. Put away *A Step of Faith (Student Edition)*. Now bring out the *Student Baptism* tract. (As you did with the first leaflet, show and dialogue about each panel of this leaflet; but do not give it to the person at this time.)

Briefly call attention to the title. Share that you will use this leaflet to help show the significance of baptism as being obedient to Jesus.

4. Open the leaflet to panel 2. Call attention to the reminder that Jesus was not ashamed of us and does not want us to be ashamed of Him. Comment that not only does baptism show we are not ashamed of Jesus, it also motivates and encourages us to confess Him publicly.

Introduce the significance of believer's baptism as an act of obedience.

Emphasize that individuals to be baptized are those who—
• already have trusted Jesus as Savior;
• understand that baptism does not bring salvation but is a symbol of what Jesus already has done for them, and thus is an expression of obedience;
• are not ashamed to follow Christ's example.
In nearly every case, new believers also are joining the church.

5. Point out panel 3: "Why be baptized?" Although you don't need to read the following information from the leaflet, be familiar enough with the reasons to be able to overview them clearly, referring to the leaflet for supporting Scriptures:
• Jesus commanded baptism (Matt. 28:19);
• Baptism is an act of obedience for which Jesus Himself, as well as His followers, set the example;
• Baptism is a picture of breaking from the past and beginning a new life with Christ;
• In the New Testament, baptism is a public testimony of faith.

6. Open the *Student Baptism* tract to panel 4; point out major concepts visualized on the front cover and in pictures inside the leaflet. Help the student realize that baptism is a picture of what Jesus has done for the believer; by pointing out elements of baptism, you clarify the beauty, symbolism, and significance of baptism.
Call attention to the fact that baptism is (__ _____) in water. The best way to understand the scriptural example (Matt. 3:5-17) and command (Matt. 28:19) is to understand the basis of the word *baptizo* (baptisma) which means to immerse in water.
Baptism also is to be in front of (_____). This is not to be a private ceremony. Christians and nonbelievers are encouraged to watch as the new believer is baptized as a testimony of his new relationship with Jesus.
Explain that most churches baptize new believers and new members in their baptismal pool as part of their worship service, with worshipers (_____ __).
Some congregations do not have facilities to accommodate baptism by immersion and they baptize new members in a pool or a river.
Baptism is conducted by the pastor or another minister as an (_____) of the church. Some churches invite other people into the water with the one who is being baptized, but most churches provide for the person being baptized to be with the minister while the congregation looks on. Either way, baptism is a meaningful experience.

7. Refer now to panel 5. Emphasize the importance of being baptized as soon as possible. Churches that follow the scriptural example emphasize the importance of being baptized only after a person has willfully accepted Jesus as Savior. Churches also emphasize the importance of persons who have experienced believer's baptism by immersion as those who can be accepted into their full membership.
This stresses the importance of baptism as something every church member has in common. Some churches require that, before a person can be baptized into their membership, he or she completes a new member training class. Other churches encourage new believers to participate in this kind of new member orientation during the weeks after baptism.

Whatever the practice of the church, it is important for a new believer to take the next steps as a Christian as soon as possible.

Will you now follow Jesus by being baptized?

8. One of the most important reasons for a follow-up visit to someone who recently has accepted Jesus is to encourage the person to make the decision to be baptized into the membership of your church.

 Call attention at this point in the visit to the question at the bottom of this panel (5): (____ ___ ___ _____ _____ __ _____ _ _____)? Use the person's name when asking the question; for example, "David, will you now follow Jesus by being baptized?"

9. Many students likely will have some questions about the reasons for and logistics of baptism in a church. As needed, use panel 6 to answer their questions. They likely will want to know such details as—

> When and with whom do I meet before the baptismal service?
> What do I wear when I'm baptized?
> Where and when will I change clothes after being immersed?
> Will I be asked to say anything during the worship service?
> How will I keep from falling while I'm in the water?

If the person has no unusual questions, refer to the information in the leaflet as something he or she may wish to overview privately. Otherwise, explain the logistics of how baptism is done in your church.

10. Invite the student to (_____ __ __ ___ _____) to be baptized on the appropriate part of panel 7. Point out the place for them to sign and to date the occasion of the commitment to be baptized. Affirm the new believer for being willing to take this next step of obedience. Indicate whether or not your church provides a baptism certificate or other special reminder of the occasion. Explain that the leaflet itself will be a significant reminder as well.

 Now ask another significant question: "Would you allow us (referring to the FAITH Team) the privilege of accompanying you as you are baptized?" Point out the spaces for the members of the FAITH Team to sign their names and to indicate their phone numbers. Indicate how, not only through support for baptism but also in many other ways, your Team wants to help the new believer grow through the ministries of your local church.

 If the student answers *yes* to the question, ask for a (_____ _____) for the baptismal service; indicate that this request will be shared, followed up on, and confirmed in a few days by a minister of the church. Also record that information on the "Appointment for Baptism" panel, which the Team takes back to the church. Indicate the location and time to meet prior to baptism; also indicate that information on the "Appointment for Baptism" card. Write down the pastor's name as well. Even though he may not be the minister who does the baptismal service, the new believer needs to know the pastor's name.

 Although most FAITH Teams cannot determine the date and time for the person to be baptized, (generally this is done by the ministerial staff after a person makes a public declaration of faith and comes for church membership by baptism) requesting a preferred date and time (morning or evening worship service) helps solidify the decision and provides the church with additional information with which to follow up.

 Make sure to record appropriate information on the Visit Assignment Card that needs to be shared with the church staff about the person's decision. Return the perforated "Appointment for Baptism" card to the pastor.

With a student who has not yet made a decision for church membership by baptism:
 If a new believer who has not been baptized makes the commitment for church membership, make sure one of the Team members indicates this information on the Visit Assignment Card. Explain the procedure (of most churches) for a new believer to declare his faith in Christ and his intention to join the church and be baptized by coming to the front of the congregation during the invitation part of the worship service.

 Make certain the student knows Team members' willingness to stand with him or her during this time (and to support them in many other ways). Explain that the minister will share specific information about the time and location to meet for baptism. Make sure this information is forwarded to the pastor. Identify additional opportunities for ministry and follow-up.

11. Give the copy of the *Student Baptism* tract to the individual. Encourage the student to think about inviting someone, perhaps an unsaved friend, to attend the baptismal service. Conclude the visit (____   _____).

If the student declines to be baptized:
 It will be rare that someone your Team visits for follow-up will choose not to be baptized. If he or she does not make a baptism appointment during this visit, ask whether there are any questions the Team might answer. Explain why waiting is not an acceptable action:
• We have no record in the New Testament about anyone waiting for baptism.
• Delay is dangerous because it gives the devil a chance to create doubt or uncertainty.
• It is always best to obey the Lord as soon as He tells us what to do.

Plan for follow-up by your Sunday School and church.

The Journey Continues
In the New Testament, baptism is for believers (Acts 2:38; 8:12-13, 37-38; Eph. 4:5). Water apart from personal commitment to Christ makes no difference in the life of anyone. In the New Testament, baptism occurs when a person trusts Christ as Lord and Savior and obeys the command to be submerged in water and raised from it as a picture of the salvation experience that has occurred. Baptism comes after conviction of sin, repentance of sin, confession of Christ as Lord and Savior. To be baptized is to preach a personal testimony through the symbol of baptism."[1]
Recall your own baptism experience. Think about the people who observed you "preach a personal testimony" through your baptism. How were conversion and baptism only the beginning in your journey of faith? How did obedience in baptism prepare you to be obedient to Christ in other, more challenging ways?

Visitation Time
DO IT
As you go . . .

Think about this:
 One Tuesday night, our FAITH visitation team called on a student who had just moved into town. Jenna's family had been transferred because of her dad's job. She was eager to meet some students and she wanted to hear all about our church and the gospel. Before we left, we had the joy of leading her to Christ.
 While in their home, our team had given her a follow-up booklet, and later Jenna's Sunday School teacher called her. But those were not the reasons she joined our church. Actually, a guy on our visitation team told his sister about the new girl who lived near the school. One morning his sister saw Jenna walking to school and gave her a ride They discovered that they both loved tennis, so they made a date to play on Saturday morning at the school's court.
 After the tennis match, they stopped for a soda and the conversation turned to spiritual matters; Jenna shared that she had received Christ during the FAITH visit earlier that week. The girls sat together in Sunday School and the worship service the next day and Jenna went down front to make her decision public and ask for baptism.
 The instructive element of follow-up is foundational, but it usually won't happen without a relationship.

Celebration Time
SHARE IT
As you return to share . . .

- Other reports and testimonies
- Session 3 Evaluation Card
- Participation Card
- Visitation forms updated with results of visits

---

[1] Johnnie Godwin, "Baptism," *Holman Bible Dictionary*, Trent Butler, Gen. Ed. (Nashville: Holman Bible Publishers, 1991), 151.

THE DAILY JOURNEY

Day One:
Read Acts 8:26-40
What a Ride

Obedience to God's leadership is an incredible thing! One day Philip was right in the middle of real life when God gently whispered to him and gave him a mission. Philip did not know the plan or the result, he only knew God had spoken and he must follow. Philip was a willing and obedient disciple. How about you?

The man in the chariot who accepted Christ was also willing and obedient. A man of his importance would have had a large group of people traveling with him. Yet, as soon as they passed a place with water, he was ready to be baptized in front of all of them. The Ethiopian man learned immediate obedience from Philip. When God leads you to action, you do it right then and allow God to handle the results of immediate obedience.

List one example of when God called you to do or not do something and you obeyed him immediately. _____ ____

Do you listen for God's voice throughout the day? Are you willing to follow Him immediately if God leads you during your day? Pray for your FAITH Team. Pray that all of you would be willing to follow God daily as He leads you. Pray also for those who have accepted Christ over the past year and have not yet been baptized.

Day Two:
Romans 6:1-14
Live the Picture

Why is it such a big deal to be put under the water when you are baptized rather than just sprinkled? Think of the picture of baptism. Going under the water is a symbol of Christ's death and burial. When you are lifted out of the water it is a picture of Jesus coming out of the tomb. It is a symbol on the outside of what happened to you on the inside when you accepted Christ.

When you accepted Christ it was as if your old life died and Jesus gave you a new life. Sprinkling or pouring water could never fully symbolize the radical change in life that occurred at salvation. It was far more than just being made clean—it was the death of your old life and lifestyle and the creation of new life in you. Are you ready to live the picture? Live life as a person changed forever by the power of Jesus' resurrected life in you? Are you willing to tell other people at school that Jesus can change their life that radically?

Name one area where your life has changed since you became a Christian.

_____

Pray for yourself and your FAITH Team. Pray that you will be bold in sharing your faith at school and that you will live your lives as a picture of Jesus' new life in you.

Day Three:
Psalm 27
One Thing

Narrow down your life to one thing. If you could pick only one thing, or one relationship or one activity that you could do, what would it be? Parents, boyfriend or girlfriend, best friend, car, sports, music, leadership? It's a hard question, but there's an easy answer. If all of life could be cleared out and only one thing remained, I would go with David's answer.

Read Psalm 27.

It's amazing to know that a king wants only one thing—to be with God. David had all the wealth, all the food, all the relationships, all the power he could ever want, but he would rather wait on God to be with Him than have any other thing or person. David certainly was not a perfect man, but he did have his priorities in order.

Now it's time to evaluate *your* priorities. What are your top ten most important relationships or possessions? List them:

_____

_____

_____

Honestly evaluate the priorities of your life as they are now by ranking them one to ten. Next to your current ranking, list another number for how you would *like* your life to be prioritized in the future. If there is any difference, spend some time in prayer asking God to guide you through changing the priorities of your life. Pray also for the life priorities of your FAITH Team.

Day Four:
Read Luke 3:21-23
Impressive Special Effects

When you were baptized, did God the Father speak audibly from heaven and affirm you with the visible presence of the Holy Spirit? Not me, either!

The day Jesus was baptized must have been an incredible day—imagine the conversation around the dinner table that night for the people who were at the river that day. "What did you do today?" "Oh, not much. I did some work, then I went down to the river to watch someone be baptized and heard God speak out of the clouds. Just another ordinary day."

Jesus' ministry was accompanied by many amazing events. But, we cannot lose track of the fact that God enjoys our obedience, even when there are no special effects to affirm our obedience. God is pleased with us when we choose to follow Him fully and to know His love more than the love of any other person or thing. Obedience is never overlooked or ignored in the eyes of God.

Is there one thing that you can do today as an act of obedience to God that would remind you again of your love and priority for Him? Record it here:

_____

Pray for your obedience and that of your FAITH Team. Pray that you would not grow weary of doing what is right just because you do not get public praise.

Day Five:
Read Acts 20:17-38
Finish the Job

Graduation Day! There is no day quite like it. The weird hat, the gown, and the diploma make it official; you are through with school! As you walk across the stage and shake hands you look across the crowd and think, *I am finished!* But as you sit down your eyes look up and down the aisles of your classmates and you realize, *I will never have a chance again to tell them about Christ.* It is a bittersweet feeling common to Christians at graduation. While you were in school, did you finish the task—did your friends and peers have an opportunity to hear the gospel from you?

Paul stood on the beach and talked to some of the people with whom he had shared Christ years before. He had returned to encourage them one last time before he left for Jerusalem and certain imprisonment. Before departing, he said an amazing thing. Paul said that he was innocent of the blood of all men because he had been faithful to complete the task that God had given him.

Are you ready at graduation day to say that you are innocent of the blood of all people because you were faithful to complete the task God gave you? If you are not ready for that day, today is a great day to start getting ready. Share Christ with your peers and fellow students. Don't put it off any longer. When your friends come to know Christ, encourage them to get involved in your church and in a consistent walk with God. If you do, in a few months they will be helping you reach the rest of the school for Christ. Finish the job!

List three people for whose salvation you will pray. List only people that you will encounter in some way over the next two months. _____

_____

Pray for the people that you listed who need to know Christ. Pray that you and your FAITH Team will not lose your priority of impacting the campus for Christ before Graduation Day.

Day Six:
Acts 11:19-26
Tough Times

Tough times can be looked at in a couple of different ways: In the beginning of this passage we read about Christians who had to move to other cities just to keep from being killed for their belief in Jesus. Instead of keeping quiet about their faith, though, they began to tell the Jews there all about who Jesus was and how they could trust in Him. They even began to tell some Greeks, people who weren't like them, the way they could know Jesus as their Lord and Savior also. These Christians took a tough situation and allowed God to use them to reach people unlike themselves. This week, watch for opportunities and situations that might look difficult at first, but can be used by God to let people know that He loves them very much.

Who is someone around you, different from you and your friends, who needs to know Christ?_____

Pray that you and your FAITH Team would not share Christ with people only like yourself.

Day Seven:
Read 2 Corinthians 5:11-21
A New Grateful Creation

Can you imagine what it would be like if you risked your life to save somebody else and when it was all over they just acted as if nothing unusual had happened? As adopted sons and daughters of God, we are called to a deeper level of gratitude for the fact that Jesus gave up His life to save us from spiritual death. Think about it—you were spiritually dead, separated from a loving, holy, caring Father; and Jesus saved you from that forever! Today you are a new creation because of God's love for you.

That same loving Father is calling many of the people you will encounter today to be His children. Look at people the way God looks at them—with loving, caring, compassionate eyes. Let those persons know that there is a perfect Father who desperately wants to give them spiritual life forever.

Who can you and your FAITH Team encourage this week to follow Christ more faithfully? Is there anyone you have visited before that may need some encouragement this week?

Pray that you and your FAITH Team will see people today as God sees them.

The Weekly Sunday School Leadership Team Meeting

Use this space to record ways your FAITH Team impacts the work of your Sunday School department or class. Use the information to report during weekly Sunday School leadership team meetings. Identify actions that need to be taken through Sunday School as a result of prayer concerns, needs identified, visits made by the Team, and decisions made by the students being visited.

Highlight needs or reports affecting your class, department, or age group.

_____

_____

Pray now for teachers and department directors.

How does preparation for Sunday need to consider needs of students or families—
- who have prayed to receive Christ through FAITH but have not yet attended Sunday School?

_____

_____

- who have not followed up by being baptized?

_____

_____

How can Sunday School leaders and members pray for and encourage students who have made a decision or other commitment during a FAITH visit?

_____

_____

How can Sunday School leaders and members encourage new believers who recently have been baptized into the membership of the church?

_____

_____

For Further Reading

Read the FAITH Tip, "The Significance of Believer's Baptism."
Read pages 91-97 in *Evangelism Through the Sunday School: A Journey of FAITH* by Bobby Welch.

For the Team Leader

This weekly feature suggests actions the Team Leader can take to support Team members, prepare for Team Time, and consider ways to improve visits. This work becomes part of the Team Leader's Home Study Assignments. Add any actions suggested by your church's FAITH strategy.

Support Team Members
❑ Call Team members and talk with them about their participation during the class training and visits. Discuss any observations they made during the visits and particularly about sharing their Sunday School testimony.
❑ Discuss ways to prepare and share evangelistic testimonies without giving away the answer to the Key Question.
❑ Encourage Team members as they memorize all of *Preparation* in the FAITH Visit Outline.

Prepare to Lead Team Time
❑ Overview "Team Time" at the beginning of Session 4.

Prepare to Lead Visits
❑ Review the FAITH Visit Outline in order to model the entire process for Team members.
❑ Be prepared to model a visit in which Team member(s) are asked to lead in sharing a Sunday School testimony and evangelistic testimony.
❑ Be prepared to model the use of the Opinion Poll in making visits.
❑ Be prepared to lead your Team to participate during Celebration Time.

Connecting to Sunday School
❑ Participate in your weekly Sunday School leadership meeting. Share pertinent information and other FAITH visit results.
❑ Does every member of your Team (including yourself) have a prayer partner from within the Sunday School class? If not, present the need to your class on Sunday.

FAITH*TIP*

The Significance of Believer's Baptism

Christian baptism is the immersion of a believer in water in the name of the Father, the Son, and the Holy Spirit. It is an act of obedience symbolizing the believer's faith in a crucified, buried, and risen Savior and the believer's death to sin, the burial of the old life, and the resurrection to walk in newness of life in Christ Jesus.

It is a testimony to his faith in the final resurrection of the dead. Being a church ordinance, it is prerequisite to the privileges of church membership and to the Lord's Supper.

The word for baptize in Greek is baptizo, which means "to dip, plunge, submerge, or immerse." Baptism in the New Testament was related to the ministry of both John the Baptist and of Jesus. John's baptism was symbolic of one's repentance from sin and of willingness to participate in the kingdom of God (Matt. 3:6-8; Luke 3:3-16).

Jesus submitted to John's baptism (Matt. 3:16) not to denote repentance but to authenticate John's ministry, to set an example for His followers, and to dedicate Himself publicly to His redemptive ministry. In so doing Jesus symbolized His death, burial, and resurrection.

Baptism translates baptisma, the meaning in the act of baptism, namely, a symbol of what Jesus did to save us—death, burial, and resurrection—and what He does in the believer—death to the old life, its burial, and resurrection to a new life in Christ.

Keeping in mind the meaning of baptisma, what is the significance of believer's baptism? Is it sacramental in nature and necessary for salvation, or is it symbolic in nature? The word itself strongly suggests the latter. The idea of baptismal regeneration did not appear in Christian teachings until late in the second and early in the third centuries. However, by the late second and early third centuries, baptismal regeneration came to be accepted by the group that later evolved into the Roman Catholic Church.

That immersion is the original form of baptism is generally agreed. Baptizo itself teaches that neither pouring nor sprinkling constitutes New Testament baptism. Because of the later belief in baptismal regeneration, the practice arose of pouring water all over a sick person. This was called clinical baptism. Later, water was poured only on the head.

It should be noted that while the verbs for pour and sprinkle appear in the New Testament, neither is used for baptism. No usage has been found where baptizo means either pour or sprinkle. The practice of sprinkling for baptism gradually replaced immersion in the Catholic Church and when it divided into the Roman and Greek branches, the latter retained immersion. It was not until the 13th century that sprinkling became the official mode of Roman Catholic baptism.

Herschel H. Hobbs, *The Baptist Faith and Message* (Nashville: Convention Press, Rev. 1996), 72-75.

ΠΟΤΕS

MAKING A FOLLOW-UP VISIT

LIBBA GILLUM

LOG: FRIDAY LUNCH—
Joshua asked Joy if she had talked to Amy since they made their FAITH visit; he wanted to know if Amy had been invited to Sunday School. Joy promised Josh that she would call her right after school.

FRIDAY AFTERNOON—
Joy checked her email and had a message from a friend she met the previous summer at Centrifuge. She wrote him a long message, telling all about events in her life, including all about FAITH. Then Joy remembered her promise to call Amy—but it was too late to call.

SATURDAY MORNING—
While Joshua was at work at the local supermarket, Amy and her mom came through his checkout line. As he bagged their groceries, he asked if they were planning to come to Sunday School the next day. He also asked if Joy had called Amy and he discovered that Joy had not kept her promise.

SATURDAY NOON—
Later that day while Joshua was still at work, Joy came into the store. He asked her "How did your conversation with Amy go yesterday?"

TEAM TIME

The team leader leads this time. Learners are primarily responsible for reciting the assigned portion of the FAITH Visit Outline and for discussing other Home Study Assignments.

Keep in mind how Learners also look to Leaders as role models, motivators, mentors, and friends. Team Time activities can continue in the car, as the Team travels to and from visits.

Check It

FAITH Visit Outline
❑ Listen as each Learner recites the appropriate portion of the FAITH Visit Outline (all of *Preparation*, adding the Key Question and Transition Statement; plus key words for *Presentation* and *Invitation*). Indicate your approval by signing each Learner's Journal. Involve an Assistant Team Leader in this part of Team Time, if you have this Team member.

Evangelistic Testimony—First Draft
❑ Review the first draft of written evangelistic testimonies, due this session. Use the criteria from Session 3 FAITHTip (*Student FAITH*). Explain why you are making your suggestions. Indicate that most testimonies undergo some revisions. Be sensitive in helping Team members develop their testimonies, keeping their stories intact. As a reminder, these are the criteria which Learners have used to develop their testimonies:
  • Define some specific event before (pre-conversion) and after your conversion (benefits).
  • Do not answer the Key Question in your testimony.
  • Keep your testimony brief (three minutes or less).
  • Do not give too many unnecessary details; instead, concisely reflect your experience.
  • Conclude your testimony with the assurance that you are going to heaven.

Sunday School Testimony—Practice
❑ As possible, provide time for Team members to practice their Sunday School testimonies. Review of the evangelistic testimony, however, should be your priority.

Session 3 Debriefing (Developing Your Evangelistic Testimony)
❑ Answer other questions Learners may have from Session 3 or as a result of their Home Study Assignments.

Help for Strengthening A Visit
❑ Identify ways Team members can improve sharing their evangelistic testimony in a visit.
❑ Help your Team, especially Learners, know how to—
  • dialogue with a student who answers the Key Question with a *faith* answer, by discussing his or her journey of faith in Christ.
  • briefly explain to a person who answers the Key Question with a *works* answer, that many people feel that doing good things gets them into heaven. Discuss the various ways such a response might be verbalized.

- look for opportunities to ask permission to share what the Bible says about how a person goes to heaven.
- look for ways to get clarification or explanation if someone shares an unclear response to the Key Question.
- prayerfully look for ways to talk with a person who indicates no opinion about the Key Question.

Notes

_____
_____
_____
_____

Actions I Need to Take with Learners During the Week

_____
_____
_____
_____

A Quick Review

You will encounter several types of FAITH follow-up situations. One of the most important is the follow-up visit in which you discuss baptism as a next step of obedience with a new convert. Test your knowledge of key truths by circling one or more answers, as appropriate:

1. Use the *Student Baptism* tract when—
    a. making a follow-up visit to someone who enrolled in Sunday School during a FAITH visit;
    b. making a follow-up visit to someone who has a ministry need, as discovered during a FAITH visit;
    c. making a follow-up visit to someone who accepted Christ;
    d. a FAITH Team member has completed sharing the FAITH gospel presentation.

2. Three words—*After, Next, Although*—help you remember an appropriate format for—
    a. elaborating on your evangelistic testimony;
    b. sharing your baptism testimony;
    c. remembering details of your Sunday School testimony.

3. Three requirements for persons to be baptized, as identified in the *Student FAITH Baptism* tract, are individuals who—
    a. already have trusted Christ;
    b. understand that baptism does not bring about salvation but is a symbol of what Jesus has done for you and is an expression of obedience;
    c. are not ashamed to follow Christ's example and command and are joining the church.

The Person God Uses

The person God uses is an encourager.

One of the characteristics of a person God uses (p. 126, *Evangelism Through the Sunday School: A Journey of FAITH*) is that of encouraging others. This seems like such a simple and obvious action. On the other hand, the importance of encouragement cannot be overlooked.

Think about how God has used other people as an encouragement to you. Consider how important it is for you to have someone who encourages you, particularly when you are facing new or challenging situations.

God has placed His hand on you to be an encouragement to other FAITH Team members, as well as to other Sunday School members. You also are making connections to individuals visited by your FAITH Team. You now are called on to demonstrate the ministry of encouragement.

Nehemiah 4 records some simple yet profound actions Nehemiah took to overcome the discouragement of the Israelites who were rebuilding the city walls. Consider these truths:

- You begin encouraging others when you recognize the potential they have to be discouraged.
- You encourage others when you join them in prayer.
- You can be used of God when you give people specific actions they can successfully take to improve their overall situation.
- You encourage others by your very presence and your confidence in them. ("You can do it," "I believe in you," and other sincere expressions.)
- God uses you meaningfully when you help people recognize how He is at work in their midst and how He is choosing to fight on their behalf. You encourage others as you remind them to "remember the Lord, who is great and awesome" (Neh. 4:14).

You will be called on by God to encourage some students as they learn to share their faith. You will be used of God to encourage others as they begin considering new directions for their lives.

Keep in mind how God has used others as a model of encouragement to you. Pray that He will use you in similar life-changing ways.

Put Yourself in Their Shoes

Put yourself in the place of a student who recently has decided to accept Jesus as Savior and Lord or to enroll in a Sunday School class. Recall your own excitement of newfound faith.

When placing yourself in this situation, think about some of the advantages of having caring people connect with you as you begin taking your new steps of faith. Think about some of the challenges for the new believer or new class member who doesn't have someone seeking to build relationships during the important first steps of discipleship.

Take the Initiative to Make Connections

Do you expect new Christians or new members to take the initiative in making connections to us, the church? In reality, most people who make a commitment to Christ or enroll in a Sunday School class need encouragement from others. Our initiative is important in helping them take steps in building relationships and in beginning to follow Christ.

The FAITH Team is a vital link in making connections to the church and students who make commitments to Christ and/or who enroll in Sunday School. The FAITH Sunday School Evangelism Strategy recognizes the importance of building relationships between these people and the Sunday School.

Instead of waiting for a new member to take the initiative, Team members—and the entire class—are motivated to reach out because they know this student and have been involved in what is happening in his or her life. Such relationship building is a vital reason for a follow-up visit.

During a FAITH follow-up visit, you will lead your Team to do these and other types of actions:

- (_____) or (_____) your team members and briefly talk about interests.
- Share the (_____) of the visit: "We wanted to spend some time talking about your recent decision to _____ (describe)."
- Dialogue with the student about his or her (_____) since making the decision. Talk about ways the Sunday School class can be helpful.
- Share some (_____) the student can take in building or strengthening his or her journey of faith.
- Share a (_____ _____) testimony to indicate the benefits that are experienced by participating with a small group in Bible study.
- Ask whether a FAITH Team member can "(_____)" the gospel presentation based on the word FAITH.
- Discuss some (_____) or challenges that might confront the student in participating in discipleship actions.
- If the student has not attended church or Sunday School since making the decision, discuss (_____) the team and class can take to encourage participation.
- Identify (_____) actions members of the class can take to assist the student in his or her journey of faith.
- (____) together.

Real People, Real Life: How Would You Help Students Connect?

Four case studies represent real situations your church might encounter and about which you always should be sensitive. Now think about specific actions your FAITH Team might take to make connections before the situation becomes discouraging for the student who made the commitment.

Case Study #1

I recently gave my life to Christ after my best friend shared with me. He encouraged me to come to Sunday School, and I really want to go. I've heard him and others in my class talk about the great Bible study and the fun stuff they do. But I don't have a drivers' license yet, and my parents don't have any desire to go to church. My friend keeps asking me when I am going to come to Bible study and I don't know what to say; I hate to admit that my parents won't bring me and I need a ride.

Principles for Connection: Follow-up seems challenging if all we are doing is seeking to get someone to come to a class. This situation calls for some creativity and flexibility.

When the FAITH Team realizes that this student has no way to get to church, they could share this concern during weekly Sunday School Leadership meetings.

It also is important that the Team share with the Sunday School class that members need to identify specific actions to connect with this student through regular ministry, fellowship, and Bible study opportunities that occur at times other than Sunday.

Case Study #2

I went with my friend Carmen to a lock-in at Greenglade Baptist Church. I had a great time and met some really nice kids. The youth minister visited me the next week, and after I went to Sunday School the teacher enrolled me in their Bible study class. I was excited—I figured they would keep giving me that attention and encouragement. Right after I signed up, my dad got hurt at work and my family and I spent several weeks going back and forth to the hospital to take care of him. I really forgot all about Sunday School. Besides, no one has checked on me. I guess it's because I didn't come back to class like I said I would.

Principles for Connection:

One reason some students do not come to Sunday School is that they don't know anyone in the class. Others go through short-term experiences in which they are not able to participate. If they have little or no contact with class members, particularly during times when they are away, many times newcomers feel unwanted. Individuals may feel let down by the class they thought really cared for them.

Although it is difficult for a class to know how to care for students who do not come, it is important that class leaders take the initiative in leading members to discover and respond to these types of challenges. Caring class members can:
* initiate prayer chains to members;
* make phone calls to students with special needs;
* plan to take meals or care packages to families in need; and
* provide transportation, a trip to the mall, or a listening ear when there is a special need.

FAITH Team members may be the best people to identify and begin making connections so some initial needs can be addressed.

Case Study #3

I started going to this church because a friend invited me. I had just broken up with my boyfriend and I really needed some hope. I was encouraged by the music and the preacher's messages. I decided to accept Jesus into my life. I know that He saved me.

But I've been disappointed with the church. When I hear other students talk, they share about how many friends they have in the church and how friendly the church is. So far, I haven't really found it to be that way. I sit with the students in worship nearly every Sunday I can attend. The people around me are OK, but I just don't feel like I fit in.

Principles for Connection:

A couple of clues in this case study should help you respond. First, if a FAITH Team follows up within a week or two of the person's commitment, members can begin building a relationship. It sounds as if this student doesn't know about the Sunday School. A FAITH Team should be careful to enroll a student in a specific Sunday School class during the first visit. Often a person is hesitant to enroll if he or she doesn't know anyone in the class. The follow-up visits give additional opportunities to emphasize enrollment and the benefits of being linked to a specific class.

If the student already is enrolled but is not yet attending, this may give opportunity to emphasize ways the student can be involved. It also should clue a Team about additional follow-up opportunities for other Sunday School members and leaders.

Case Study #4

It hasn't been long since I prayed to receive Christ into my life. I could tell that my life had new hope and joy, which I had never felt before. But, you know, it just hasn't lasted like I thought it would.

Maybe I've been too busy or too scared to go to church like I know I should. Maybe I feel like I'll go to Sunday School and ask a dumb question or say something really stupid to the kids who have been going for a long time.

Principles for Connection:

Every Christian needs to take actions that assist and enhance spiritual growth. It is nearly impossible for a Christian to grow in isolation from other believers.

This student, like every other Christian, needs to participate in Bible study and worship. This student needs opportunities to apply God's Word. Many people will feel intimidated by participating in a Bible study or discipleship group where they think they will be put on the spot or be made to feel uncomfortable. It is important that students in the class encourage new believers and nonattenders to participate in a variety of experiences designed to enhance Christian growth.

Many resources are designed to help new and young Christians develop Bible study, prayer, worship, and ministry skills. Since many newcomers initially may feel that they would not fit into an existing group, starting new groups periodically and targeting individuals who do not participate will increase the possibility of their participation.

The FAITH Team needs to be aware of these types of needs and to communicate the needs and potential actions through Sunday School leadership meetings, as well as in class gatherings.

In some cases, a student thinks he or she will have to do something in class—something that might be embarrassing if he or she does it incorrectly (for example, reading Scripture aloud when the Bible is not familiar to them). Providing current Bible study materials to the new believer ahead of time helps that student know what to expect and eases assimilation into the class. Also, sensitizing teachers to the presence of new members and to ways of involving them appropriately can help the entire class be more open to new people.

What are some additional actions that can be taken during and after a FAITH Team visit to make connections to students who are not attending worship, Sunday School, and/or discipleship opportunities?

Visitation Time
DO IT
As You Go . . .

Be sensitive to opportunities to connect with people who already may have had some contact with your church. You may not know all the details behind their lack of response or participation. With sensitivity and without being judgmental, attempt to find out more about the situation so your church can be responsive. Always be aware that you and your Team represent Christ and the church in someone's life. Even people with whom God is working may be unaware of their spiritual need or may be reluctant to seek out someone in the church. Your FAITH Team can make the connection that may enable someone to begin his or her journey in faith.

Are you and your Team experiencing opportunities to share FAITH in daily life?

Celebration Time
SHARE IT

As You Return to Share . . .
Celebrate every victory, even the small ones. What seems minor or insignificant at the time, may be a major inroad in the life of an individual or a family. Celebrate the faithfulness of participants to train and to visit.

• Other reports and testimonies
• Session 4 Evaluation Card
• Participation Card
• Visitation forms updated with results of visits

The Daily Journey

Day One:
Read Matthew 5:13-14
Salt and Light?
Did you ever notice that a call to follow Christ is a call to be noticed? We're encouraged to be "light" and "salt." Think for a minute about what it means to be a light. Darkness is the absence of any light. We can complain about living in a dark world, and about how most of the people we know don't seem to care about spiritual matters or we can get excited about the opportunity God has given us to shine in the darkness. People will know where to find the light as God's Spirit draws them to Jesus and they see the light in you.
 As you and your team encounter people this week, don't be put off by the apparent darkness of some people and situations—be excited about being the light that God will use to show them the way!
 How can you show the students in your school this week that Christ has made a difference in your life?
 Pray that you and your FAITH Team will show the light of God in a bold and loving way this week.

Day Two:
Matthew 28:18-20
Distorted Disciples
Mountain lakes are cool to look at. They are usually crystal clear and surrounded by one or more massive peaks that reach to the sky. The really cool thing is that, if there's nothing disturbing the water, you can look at the surface of the lake and see the exact reflection of the mountain. Only when something disturbs the water do you get a distorted view of the mountain. God has called us to be His reflection in this world. A disciple reflects God in his or her life. If there is sin in our life, it causes ripples that give other people a distorted view of God. As we fulfill God's command to "go and make disciples," we have to be right with God. Agree with Him today about the things in your life that are sin, confess them and allow Him to cleanse you of them. Then you will reflect who He is to the people around you. As your friends follow your example, they, too, will become disciples of the living God.
 Is there an attitude, action, or relationship in your life right now that is causing people around you to get a distorted view of God? If so, spend time with the Father and cleanse your life of that distortion.

Day Three:
Read Colossians 4:2-6
A Page from the Cookbook
Today's recipe is for a "power-filled" life. Take a large portion of prayer devoted to others and yourself; add to your prayer a deep concern for people who need to know about Jesus. (They are, after all, one of the main reasons

we are still living here instead of heaven.) Top it all off with uplifting, positive speech—speech full of wisdom and kindness so that those without Christ will hear His voice through you. Bake all three parts deep into the fabric of your being and watch what God will do!

Re-read Colossians 4:2-6 and identify the areas in which you are doing best and the areas in which you are doing worst. Spend some time with the Father evaluating what needs to happen in your life for the recipe to turn out more successfully.

Pray for the lost around you at school. Pray especially for you and your FAITH Team to be faithful to share when God gives you the opportunities.

Day Four:
Read Philippians 3:7-11
More Than Just Show

Each of us has a choice to make that will affect how we live as a Christian. We can live so that we look righteous in the eyes of other Christians—people will think we're special because of our morality, but with such an attitude, we may never interact with God Himself. Christ's call to discipleship is a difficult one.

Philippians 3 deals with something much deeper. Christ's life on earth was a mixture of great happiness and deep hurts, the greatest of compliments and the cruelest of insults. Paul described a relationship with Christ where he would experience the same kind of power that Jesus experienced during His lifetime—the power to walk with God in spite of hateful people, difficult situations, and tough decisions; the power to set his own life aside because of a deep love for God and other people.

The decision to live one's life just to impress people with your morality is much easier, but there are not many spiritual rewards. Walking with Christ is a much more difficult task, but the reward is an intimate relationship that will go beyond what you could ever imagine. The choice is yours, and you get to make it today.

What is holding you back from an intimate relationship with God? If there is any action, attitude, or life choice that is preventing your intimacy with God, deal with it now. If your relationship with God is going great today, continue to dig deeper into Who He is and how you can know and follow Him.

Day Five:
1 Thessalonians 1 (especially verses 6-7)
Wilderness Guides

If you decided to send someone on a wilderness trip into a remote area, you could do it a couple of different ways: (1) You could find an experienced guide who would lead the way for them, and the guide would let them know what they need to take, what they need to leave behind, where the danger spots were, and where the most spectacular scenery could be found. Or (2) you could make them strike out on their own and hope all goes well. The first is by far the better choice.

It is the same in your Christian life as you relate to new believers. You can choose to help them as their guide, showing them things they will need and things they will want to leave behind. You can show them the danger spots as well as the benefits of walking with God and having a perfect, loving Father. Or you can just abandon them and let them try to find their way with God on their own. If you will guide them through the beginning stages of walking with God, you will be challenged to examine your own walk and encouraged every time they make a new discovery about the majesty of our God. That's a whole lot better than letting them strike out on their own, hoping they survive!

Look back at session three, day seven to see if you have taken care of the person named there in the past weeks. Spend time praying about your role in encouraging them to know and follow God.

Day Six:
Read Matthew 9:35-38
Through His Eyes
People with certain hobbies and interests can sometimes seem pretty different. They can be so into their sport, hobby, or activity that it affects everything else they do. It makes them seem strange to people who don't enjoy or understand that particular activity. But, if you could ever step inside their head and look through their eyes you would understand them and the way they act would make sense to you. It might even influence the way you act!

In this passage, we have the opportunity to look at people through the eyes of Jesus. When we see through His eyes, we do not see a harsh Jesus, we see compassion—a loving God who poured out His life for the people we pass every day. Look at the people you encounter today through the eyes of Jesus and see if it doesn't change the way you live life and the way you react to the people whom Jesus died for.

What does it mean to you to see people through Jesus' eyes?

Pray that you and your FAITH Team would see people this week with the eyes of Jesus rather than eyes that condemn, neglect, or discourage.

Day Seven:
Colossians 3:12-17
Pleasing the Father
As a Father, I have fun watching my kids go through life. It is a blast to watch their games, listen to them talk with their friends, and just live life. I am the most pleased when they do something that reflects the values we have stressed as a family—being kind, caring for others, or being a good winner or loser.

Colossians 3 teaches us several things about the kind of values that God desires for us. He wants us to be holy, compassionate, humble, kind, gentle, patient, and forgiving. Imagine how excited He gets as He watches us treat other people with these God-like qualities. Let God fill you with these qualities today and remember that He is excited about having you as His child.

What characteristic in your life brings (or brought) God joy today? List some things that are going well in your character development._____
_____

List some things you need to work on. _____
_____

Pray that you and your FAITH Team would exemplify the character of God this week.

The Weekly Sunday School Leadership Team Meeting

Use this space to record ways your FAITH Team impacts the work of your Sunday School department or class. Use the information to report during weekly Sunday School leadership team meetings. Identify actions that need to be taken through Sunday School as a result of prayer concerns, needs identified, visits made by the Team, and decisions made by the persons being visited.

Highlight needs and reports affecting your class or department.

_____

_____

Pray now for teachers and department directors.

How does preparation for Sunday need to consider needs of individuals or families who have agreed to enroll in Sunday School but have not yet attended Sunday School and/or worship?

_____

_____

How can Sunday School leaders and members follow up on people who have made a decision or commitment during a FAITH visit?

_____

_____

For Further Reading

Read pages 62-72 in *Evangelism Through the Sunday School: A Journey of FAITH* by Bobby Welch. Are any of these results becoming apparent in your church? In your Sunday School class? Pray that God will change your Team and your church.

For the Team Leader

This weekly feature suggests actions the Team Leader can take to support Team members, prepare for Team Time, and consider ways to improve visits. This work becomes part of the Team Leader's Home Study Assignments. Add any actions suggested by your church's FAITH strategy.

Support Team Members
❑ Call Team members and dialogue with them about their participation in class training and in visits. Talk about observations they made during the visits and particularly as they shared their Sunday School testimonies. Discuss ways to prepare and share their evangelistic testimony without giving away the answer to the Key Question. Encourage them as they are memorizing all of Preparation of the FAITH Visit Outline.

Prepare to Lead Team Time
❑ Overview "Team Time" at the beginning of Session 5.
❑ Be prepared to evaluate the written evangelistic testimonies. Use these criteria:
  • Define some specific event before (pre-conversion) and after your conversion (benefits).
  • Do not answer the Key Question.
  • Keep your testimony brief (three minutes or less).
  • Do not give too many unnecessary details; instead, concisely reflect your experience.
  • Conclude your testimony with the assurance that you are going to heaven.

Prepare to Lead Visits
❑ Review the FAITH Visit Outline to be able to model the entire process for Team members.
❑ Be prepared to model visits in which Team member(s) are asked to lead in sharing a Sunday School testimony and/or evangelistic testimony.
❑ Be prepared to model the use of the Opinion Poll in making visits.
❑ Be prepared to lead your Team to participate during Celebration Time.

Connecting to Sunday School
❑ Participate in weekly Sunday School leadership meetings. Share pertinent information and FAITH visit results.

NOTES

USING THE
OPINION POLL

LIBBA GILLUM

CRANDALL RANG THE DOORBELL. There was complete silence inside the house. He rang it a second time—still no answer. Then he knocked on the door, just in case the doorbell was broken. Still no answer, so he placed a door hanger on the doorknob and the FAITH Team headed back to the car.

The same thing had happened at five other homes—no answers! This was the fourth week in a row they had gone on FAITH visitation and found no one at home.

Frustration was at an all-time high for Liza Rae and Crandall. They knew it was important to visit and contact people, but never finding anyone at home was getting old! They went to a local fast-food restaurant to kill the rest of the time before they went back to the church for Celebration Time.

"Some Celebration Time we'll have tonight," Crandall griped. "I can hear our report now, 'For the fourth week in a row, we went, we knocked, and we practiced sharing the FAITH outline to a closed door. The closed door had no opinion when it came to the key question.' "

"I'm almost to the point of just going anyplace with a light on and knocking on the door so we can say we at least talked to someone."

"If we did that, how would we introduce ourselves? What would we say?" asked Crandall.

As Mr. Blanton listened to the conversation, he reached into their FAITH team bag, and pulled out a copy of the Opinion Poll. Showing it to them, he asked, "Do you think something like this would work?"

TEAM TIME

The team leader leads this time. Learners are primarily responsible for reciting the assigned portion of the FAITH Visit Outline and for discussing any Home Study Assignments.

Keep in mind how Learners also look to leaders as role models, motivators, mentors, and friends. Team Time activities can continue in the car, as the Team travels to and from visits.

Check It

FAITH Visit Outline
❑ Call on each Learner to recite the assigned portion of the FAITH Visit Outline (all of *Preparation,* plus key words in *Presentation* and *Invitation*). Indicate successful completion by signing your name or initials in each Learner's Journal. Be prepared to answer any questions Learners may have. Make suggestions for improvement.

Final Draft of Evangelistic Testimony
❑ Call for final written copies of Learners' evangelistic testimonies. Congratulate Team members for achieving another important milestone.

Make sure any revisions include criteria discussed in Sessions 3 and 4 (not answering the Key Question with your testimony, and so forth). Ask for permission to print these testimonies in church materials that publicize the FAITH strategy or that encourage students to share their faith.

Emphasize to Team members the importance of sharing their testimonies naturally, in their own words, in actual visits.

Practice Key Question/Transition Statement
❑ Practice the Key Question/Transition Statement, helping Learners use their hands naturally to spell out the word FAITH.

Other Home Study Assignments
❑ Look over Learners' Home Study Assignments. Are they on track? Clarify or emphasize key points from FAITH Tips and/or *Evangelism Through the Sunday School: A Journey of FAITH* as needed.

Session 4 Debriefing (Making A Ministry Visit)
❑ Review the importance of and approach for making Sunday School ministry visits. Help Team members understand how such visits "reconnect" many inactive students to church life. Highlight ministry visitation assignments and indicate why certain comments are made during different types of ministry visits (to absentees, nonattenders, members with ministry needs). As inactive members return to the Sunday School or church, remind Team members they had a part in their return.

Ask any questions you feel would solidify Learners' understanding of Session 4, including questions that will appear on the final written review.

Help for Strengthening a Visit
❑ Be prepared to discuss ways to strengthen a visit based on what has been discovered in previous sessions.

- ❏ Be prepared to model an Opinion Poll visit during Visitation Time.
- ❏ Identify which Team member(s) will take the lead in sharing a Sunday School testimony. Ask another Team member to be prepared to share his or her evangelistic testimony. With sensitivity to Learners and person(s) being visited, be prepared to resume the visit after Team members have shared.

Notes

_____

_____

_____

_____

Actions I Need to Take with Learners During the Week

_____

_____

_____

_____

A Quick Review

A new Christian needs a strong connection to a life of discipleship and spiritual growth. Your Sunday School class can form a vital connection to a student who has been reached for Christ. In some cases, your class can connect an entire family to the church.

If a follow-up visit is appropriate, that information will be on your FAITH Visit Assignment Card. You can know that your FAITH Team, if a part of leading a person to Christ, also will have the privilege of following up on that individual and his or her decision. You can help a student—

- clarify his or her decision;
- understand why a public profession of faith is important;
- realize how Bible study and worship experiences can start a new Christian on the right road; and
- explain baptism and discipleship as important steps of obedience.

Your Team also may uncover unique needs or situations by making a follow-up visit into the home. This information affects how you relate to the student and his or her family. Sensitive, caring follow-up can make the difference in how someone's new journey in faith begins.

Returning the Word *Go* to the Great Commission

We have been appropriately taught that for every three unsaved people we enroll and cultivate in our Sunday Schools, at least one person is likely to be saved within a year. That's wonderful and encouraging, and it motivates us to continue our efforts.

However, it's obvious that on any given week many people choose not to participate in any church's worship or Bible study experience. For every 3 people we enroll there likely are 30, 300, 3,000—or even more in highly populated areas—who are not interested in attending any Bible study group.

How do we reach those people?

Once again, the Great Commission gives us our focus and mandate. Review the first part: "Therefore *go* (italics added) and make disciples of all nations, baptizing them . . . ." (Matt. 28:19-20). This mandate appears in all four Gospels and in the Book of Acts, indicating its priority to our Savior.

But a strange thing has happened in many churches today: the word *come* has been substituted for the word *go*. Have you noticed this shift?

As important as it is, inviting people to come to church, to come to Sunday School, to come to our homes for Bible study, to come to special events is not sufficient. We must (__) into our communities with the gospel, not waiting for people to come to us.

(_____) is how Jesus related to people, and it is how we are to relate. Going reflects our awareness that students are lost without Christ. It reflects our urgency and commitment to share the good news. As obedient Christians, we must intentionally go into our communities to share the good news.

This session will help you train Team members to use the Opinion Poll—one way we have of putting the word *go* back into the Great Commission. It also will help you discover some unique opportunities to make connections between your church and your community.

Important Opportunities

When you first were asked to participate in FAITH training, you likely became excited about the possibility of sharing the gospel with and ministering to students assigned to your Sunday School department or class. You may feel more comfortable visiting your peers than you would visiting people you have never met or about whom you have no information. Then you heard about the Opinion Poll.

Many participants in FAITH training are apprehensive about the Opinion Poll until they see it work. Likely your FAITH Team members will feel just as uneasy until they see how God uses students to make connections through this simple tool. The Opinion Poll gives your FAITH Team some important opportunities:

1. Your Team can help fulfill the (_____ _____) by intentionally going to students who have not necessarily expressed interest in any church's Bible study or worship.
2. The Opinion Poll helps your FAITH Teams go to students who likely would not be contacted or reached by another evangelical congregation.
3. Teams potentially can make a large number of (_____) and students will learn of our interest in them.
4. The Opinion Poll allows your Sunday School to discover and receive information, potentially on a large number of (_____). A growing FAITH ministry demands a large number of prospects for visitation assignments. Since it is preferable to have at least three prospects for each Team each week, it is obvious that Opinion Poll visits will be a great asset to any Faith ministry.
5. Through Opinion Poll surveying, your FAITH Team can help locate (_____ ____ ___ _____).
6. The Opinion Poll helps identify (_____ ___ _____) ways to share the

gospel with people you ordinarily would never encounter.

7. Use of the Opinion Poll will help you grow (____ _____) in talking about spiritual matters and in sharing the gospel with strangers.

This is another major reason we include Opinion Poll visits in FAITH training—for the benefit Team Leaders and members receive. Using the Opinion Poll builds confidence because it places you and your Team with students you don't know and gives you a usable format to dialogue with and get information from persons.

8. The Opinion Poll gives greater opportunity to experience (_____ _____) with students who need to hear the message of the gospel.

Opinion Poll: a Team Effort

As is true with other visits, Opinion Poll visits are a Team effort. The team prays for one another, and each member takes different responsibilities. In general, follow these guidelines when making Opinion Poll visits:

When approaching houses, encourage all Team members to have pleasant expressions on their faces. As your Team approaches each door, make sure one person has been designated to (_____), (_____ _____), and (_____) your church and Team members by first names. Designate one person to record (_____) to the survey on the form.

1. The spokesperson on the Team should be prepared to—
   • state the purpose of this brief survey: to help your church be more responsive to needs in the community;
   • ask permission for them to give their opinion on several brief questions; and
   • (if permission is given), continue by asking the questions.

2. (____ _____) should be prepared to—
   • listen for clues regarding spiritual needs or interests;
   • talk about interests and church involvement;
   • follow up responses to the Key Question in the same ways that were learned in earlier FAITH training.
   (If a *faith* response is given, say something like, "That's wonderful; we're so glad you have trusted Jesus as your Savior. Are you participating in a local church?" If not, offer to enroll him or her in Sunday School and give directions and information about your church. If the person responds with a *works* answer, ask permission to share how the Bible answers the question and move into the gospel presentation.)
   • record as much information as possible about the student and family, including name, address, approximate age, and follow-up opportunities.
   • If a student makes a decision, indicate the decision on the appropriate panels of *A Step of Faith (Student Edition)*. Provide the information needed for the student to know where to attend Sunday School and worship.

The Team member responsible for recording information may need to write rapidly. Data may need to be rewritten on another card after the visit to make sure persons at the church can easily read and transfer this information for follow-up.

Realize that many people will not be at home. Some of the ones who are will not permit you to begin a conversation. In most situations, responses will be shared at the door without the Team's entering the house. However, some people will invite the Team inside.

Always be cordial and respectful. If a person chooses not to participate in the Opinion Poll, be gracious. Note all information discovered (even refusals) on the Opinion Poll.

Even if someone provides partial or incomplete information—for example, only answering two questions or not having time to dialogue—he or she may represent a prospect or prospect family for your church. "Success" in Opinion Poll visits not only occurs when a person accepts Christ during a visit, but also when Teams are sensitive to new prospects and to the potential the church has to strengthen connections to them in the future.

With this perspective, Celebration Time becomes a wonderful opportunity to celebrate Opinion Poll results and their potential for the future. Celebrate—
- changes in how you and your Team view Opinion Poll visits;
- getting information to help your church be more effective in its ministries;
- new prospects and prospect families discovered; and
- individuals who accepted Christ or for whom a word from the Lord was planted.

Celebrate . . . and now begin to follow up!

Using the Student Opinion Poll

The Student Opinion Poll is similar to the Opinion Poll—but the questions are worded so that it is more student-friendly. The Student Opinion Poll is designed for a different purpose, however. The Opinion Poll is to be used as an introduction when FAITH Teams visit door-to-door in a neighborhood. The questions are more general because the person who answers the door may be of any age.

The Student Opinion Poll is created to be used in one-on-one situations between students. There are times when students may be at school, at the mall, a party, or other places where they have an opportunity to get into the FAITH presentation to share Jesus with their friends. It is suggested that the Student Opinion Poll be printed on heavy paper or laminated so students can carry it with them in their wallets or backpacks. Then, when they sense an opportunity to lead the conversation toward spiritual things, the Student Opinion Poll may be used as a basis for dialogue and information, just as the door-to-door Opinion Poll is used.

Jesus Went to People

Jesus frequently engaged people in a discussion of spiritual matters. He often made Himself available and experienced what we might call divine appointments. A classic example is that of the woman at the well (John 4).

Jesus had to go through Samaria (v. 4), to a place where He knew He might not be welcome. He established common ground with the woman. He made transition to spiritual matters. He let the woman know how her most pressing need could be met.

When you think about it, this is the only way that most people will have a chance to hear the gospel. Since they are not coming to us, we must go to them. Remember, this is how Jesus communicated.

Visitation Time
DO IT
As You Go . . .

A Team member once commented there were not enough prospects to visit. One wise Team Leader assigned this student to his Team for one evening. When other Teams got into their cars and headed out for visits, this Team began to walk toward the end of the block. When the girl asked why, the Team Leader said he wanted the Team to see that prospects were everywhere.

Before they reached the corner they met a couple of students walking toward them. The Team Leader greeted them and began a conversation that resulted in the couple's praying to receive Christ. The Team member got the message!

Have you gotten the message? People are lost without Christ and our command is to go to people, just like Jesus did. Prayerfully participate in intentional visits to share the gospel and to find out more about who people in your community are and what they need. Especially observe and pray for the outcome of Opinion Poll visits in this session.

Celebration Time
SHARE IT
As You Return to Share . . .

- Especially highlight "successful" Opinion Poll visits. Does your church have some new opportunities to make connections?
- Other reports and testimonies
- Session 5 Evaluation Card
- Participation Card
- Visitation forms updated with results of visits

The Daily Journey

Day One:
Isaiah 61:1-3; Luke 4:14-30
Hometown Opinion
When you read Luke 4 after reading Isaiah 61 do you get the connection? The Jews had been reading Isaiah 61 for hundreds of years by the time Jesus read this Scripture in Nazareth. People had waited their whole lives for the Scripture to be fulfilled; but when it was, they rejected Christ. Why? The answer is probably a mixture of things, but certainly one of the issues for them was the fact that they knew Jesus so well; He had grown up with them. He had always been around them—how could *He* be the Messiah? (See Luke 4:22.)

Some members of your church may still see you as a child who ran in the hallways and spit up on them in the nursery. Some of your peers at school will remember all the crazy things you did in the past and they will ask you why Jesus is so important to you now. You must be faithful to share and encourage others to know Jesus. God has placed you in their lives to allow them to see the difference He can make. But, you should also be faithful to talk to people who do not know you or your past. Share the gospel with strangers on the street or go house-to-house. These individuals need to know who God is in your life. Sometimes it's easier to talk to a stranger about Jesus than talk to a friend. Which one would you rather do?

Spend some time praying for the area of evangelism that is most difficult for you. Pray that you and your FAITH Team would not just do what is easiest, but that you would do what God wants.

Day Two:
Read Daniel 1
Consistency Out of Sight

It is one thing to do what is right in front of your parents and at church; it's another thing to do it when you are alone or only with your friends. Daniel could have done whatever he wanted when he was in Babylon. He and his friends could have rejected everything they had ever been taught, but they didn't. Did you notice that Daniel made the hard choices to fully obey God, and because of that he was blessed by God? God is the one that takes care of us and guides us, not our parents. We need to live our lives for God, not others.

Another important point in this passage is the change in the heart of the king and the guards when Daniel and the others were faithful to God. You may not see this kind of change in the leadership around you, but if you will live for God in front of strangers, family and friends, God will use your faithfulness to change their lives as well. Are you willing to be used by God to change the life of strangers, family, and friends?

What is the most difficult area of your private life to give over to God? What part of your private life has God changed in the past that has radically affected who you are now?

Pray that you and your FAITH Team will live consistent lives before each other, your families, your church, and total strangers. Pray that your attitude and actions will not distract anyone from hearing and receiving Christ.

Day Three:
Acts 4:32-37
Son of Encouragement

An elderly lady now lives alone. Her husband died years ago and she cannot go many places because she doesn't drive—she is totally dependent on others. But none of her caretakers is a Christian, and she misses going to church and she longs for someone to encourage her in her faith. One evening she hears a timid knock at the door. She greets an adult and two teenagers who are standing there with an opinion poll. She answers the questions and then spends over an hour talking with them about Jesus and her great love for Him.

That is a true story of an opinion poll visit. The FAITH Team thought they were going door-to-door to find a person who needed to hear the gospel. But God wanted to encourage one of His elderly saints and He chose one of His youthful FAITH Teams to do it!

When you are faithful to follow God each day, you never know what He may do through you. Our choice is to be available to God; His choice is how to use us that day to accomplish His plan in the world. Be ready—God may want you to be an encourager today with your time, words, money, smile, friendships, and so on.

What is one way you can encourage other believers today?

Pray that you and your FAITH Team do not become so focused on evangelism in your FAITH visits, that you overlook God's passion for encouraging people.

Day Four:
1 Corinthians 1:26-2:5
An Incredible Formula!

. . . Another evening knocking on doors with no response! Before the FAITH team headed back to the church, they decided to stop and get a soft drink. At the market, one of them thought, *Why not ask the guy behind the counter to answer the opinion poll?* Guess what happened? A divine appointment occurred!

God's Power + A Divine Appointment = An Incredible Event! When you take the power of God's Holy Spirit during a divine appointment, then you are involved in a "God moment" that will reaffirm your faith in Him and your belief in His power. That may happen as you use the opinion poll. It may seem like the "assignment" you started out on just isn't working, but God could have another appointment for your team. If so, make sure to take advantage of it as you watch Him pull events and people together for a divine appointment that will change the lives of everyone involved.

Think back through the last few weeks and write down a "chance encounter" that you now see was really a divine appointment.

Pray that you and your FAITH Team members will be sensitive to watch for divine encounters in everyday life and when they occur you will be bold enough to speak.

Day Five:
Read Colossians 3:1-17
Putting on a New Life

Picture this: A hot summer day, a lawnmower, and you. Sound sweaty? It always feels great to get out of the summer heat and into a shower. You take off your sweaty, smelly, shirt and put on a fresh, clean shirt. Colossians 3 creates a picture of taking off our old "smelly" life and lifestyle and putting on a new life with God.

As a Christian, your life is focused on walking with God and doing everything in life to please Him. You have taken off your old life and put on a new life. So if you date, study, eat, play, work, or talk, you do it for the glory of God. That is who we Christians are in this world.

If there is any part of your life that needs to be "taken off" write it here._____ Spend time praying for God's help in taking off the old life and putting on the new life with Him.

Pray for yourself and your FAITH Team. Pray that you will be faithful to please God in every part of your week. Pray that your life will draw other people to be interested in hearing more about Jesus.

Day Six:
Read Galatians 5:16-26
It is Obvious

You come home from camp, a retreat, or a significant worship time at church and you are more committed than ever to serving Christ and being faithful to His commands. But two weeks later you find yourself in some of the same sins and even more guilt. Why did that happen? Was your devotion insincere? Probably not. You are learning that the Spirit of God within you is at war with your old desires. Whoever you follow at that moment is who wins the war.

Imagine you are playing a game of "Follow the Leader." In front of you, however, are two leaders and they are both encouraging you to follow them. If you follow one, you will walk through life producing impurity, hatred, jealousy, envy, sexual sins, and more. If you follow the other, He will guide you through a life that will produce peace, joy, love, patience, and blessings. Each moment of each day you choose whom you will follow and what your life will produce. In everything you do, keep in step with the Spirit of God today.

List one area where you have followed God's lead and you have seen the benefit of trusting God.

Pray that you and your FAITH Team will walk in step with the Spirit of God today and that the fruit of that relationship will be evident to the people around you. Pray also that you will have opportunities to share the FAITH outline with someone in the next 24 hours.

Day Seven:
Read Hebrews 9:11-15
Costly Forgiveness

When you think about Jesus' sacrifice do you think about the cross only? Most people do. In the Old Testament clean and healthy bulls, sheep, birds, and so forth were sacrificed in the Temple to transfer God's judgment onto the sacrifice for the sins of the person offering the sacrifice.

Because sin is so destructive, forgiveness has always required blood. When Jesus died on the cross He paid the ultimate price—He gave His life. When His blood was poured out on the altar of heaven, He made a way for each person to come to God through His blood, rather than the blood of animals. His sacrifice was enough to take away the sin of every person who has ever lived or ever will live. In Old Testament times not every person was righteous. Some people refused to go to the Temple and offer their sacrifice. So, their guilt remained upon them. They had a choice: either allow the blood of the animal to pay for their sin, or they could pay with their own blood at their death. The same choice exists today: We can either allow Jesus' blood to pay our debt for sin, or we can pay with our own blood at our death. Allowing Jesus to pay brings life in heaven, but paying your own debt results in eternal hell.

What is the hardest part about sharing Christ with the people around you?

Pray for the people around you who need to respond to the offer of forgiveness Jesus provides. Pray that you and your FAITH Team will be bold and loving as you share this week.

The Weekly Sunday School Leadership Team Meeting

Use this space to record ways your FAITH Team impacts the work of your Sunday School department or class. Use the information to report during weekly Sunday School leadership team meetings. Identify actions that need to be taken through Sunday School as a result of prayer concerns, needs identified, visits made by the Team, and decisions made by the students being visited.

Highlight needs and reports affecting your class, department, or age group.

_____

_____

Pray now for teachers and department directors.

How does preparation for Sunday need to consider needs of students or families visited through FAITH?

_____

_____

How will the class begin to follow up on students discovered through the Opinion Poll?

_____

_____

Indicate ways Sunday School leaders can help you and Team members in FAITH.

_____

_____

What areas in your Sunday School do you need to start or strengthen based on input from Opinion Poll visits?

_____

_____

For the Team Leader

This weekly feature suggests actions the Team Leader can take to support Team members, prepare for Team Time, and consider ways to improve visits. This work becomes part of the Team Leader's Home Study Assignments. Add any actions suggested by your church's FAITH strategy.

Support Team Members

❏ Pray for and personally follow up on any Learner who may need personal encouragement.

❏ Contact Team members during the week to remind them you are praying for them and to discuss their participation in FAITH. Seek to encourage Learners. Remember, Learners have overviewed the entire gospel presentation in Session 5 and may have questions about their role in making a visit. Record specific needs and concerns in your Journal margin.

❏ Think of appropriate ways to involve an Assistant Team Leader, if assigned to your Team.

Prepare to Lead Team Time for Session 6

❏ Overview "Team Time" for Session 6.

❏ In a review of Session 5, be prepared to overview the entire gospel presentation.

Prepare to Lead Visits

❏ Review the FAITH Visit Outline.

❏ Do you need to begin gently "pushing" some Learners out of their comfort zones during evangelistic visits? Some may be hesitant to participate fully without some encouragement.

❏ Be prepared to model a visit in which a Team member is asked to lead in a visit—up to asking the Key Question. Think about who might be ready for this opportunity or to share an evangelistic or Sunday School testimony.

❏ Pray for sensitivity as you involve different members in visits and pick up your part of the presentation appropriately and naturally.

❏ Prepare to lead your Team during Celebration Time.

Connecting to Sunday School

❏ Participate in your weekly Sunday School Leadership meeting. Share pertinent information in this meeting and FAITH visit results.

REVIEWING THE FAITH VISIT OUTLINE:

FORGIVENESS AND AVAILABLE

LIBBA GILLUM

AS CORTEZ WALKED PAST THEIR LUNCH TABLE,

Jared and Tony gave him a friendly nod. They watched him as he walked over to a table of new friends and sat down.

"We've known Cortez for a long time now. Remember when we were in third grade and he filled Shay's coat pockets with ketchup?" commented Jared.

"Or the time he hid everybody's socks during P.E?" asked Tony.

"How about the time he went home sick just so he could go watch an early afternoon baseball game?" countered Jared. "To this day, I still don't know how he made that look so real!"

"Those were the days," Tony continued. "But he isn't the same old Cortez any more. He's always doing something to help people. I heard yesterday that he is going on a two-week trip this summer to help build a Habitat for Humanity house. I even heard he was raising money to pay his own way."

Jared interrupted, "He always seems so happy now—I just don't get it. What do you think has made him change? He used to be the best practical joker in our class, but now he seems to be going in a different direction."

TEAM TIME

The team leader leads this time. Learners are primarily responsible for reciting the assigned portion of the FAITH Visit Outline and for discussing any Home Study Assignments.

Keep in mind how Learners also look to leaders as role models, motivators, mentors, and friends. Team Time activities can continue in the car, as the Team travels to and from visits.

Check It

FAITH Visit Outline

❑ Listen while each Learner recites all of *Preparation, Presentation* through the FORGIVENESS statement and verse (Eph.1:7*a*), as well as other key words in *Presentation* and in *Invitation*.

Other Home Study Assignments

❑ Check to see whether Learners shared their evangelistic testimony with two different believers. Briefly discuss how these two believers responded to the testimony.

❑ Discuss benefits Learners are discovering from assigned reading material in *Evangelism Through the Sunday School* and in the FAITHTip, "Nurturing a New Christian."

❑ Make sure Learners are writing in their Journals and keeping up with "The Daily Journey."

Session 5 Debriefing (Overviewing the Gospel Presentation)

❑ Learners have heard the entire gospel presentation by viewing the videotape, hearing the presentation during visits, and overviewing it in Session 5. Ask Learners to share how comfortable they are becoming with understanding the significance of sharing the complete gospel presentation.

❑ Remind Learners that although the gospel presentation is built on the letters in FAITH, *A Step of Faith (Student Edition)* is used to help lead a person to make a commitment to Christ and enroll in Sunday School.

Indicate that each of the following six sessions will focus on letters of the gospel presentation and on how to use the leaflet in leading a student to make a decision to follow Christ.

Help for Strengthening a Visit

❑ Encourage Learners to be constantly in prayer for each other and for the persons being visited. Emphasize the importance of looking for opportunities to make connections that allow us to share the gospel while, at the same time, being sensitive to the needs of the person being visited. Call attention to the fact that many times a Team might inadvertently close a door to receptivity to the gospel because they come across as "pushy."

❑ Remind Team members of the importance of being available to the Holy Spirit and of relying on Him to prepare a student for the gospel. We are to be prepared to share and to know how to compassionately lead someone to make the commitments that will forever change his or her life.

Notes

_____

_____

_____

_____

Actions I Need to Take with Learners During the Week

_____

_____

_____

A Quick Review

1. Which of the following statements is (_____)about using the Opinion Poll?
    a. Use the Opinion Poll when your FAITH ministry needs more prospects to visit.
    b. Ask Opinion Poll questions if you discover a person is already a Christian or a church member.
    c. A Team can ask Opinion Poll questions while standing at the door, rather than entering the house to take the brief survey.
    d. Even if a person chooses not to answer the questions, try to get basic information to help make a connection between him or her and the FAITH Team, your Sunday School class, and department.

2. In the space provided, describe the purpose you share for the Opinion Poll with the person you are visiting.

_____

_____

3. Place a checkmark beside the correct response(s) to the following question: What should you do if a student answers the last question on the Opinion Poll with a _faith_ answer?
    ___ a. Celebrate his or her response, ask that he or she briefly share what Jesus means to them, and ask for prayer for your church's ministry.
    ___ b. Try to enroll the student in the appropriate Sunday School class if not participating in any ongoing Bible study group.
    ___ c. Respond with a loud "Amen!" and jump up and down in celebration.

4. Place a checkmark beside the correct response(s) to the following question: What should you do if a student answers the last question on the Opinion Poll with a _works_ answer?
    ___ a. Record the response, thank him, and move on to the next house.
    ___ b. Tell him he is going to hell without Jesus, invite him to Sunday School, and leave.
    ___ c. Ask for permission to share what the Bible says about answering that question. With permission, share the FAITH gospel presentation and use A Step of Faith (Student Edition) to ask whether the person is willing to accept God's forgiveness.

God's Forgiveness:
Vital to the Gospel

It's important that you have a growing grasp of the biblical concept of God's forgiveness being available to all—but not automatic. You may encounter someone who does not understand the need for God's forgiveness. You might talk with a student who does not realize that God loves and is willing to forgive him or her. During this session we will identify information designed to help supplement your understanding of forgiveness and to be prepared to further explain it if needed.

First, let's focus on God's forgiveness. Ephesians 1:7*a* is the verse we quote to highlight Forgiveness: "In Him (meaning Jesus) we have redemption through His blood, the forgiveness of sins" (NKJV).

Several significant words in this verse need to be highlighted to build on our understanding of God's forgiveness. While most presentations of the gospel will go smoothly and without interruption, in a few cases these words might trigger a question. For example, what would you do if a student asked for clarification of the word *redemption*?

• Redemption—"To redeem is to (___ ____ _____). God paid the ransom to himself in order to satisfy the demands of his holy, righteous nature. This he did through Jesus' death and resurrection. 'God was in Christ, reconciling the world unto himself'
(2 Cor. 5:19)."[1]

First Corinthians 6:20*a* says, "You were bought at a price" (NIV). This profound statement introduces us to the concept of being redeemed.

One picture that illustrates redemption is a slave market where persons were sold and bought. *Redemption* describes the action God took in purchasing you from the "slave market of sin." He paid for your (_____ ____ ___) by sacrificing His own Son on the cross.

• Blood—Jesus purchased, or redeemed, us and He did so with His own blood (1 Pet. 1:18-19). Hebrews 9:22 declares, "Without the shedding of blood there is no forgiveness" (NIV). Likewise, from 1 John 1:7*b* we read, "the blood of Jesus, his Son, purifies us from all sin" (NIV).

God requires payment for sin, and that payment is death (Rom. 6:23). The cross of Jesus Christ is central in understanding God's forgiveness and salvation. Jesus was put to death for our sins (Rom. 4:25). He came specifically to die for our sins. His blood was shed "for the forgiveness of sins" (Matt. 26:28b, NIV).

"The cross of Christ will never be understood unless it is seen that thereon the Saviour was dealing with the sins of all mankind."[2] The reality is that Jesus was crucified. Spikes were driven through His flesh to suspend Him on the cross. He bled and died and was buried. All four Gospels (Matt. 27:33-61; Mark 15:22-47; Luke 23:23-56; John 19:16-42) describe the brutal execution Jesus endured. Hebrews 9:11-14 is one of many passages that remind us of the significance of Jesus' shedding blood for salvation.

• Forgiveness—Peter climaxed one of his sermons with this declaration: "All the prophets testify about him (Jesus) that everyone who believes in him receives forgiveness of sins through his name" (Acts 10:43, NIV). Forgiveness is defined as "an act of God's (_____) to forget forever and not hold people of faith accountable for sins they confess; to a lesser degree the gracious human act of not holding wrong acts against a person."[3]

In the Old Testament, God required the sacrificial system of the covenant relationships to show the seriousness of and payment for sin. "The forgiveness of God, channeled through the sacrificial offering, was an act of mercy freely bestowed by God, not purchased by the one bringing the offering. . . . Jesus is the perfect and final Sacrifice through which God's forgiveness is mediated to every person."[4]

Jesus taught His disciples to pray by emphasizing God's forgiveness as well as our forgiving others (Matt. 6:14). Likewise, Jesus demonstrated a portrait of God's forgiveness when He said, while nailed to the cross, "Father, forgive them, for they do not know what they are doing" (Luke 23:34, NIV).

• Sin—In the Bible *sin* always refers to the actions and attitudes of rebellion against God. The results of sin "are guilt, separation from God, loss of fellowship [with God], and a life of hardship, anxiety and death lived under the wrath of God."[5]

Many people have a difficult time seeing themselves as sinners. The downplay of the concept of sin by certain groups today—who refer to such factors as sickness, heredity, or other forces beyond our control rather than to rebellion against God—has all but stripped the word of its real meaning. The reality is that (_____ __ _____ __ ___ _____ ___), and the punishment for sin is separation from God.

If, during a presentation of the gospel, someone protests that he is not a sinner, ask whether you can talk more later. You will be talking much more about humanity's sinful nature when you come to I (IMPOSSIBLE).

If an explanation is requested at the time, suggest this way of thinking: Most people can identify themselves as sinners when they hear three categories of sins: *sins of commission* (those actions you commit against another, including against God); *sins of omission* (those good things you fail to do); and *secret sins* (those attitudes that are against another person or against God).

It is almost impossible to separate the truths of God's forgiveness and love from reference to our sins. We realize how great is His love for us when we learn what He did to redeem us from the consequences of our sins.

Psalm 103:10-12 reminds us: "He does not treat us as our sins deserve or repay us according to our iniquities. For as high as the heavens are above the earth so great is his love for those who fear him; as far as the east is from the west, so far has he removed our transgressions from us" (NIV).

God's Forgiveness: Based in His Great Love and Mercy

God's forgiveness is available to all! John 3:16 announces, "For God so loved the world that He gave His only begotten Son, that whoever believes in Him shall not perish but have everlasting life" (NKJV).

The Bible speaks of God's forgiveness as being an expression of His love. Many passages refer to God's loving us so much that He was willing to provide the sacrifice to save us from the serious consequences of our sin. Here are but a few verses that remind us of God's love for the redeemed:

• John 15:13, NIV—"Greater love has no one than this, that he lay down his life for his friends."
• Romans 5:8, NIV—"But God demonstrated his own love for us in this: While we were still sinners, Christ died for us."

- Ephesians 2:4-5, NIV—"But because of his great love for us, God, who is rich in mercy, made us alive in Christ even when we were dead in transgressions—it is by grace you have been saved."
- First John 3:1, NIV—"How great is the love the Father has lavished on us, that we should be called children of God!"
- First John 4:10, NIV—"This is love: not that we loved God, but that he loved us and sent his Son as an atoning sacrifice for our sins."

Read John 3:16 once more. "For God so loved the world that He gave His only begotten Son, that whoever believes in Him shall not perish but have everlasting life" (NKJV). As simple and straightforward as this verse is, it seems there could be no misunderstanding that God's forgiveness is available to all but is not automatic.

Why "Available But Not Automatic" Is Essential to the Gospel

Many people do not believe that a belief in Jesus Christ is the absolute requirement for salvation. This belief system teaches that ultimately all people will be allowed to enter into heaven; this is called universalism. "All religions lead to God" is the supposed motto of this belief system. It is inclusive because it accepts all beliefs as long as a person is sincere.

Such people share no concern about evangelism and about seeing people come to Christ. There is a major danger in (_____) Scripture in this way.

"Christianity is inclusive in that God meant everyone when He said 'whosoever' in John 3:16. Even so, Christianity is exclusive as Jesus Christ is the only way to the Father and heaven . . . (John 14:6). Any other worldview of Christianity is unbiblical and killing to the church of Jesus Christ and world evangelism."[6]

Many religious groups worship God or include Him as a major part of their belief systems. What they fail to recognize—and what is the distinctive of Christianity—is that Jesus is the only way to God and the only means of receiving God's forgiveness and salvation.

Another way many people overlook the *But Not Automatic* part of God's forgiveness is summed up with a (_____) answer to the Key Question. These people cannot accept the fact that salvation is not attained by their own effort, by being good to others, and by refraining from doing extremely bad things.

According to some current polls, most people see themselves as acceptable to God because they are not bad people. There is no evidence in Scripture to support this erroneous view.

In reality, this view is exactly opposite to what is declared throughout the Scripture. Jesus said: "Enter through the narrow gate. For wide is the gate and broad is the road that leads to destruction, and many enter through it. But small is the gate and narrow the road that leads to life, and only a few find it" (Matt. 7:13-14, NIV). This verse identifies for us the main reason we must give emphasis to the *But Not Automatic* point in the FAITH gospel presentation.

This may be the most misunderstood point in the gospel. Many people seem to believe that entering heaven when we die is more or less automatic.

Second Corinthians 4:4 is very instructive at this point: "The god of this age has blinded the minds of unbelievers, so that they cannot see the light of the gospel of the glory of Christ, who is the image of God" (NIV).

The blindness mentioned in this verse refers to those who do not believe the glorious gospel of Christ.

The longer you are involved in the FAITH evangelism strategy, the more you will realize the truth of this verse. It seems that the reason most people think they are OK is that they judge themselves (horizontally) in comparison to their neighbors—and so feel they are as good as other people. The reality and problem is that we are judged (vertically) by the absolute requirements of a Holy God.

The *all* of the gospel is like a two-edged sword; it (____ ____ ____). All have sinned (Rom. 3:23), but all may be saved (John 3:16). The qualifier is belief in the saving work of Jesus. Without belief in Him there can be no salvation. God's forgiveness is available to all, but it is not automatic.

The following is a familiar illustration of this concept, but it is still a good one:

A highwire artist displayed his skills before a large audience. Several times he walked a tightrope from one point to another high above the floor. He then asked the audience if they believed he could roll a wheelbarrow across the high wire. Everyone raised their hands, but when he asked for a volunteer to sit in the wheelbarrow as he rolled it across the high wire, he had no one to volunteer. This means, of course, that no one truly believed he could do it.

All who truly believe in Christ will enter heaven.

---

[1] Herschel H. Hobbs, *The Baptist Faith and Message* (Nashville: Convention Press, Rev. 1996), 49.

[2] *The Illustrated Bible Dictionary* (Inter-Varsity Press, 1980), 148.

[3] Earl C. Davis, "Forgiveness, "*Holman Bible Dictionary* (Nashville: Holman Bible Publishers, 1991), 509.

[4] Ibid, 510.

[5] Ibid., 510.

[6] Bobby Welch, *Evangelism Through the Sunday School: A Journey of FAITH* (Nashville: LifeWay Press, 1997), 142.

Visitation Time

DO IT

As you go . . .

Be aware that many people expend a lot of effort to look good, act good, and appear better than their neighbors. The Scriptures tell us no one is good, not even one. People are lost without Christ, just as you were until you decided to accept God's forgiveness in Christ.

Just as this is a significant point in the gospel presentation, so are you at a significant time in your FAITH training and in your growth as a Great Commission Christian.

Celebration Time

SHARE IT

As you return to share . . .

Reports can help Learners clarify ways to respond to how a student answers the Key Question. Also handle—
• Reports and testimonies
• Session 6 Evaluation Card
• Participation Card
• Visitation forms updated with results of visits

The Daily Journey

Day One:
Read Colossians 1:13-20
Who is That Guy?
You are sitting at a restaurant enjoying your meal when you look up and see the greatest player to ever play the game. You choke on your food when you see him and nearly pass out when you realize it really is him. You want to talk to him (really, you want your friends to know that you talked to him!) but you think there is no way that guy would ever speak to you.

Now change the scene a little: It's the same restaurant and the God who spoke and made the greatest player ever to play the game walks in. Before you realize what is happening, God himself sits down at your table, calls you by name, and asks about your day. Seem far fetched?

God Himself rescued you from your old life and has given you new life in Jesus. Jesus is the image of the invisible God. He is the one who has all authority and power, but He still desires a relationship with you. He holds the whole universe together, but He wants to forgive you of every sin you have ever thought. He is the head of the church, but He is available to you and all of your friends.

If Jesus were to physically sit down with you right now, what would you say to Him?

Pray that you will not become distant from God and lose track of the availability of a close relationship with Him. Pray that your FAITH Team will remember that people around you need to hear and know about who Jesus is.

Day Two:
Read Galatians 3:10-14
Obey Everything

In Old Testament times everyone lived under the curse of disobedience. And that remained the case until Jesus took the curse of mankind with Him to the cross. Now we no longer need to follow a set of laws and rules to gain God's approval; our task is to follow Jesus because He paid our debt. The Holy Spirit lives within each of us who has accepted Christ and He guides our daily life as we listen and obey Him. We Christians are people who have been forgiven and set free from the law and the curse of disobedience to the law. We live as forgiven people, not because of what we have done, but because of what Jesus did in our place. The Holy Spirit within us is our guarantee of the promise of forgiveness and guidance.

Have you done something in your life that you feel sure God will not forgive you for doing? Write that sin in this space then allow God to explain to you how much He loves you and how He has or will forgive you of that sin.
_____There is no sin too big for God to forgive.

Thank God right now for the forgiveness of sin in your life. You have been taken out from under the curse of sin when you accepted Christ. Pray that you and your FAITH Team can clearly communicate this truth to people who are still trying to work off the curse of disobedience.

Day Three:
Read Luke 23:39-43
What Do I Do to Get Forgiveness?

If God is going to forgive you, you better do something *really big* to earn His forgiveness, right? You should clean up your life and prove to God that you really mean it when you ask for forgiveness, right? Wrong, wrong, and really wrong!

Read part of the crucifixion account in Luke 23:39-43. Three men were dying that day—two of them for their sins, and the other for the sins of the two men. It's ironic that one of the men rejected Jesus' forgiveness to the very end, but the other man accepted Jesus with his dying breath. It is amazing to hear Jesus pour love and encouragement on the criminal who received Him, even though the man was a criminal and he could do nothing to prove himself to God in the final moments of his life.

The criminal on the cross is one of the greatest examples that forgiveness is not about how good you are or how much you clean your life up; it is about trusting Christ only. Forgiveness is because of God's great love, not our great effort.

Have you tried to "earn" God's forgiveness in some way for a past sin? If so, listen again to the voice of Jesus assuring the criminal on the cross that it was not the man's actions, but Jesus' grace that brings forgiveness. Write down any action that you have done to try to earn forgiveness. When you finish, release those areas to God. _____
_____

Spend some time today asking God to show you the areas of your life that are inconsistent with the life of Christ. Understand that God will still forgive you of those sins just like He forgave your sin when you accepted Him. Pray that you and your FAITH Team will live today as a great example of God's forgiveness to other people.

Day Four:
Read Luke 7:36-50
Who Loves More?

Sometimes those of us who have grown up in church and live around Christians forget how much we have been forgiven. That can cause us to live a life with very little gratitude. Forgiveness is a big gift. The woman at Jesus' feet did not have to prove her love to get Jesus' forgiveness, she was only expressing incredible gratitude for the love and forgiveness she has already received from Him. Stop for a few minutes and reflect. How much have you been forgiven? Do you love much because you remember how much you have been forgiven or do you love Jesus little because you think you do not need his grace very much anymore?

Write a day or time in your life when you sinned much and needed much forgiveness. Reflect on your desperate need for Jesus' grace and allow the quantity of your sin to remind you of the quantity of His love. Love much today because you have been loved and forgiven of much.

Spend some time reflecting on how Jesus has forgiven you. Pray that you and your FAITH Team would live lives of gratitude this week.

Day Five:
Read Matthew 7:13-14
Available, But Not With Luggage

The sign on the door says, "One person at a time—no luggage." As you approach the door, you think, *No kidding! Look how narrow that door is!* Then you see a man walk up wearing a backpack. He wants to go through the door, but not if he has to leave his backpack, so he begins looking for another way in. Next come three girls—one of them wants to go through the door, but she will not go unless her friends go. Her friends choose not to go because they would have to leave their purses, so all three walk away.

It's a safe bet that you know students who want to go to heaven, but not through accepting Jesus—that would mean they would have to set aside their old life, lifestyle, and sin. Or they will not accept Christ because their friends don't follow Him. It's amazing that the doorway to heaven is always open, but few people go through it because of their luggage. They hope there is another way to heaven that allows them to do what they want, when they want. They ignore the door that says, "One person at a time—no luggage."

What lifestyle, attitude, or habit are you carrying around? Have you walked through Jesus' door, then tried to pick up some "luggage" on the other side of the door? Write down any habit, attitude, action, or words in your life now that do not honor Jesus.

Pray that you and your FAITH Team will not become discouraged as you share Christ with other people. Sometimes people reject the truth right in front of them. Don't give up—many people desperately need directions to the door that is Jesus Christ.

Day Six:
Read Hebrews 12:14-17
Impossible Is a Big Word

How do you get back something you have lost? In the Old Testament Esau gave away his rights as the firstborn son (all the money, privileges, and blessing) to his younger brother Jacob in exchange for a meal. Sound crazy? It was crazy! Even though Esau regretted it for the rest of his life, he could never get his birthright back because it was gone.

Hebrews 12 tells us that without holiness no one can see God. The problem is, all of us gave away our holiness when we committed our first sin; although we wish it could be different, it is not. Can you clean your life up enough to erase what happened in the past? No. It's impossible. You won't go to heaven because you have turned your life around—you will go to heaven because when you accepted Christ, God forgave you, and the holiness of Jesus was placed on you. Without that gift, you could never see God no matter how many good things you did or how many semesters of FAITH you took. God loves you and He has placed holiness on you because of His great love and your acceptance of Him.

Write a prayer of thanks to God for the incredible grace He has placed on you._____

_____
_____

Pray for yourself and your FAITH Team. Pray that you will not become arrogant or conceited in your mission. Pray that you will not forget that it is not your actions that make you holy, it is the holiness of Jesus that gives you entrance into heaven and connection to God through the Holy Spirit.

Day Seven:
Read 1 Timothy 2:1-6
It is Impossible

What if someone pushed you overboard in the middle of the Pacific Ocean with no lifejacket? It's a horrible thought because it would be thousands of miles to shore and it's impossible for a person to swim that far. Your strength is limited, so your only hope is that someone comes to rescue you. It is like that with God—people spend their whole lives trying to earn their salvation and swim out of the ocean of sin. In reality, their only hope is to have a Savior.

In Paul's letter to Timothy, he gives a picture of God's desire for people. God wants everyone to be saved. He is seeking all people because there is only one way to heaven and a personal relationship to God—through Jesus. We must pray for all leadership, peers, and strangers that they will open their hearts to the gospel since we know that without a personal relationship with God, it is impossible for any person to go to heaven.

Write down the name of someone you know who is trying to be good enough to go to heaven. Pray that they will realize the magnitude of their sin this week and respond to Jesus._____

Pray for teachers and other people in authority that need to be saved. Pray that you will honor God by honoring them. Pray also that you and your FAITH Team will not fail to share the truth and love of God with people around you this week.

The Weekly Sunday School Leadership Team Meeting

Use this space to record ways your FAITH Team impacts the work of your Sunday School department or class. Use the information to report during weekly Sunday School leadership team meetings. Identify actions that need to be taken through Sunday School as a result of prayer concerns, needs identified, visits made by the Team, and decisions made by the students being visited.

Highlight needs and reports affecting your class, department, or age group.

_____

_____

Pray now for this important meeting.

What are ways the department or class can seek to impact the lives of students who do not realize both the availability and the requirements of God's forgiveness?

_____

_____

How does preparation for Sunday need to take into consideration that some students who attend might consider themselves going to heaven because they are good people (a *works* answer)?

_____

_____

For Further Reading

Read pages 140-45 of *Evangelism Through the Sunday School: A Journey of FAITH* by Bobby Welch. If you had had the experience with the cab driver (described on p. 141), what would you have said?

For the Team Leader

This weekly feature suggests actions the Team Leader can take to support Team members, prepare for Team Time, and consider ways to improve visits. This work becomes part of the Team Leader's Home Study Assignments. Add any actions suggested by your church's FAITH strategy.

Support Team Members
- ❑ Contact Team members during the week. Remind them you are praying for them. Discuss prayer concerns and answers to prayer.
- ❑ Record specific needs and concerns of Team members in the space provided.

Prepare to Lead Team Time
- ❑ Review Home Study Assignments of Team members.
- ❑ Review "Team Time" for Session 7.

Prepare to Lead Visits
- ❑ Review the FAITH Visit Outline.
- ❑ Be prepared to explain the significance of God's forgiveness.

Connecting to Sunday School
- ❑ Share information from the weekly Sunday School leadership meeting.

NOTES

Reviewing the
FAITH Visit Ouline:
impossible
and Turn

LIBBA GILLUM

PATRICIA COULD HARDLY WAIT for the first day of school. She prayed for an opportunity to share Jesus with others at school. Her first class was a science class and lab partners were being assigned.

Meet lab partner number one: Buddy. He's your basic nice guy. He always gets his homework done and everyone likes him. His name really fits him because he makes friends easily and never causes any trouble. He comes from a good family, but they never go to church. In some ways, Buddy doesn't see the need for church; he is more well-behaved than most of the people he knows who go to church anyway.

Lab partner number two is Tara. Her name also seems to fits her (terror!). She is the roughest girl in school. She has been in and out of trouble. Her all-black wardrobe can intimidate just about anyone, not to mention her ability to out-curse most grown men. Her family has pretty much given up on her, and they are waiting for her to graduate and move away.

As Patricia heard the names of her lab partners, she thought of something from her FAITH training—*I is for impossible; T is for turn*.

TEAM TIME

The team leader leads this time. Learners are primarily responsible for reciting the assigned portion of the FAITH Visit Outline and for discussing any Home Study Assignments.

Keep in mind how Learners also look to leaders as role models, motivators, mentors, and friends. Team Time activities can continue in the car, as the Team travels to and from visits.

Check It

FAITH Visit Outline
❑ Listen while each Learner recites all of *Preparation;* all of F and A— FORGIVENESS and AVAILABLE; the key words for I, T, and H in *Presentation*; and the key outline words in *Invitation*.   Indicate your approval and any suggestions for improvement.

Practice
❑ Give Learners an opportunity to practice reciting the portion of the FAITH Visit Outline they have learned up to this point.

Other Home Study Assignments
❑ Check to see whether Learners listed two or three students who might have a particular interest in knowing that God's forgiveness is available for them. Discuss how your FAITH Team can impact their lives with the gospel and with ministry. Also discuss the reading material that was assigned. Encourage Learners to continue writing in "The Daily Journey" (their journaling section).

Session 6 Debriefing (F is for Forgiveness)
❑ Learners are beginning to learn the gospel presentation. God's forgiveness becomes the foundation upon which the rest of the gospel is shared. It is vital to understand that God's forgiveness is based on the free gift of grace that God gives because of the sacrificial death of Jesus. As part of the gospel presentation, each letter is accompanied by at least one verse.

Help for Strengthening a Visit
❑ Many people will not be aware of the free gift of forgiveness that God offers. Some are living with guilt and remorse because of sin in their lives. Others are insensitive to the fact that they are sinners who reject God's love and rebel against Him. The message of forgiveness may be an unfamiliar one to them.

Emphasize the importance of showing compassion and understanding with each person being visited. It helps to remember that your Team is not going to be judgmental but to share that there is real hope because God provides forgiveness through faith in Jesus.

❑ Have Learners had opportunity to practice parts of the gospel presentation in home visits? In visiting a Sunday School member or fellow Christian, sometimes practice becomes an option.

❑ Have Learners seen someone come to know Christ in a home visit?

Notes

_____
_____
_____
_____

Actions I Need to Take with Learners During the Week

_____
_____
_____
_____

A Quick Review

The longer you are involved in the FAITH evangelism strategy, the more you will realize the truth of this verse: "The god of this age has blinded the minds of unbelievers, so that they cannot see the light of the gospel of the glory of Christ, who is the image of God" (2 Cor. 4:4, NIV).

Many students you will visit think they are OK. They don't recognize themselves as sinners because they are trying to live right and feel they have not done extremely wrong or harmful acts. They judge themselves in comparison to their neighbors and so feel they are as good as others. The reality and problem is that we are judged by the absolute requirements of Holy God.

The _all_ of the gospel is like a two-edged sword; it cuts both ways. All have sinned (Rom. 3:23), but all may be saved (John 3:16). The qualifier is belief in the saving work of Jesus. Without belief in Him, there can be no salvation.

God's forgiveness is available to all, but it is not automatic.

It Is Impossible for God to Allow Sin into Heaven

This is a startling statement, particularly when people think that their "presumed innocence" gets them into heaven. Many people automatically think that heaven is the destination of everyone who has not committed the most horrible of crimes.

Think about how our culture refers to deceased persons as "up there," "at rest," or even "with God." Some people casually refer to heaven as the next automatic destination. _Certainly, God would not keep any good person out of heaven,_ they seem to think.

Look at the statement for the letter I (IMPOSSIBLE) once more: "It is impossible for God to allow sin into heaven." We already have learned (in Student FAITH Basic) that it is impossible because of who God is and because of who we are. Let's investigate these realities in more detail.

It is impossible because of who God is.—

God is (_____). We easily acknowledge this fact by reciting the wonderful truths of John 3:16. The Bible expresses over and over the fact that God not only loves us but that He _is_ love (1 John 4:16).

God's love is (_____). He loves us no matter what actions we take.

Imagine a loving, caring parent who has a rebellious child. With few exceptions, such a parent will love and cherish the child no matter how old he or she is and no matter what actions the child might take. It is hard for us to realize unconditional love since we often are influenced by people who love "with strings attached."

God's love (_____ ___ _____ ___ __). God's love also provides us with a choice of whether to obey or reject Him.

Love is the attribute of God that almost everyone likes and with which almost everyone agrees. It also is this attribute that causes some people to question, "If God is a God of love, how can He not want everyone to go to heaven and be with Him eternally?"

There is more to God's nature than just love. Just as a beautifully cut diamond has more than one facet, so does God have more than one dimension. Each attribute is complete and helps us understand the entire picture of God.

Yes, God is love; but God also is (____ ___ ____). Many cults can be traced to a distorted emphasis on one of the attributes of God to the exclusion of others that are vital. God cannot allow sin into heaven because sin is completely opposite to His perfect (_____ ___ _____).

God is holy. Nothing in our mind can possibly begin to comprehend the holiness and perfection of God. Words do little to express such grandeur. Pictures help us only a bit.

The Old Testament is full of imagery describing the holiness of God and the consequences of any (unholy) thing or person being in His presence. The entire sacrificial system was to help people realize the need for their sins to be paid by an unblemished lamb before they could be acceptable to God. The Temple was designed to help show the need for humanity to have a mediator go into God's presence (then separated by a symbolic curtain).

God is so holy that no one could survive a look at His presence. Isaiah 6:1-5 is a magnificent passage describing Isaiah's dream of being in the holy presence of God. One observation from this passage is that when we come into God's presence our first response is, "I am ruined! For I am a man of unclean lips" (v. 5a, NIV). A further response is, "Here am I. Send me!" (v. 8b, NIV).

God is just. It is important to gain an awareness of God's holiness to understand that God's justice simply *cannot* allow sin into heaven.

God cannot ignore or condone evil. Just as a court judge must pronounce sentence based on the laws of the land, so is God the Almighty Judge Who will judge every person according to his or her sin (Rev. 20:4).

(___ _____ __ _____ ____); it does not compromise based on the truth. Every sin is intolerable by God, and He demands that all sin be punished.

(___ _____ ___ ____) by becoming the Sacrifice to pay for sin for all time. The Bible is clear that whoever believes in Him as that Sacrifice on his or her behalf (John 3:16) will be judged as righteous because of the righteousness of Christ.

God's great love for us does not stop even when we rebel and sin against Him, but the fact remains that His judgment regarding sin is without mercy. Unless a person has accepted Jesus' blood sacrifice and acknowledged Him as his or her Savior, there is really no mercy in judgment. The stark reality is that when a person dies in unbelief, God's judgment will be without mercy. (See John 3:36; Heb. 9:27.)

God cannot allow sin into heaven because of who we are.

Is there any student in this FAITH training who is without sin? The message of Romans 3:23 is to us as well as to the students we are assigned to visit. It is obvious that we are all sinners by nature and that we are visiting people who are sinners by nature. The difference for us (and for the Christians your Team visits) is that we have realized that we are sinners and cannot do anything to be saved—apart from acknowledging that Jesus paid the penalty for our sins.

Many Christians have learned that sin is "(_____ ___ ____)." Although we have only one word for sin, the Bible uses many different words to describe the different aspects of sin. Consider some of the following meanings and examples from Scripture.

Old Testament concepts include:
• moral and spiritual badness (Prov. 21:10);
• ethical wrong (Zeph. 3:4);
• moral or spiritual failure (Ex. 10:16);
• refusal to obey a command (Ex. 7:14);
• rebellion or transgression against God (Hos. 14:9);

New Testament concepts include:
• some wrong done to someone else (Heb. 8:12);
• a departure from that which is right (1 John 5:17);
• a lack of belief (Matt. 13:58);
• unfaithfulness or the betrayal of a trust (Rom. 3:3);
• a description of those whose purpose in life is to satisfy desire (Eph. 4:18);
• covetousness (Mark 4:19);
• a desire for something forbidden as in lust (2 Pet. 2:10);
• a hatred or enmity against God (Rom. 8:7)

Be very careful when you are visiting that you (__ ___ ___ _____ __ _____ __ _____). Remember, you can identify with the worst sinners. Until you chose God's way over your own, you were just as guilty as they!

It is virtually impossible for an unsaved person to be open to the gospel until he or she understands themselves to be a sinner and in need of redemption. Romans 3:10 states that there is no one "righteous, not even one" (NIV). When you identify yourself with the truth of the verse, it makes it easier for the student you are visiting to see himself in that same condition.

But how can a sinful person enter heaven, where God allows no sin?

To Turn Means to Repent

The Bible teaches the necessity of changing our attitudes and actions from rebellion against God to submission and obedience to God. The words used most often to describe this change are (_____ __ _____). The reason we share the illustration about the car in the FAITH Visit Outline is because *repent* basically means *to turn*.

Repentance is an (_____). A definition of repentance is "a feeling of regret, a changing of the mind, or a turning from sin to God."[3] There must be a remorse for sin and a true decision to change, an intentional desire to turn from sin to follow Christ.

Repentance is also an (_____). Unless a person changes the actions of sin and turns to living in obedience to the instructions of God, there has been no real repentance. Jesus preached repentance and associated it with one's acceptance of Him. Those who were unrepentant were those who rejected Him; those who received Him were truly repentant. Paul's preaching virtually identified repentance with belief in Christ.

Jesus gave a wonderful description of repentance when He shared the parable of the prodigal son who returned to the father (Luke 15:11-32).[4]

The letters I (IMPOSSIBLE) and T (TURN) are the crux of the gospel message. You are briefly sharing the bad news/good news, both of which must be understood. We move from a hopeless state (as a result of our sins) to a hopeful result (because of Christ, we can turn from sin and turn to Christ.)

T also stands for (____ _____ ____). Jesus said that unless we become as little children, we will not be able to see the kingdom of heaven. Just as *repent is* both an attitude and an action, so does trust describe both attitudes and actions.

A person who trusts Christ believes Jesus is who He says He is. FAITH Teams may encounter any number of misconceptions about who Jesus is, including that He was merely—
- a miracle worker;
- a great person;
- an esteemed teacher;
- the one who established Christianity;
- leader of the Jews; and/or
- a prophet.

While all of these characteristics are true, they do not fully describe who Jesus is— the only Son of God, fully human and fully divine. Scriptures affirm Jesus to be virgin-born (Matt. 1:18); tempted as we are, yet sinless (Heb. 4:15); the Sacrifice who makes possible our salvation (1 Cor. 15:3b); and our risen Lord (1 Cor. 15:4a). He intercedes for us even now (Rom. 8:34) and promises to come again for us (Acts 1:11).

While Teams will not be able to get into all of the significant biblical doctrines, someone who trusts Jesus is expressing belief that Jesus is Who He says He is—the Son of God and the only One able to save. A person who trusts Christ believes Jesus means what He says about His dying on our behalf, being raised by God from the dead, and returning in glory to claim us as His own for eternity.

A person who trusts Christ does what Jesus teaches, even though he does not understand all the implications. Many people use the words *trust* and *faith* as synonyms. Reflect on the following story to illustrate trust:

Identical twins grew up in a loving family. Most people could not tell them apart. As they grew older it became obvious that though they looked alike, their actions were quite different. One (John) was good and always showed a concern for others, while the other (Ron) was disobedient and seemed to care for the needs of no one but himself.

When they were grown they went their separate ways. John was good and compassionate, and a helper to others. Ron, on the other hand, lived a lawless lifestyle that always kept him in trouble. One night Ron was involved in a failed bank robbery in which he killed someone. He was caught, tried, and sentenced to death.

When John learned of his brother's plight, he knew he must try to save Ron.

When John learned that Ron would be in a local hospital for tests, he developed a plan. He entered the hospital, changed into prison clothes, and at the right moment allowed his brother to escape while taking his place as the prisoner.

The day for the execution came, and John was put to death instead of Ron. Later, the weight of guilt became unbearable for Ron. He regretted the actions he had taken and his good brother's death in his stead. Ron confessed what had happened. He was told he was free because the sentence for his crime had been carried out.

In a sense, this is what happens for the person who accepts the salvation that Jesus provides. We can be set free only if we will believe that "Christ died for our sins according to the Scriptures, and that He was buried, and that he rose again the third day according to the Scriptures" (1 Cor. 15 3b-4, NKJV). Likewise, "If you confess with your mouth the Lord Jesus and believe in your heart that God has raised Him from the dead, you will be saved" (Rom. 10:9, NKJV).

[1] Adapted from Bobby H. Welch, *Evangelism Through the Sunday School: A Journey of FAITH* (Nashville: LifeWay Press, 1997), 123.

[2] C. B. Hogue, The Doctrine of Salvation (Nashville: Convention Press, 1978), 22-43.

[3] Naymond Keathley, "Repentance," *Holman Bible Dictionary*, Trent Butler, Gen. Ed. (Nashville: Holman Bible Publishers, 1991), 1175.

[4] Ibid, 1174.

Visitation Time
DO IT
As You Go . . .

We've talked about universalism and beliefs you may encounter when you visit someone with this philosophy. "Do you know anyone in your church who claims to be a universalist, that is, a person who truly believes that everyone's going to heaven? We live in a society of universalists. U.S. News and World Report ran a cover story on hell. A survey was included revealing that 60 percent of Americans believe in a literal hell while only 4 percent think they'll go there.

"Unfortunately, Christians act like universalists if they never share their faith. If we fail to witness, we demonstrate the attitude that all will go to heaven, and this simply is not the case."[1]

As you participate in FAITH visits and FAITH training, you help many students whom you visit change their thinking and realize that separation from God and hell are realities unless they make a distinct choice. In addition, by your example and your experiences you challenge church members who, for whatever reason, fail to share their faith.

Pray not only for prospects you will encounter, but also for church members who may need a greater sense of urgency to share their faith. Pray that the Lord of the harvest will motivate and use them.

[1] David Self, *Good News for Adults: The Power to Change Lives* (Nashville: Convention Press, 1998), 14.

Celebration Time

SHARE IT

As you return to share . . .

- Other reports and testimonies
- Session 7 Evaluation Card
- Participation Card
- Visitation forms updated with results of visits

The Daily Journey

Day One:
Read Isaiah 55: 6-11

Turning to a Different Way of Thinking

God's Word is strong enough to accomplish His purpose in our lives. Many times we fall into the trap of thinking that we have to convince people to turn from their sin and lifestyle and turn to God. Our real task is to share the truth of the Scripture and allow the Holy Spirit to use the Word of God in the heart of the person. Obviously we are not to be rude or arrogant as we share, because we don't want to distract from the clear message of the gospel. But, we do not save persons, we are only God's instruments to deliver His word to the life of someone He loves. You should study, pray, share, and be faithful to God's passion for your life and then allow God's Word to accomplish His purpose in their life.

Write down a time that you have shared and allowed the Word of God to minister to someone's life. Also, write down a time that you have shared out of your own skill and strength. Be prepared to talk about these experiences with your team this week. _____

_____

Re-read Isaiah 55:6-11. Ask God to show you which verses are for you today and which verses are for your friends. Pray that you and your FAITH Team will not start believing that your words and wisdom can save people. Pray that you will remain humble vessels that God can use.

Day Two:
Read Acts 3:1-19

Turn Means Repent

In this Scripture, it was an amazing day for the beggar and the crowd! Peter and John were used by God to heal a man who had been crippled since birth. But the greatest blessing that day was not that a man was healed, it was that a group of people turned from their sin to Christ. Peter and John were confident in Christ and in the necessity of people turning from their sins and turning to Christ. Sometimes it is easier for us to tell others to pray to accept Christ and leave out (or skim over) the part about repentance. But, refreshing does not come from just verbalizing that Jesus is Lord, refreshing comes from turning from sin and self, to Christ.

Do you think the process may be the same even after you accept Christ? Sure it is! If you are doing something you know dishonors God, you should spend time right now repenting of your sin so that you can be refreshed by the Holy Spirit.

Name a sin that you turned from when you accepted Christ. _____ If turning from your sins to accept Christ was essential to your salvation, do you think it may still be essential to the salvation of others?

Pray about the last two weeks. Is there any action or attitude that needs to be confessed before God so you can be refreshed? Pray that you and your FAITH Team will live pure lives so that you will not distract others from the gospel by your words, attitudes, or actions.

Day Three:
Read 2 Chronicles 7:11-14
National Sin

Solomon spent years building the Temple for Israel. During Old Testament times, the Temple was the place where sacrifices would be made for forgiveness and people could come to talk with God. The dedication services were in full swing late one night when God spoke to Solomon and gave him the rules for repentance. But this was not an instruction for lost people to repent, this was for God's people.

If our nation or your school is in trouble, we shouldn't blame God—we should first look at the actions and attitudes of our lives. God's desire is to forgive sin, but that forgiveness won't occur without humility, prayer, and repentance. This is not a prayer to accept Christ, but a call on God's people to live holy lives devoted to God. God's people should lead the way in repentance.

Rewrite 2 Chronicles 7:14 to apply to your life and your school:_____
_____
_____

Spend a few minutes thinking about sin and the results of sin at your school. Pray that you and your FAITH Team will lead the way at your school in repentance. Be honest with God about your own sin, then be faithful to love and encourage others to follow God as well.

Day Four:
Read 2 Corinthians 5:16-21
Overseas Ambassador

When you travel to a foreign country an interesting thing to do is to visit the American Embassy and meet the American ambassador. He lives full-time in that country representing the desires, lifestyle, and voice of the American people. Much of what other governments and people know about America is derived from the life and lifestyle of the American ambassador. Not only that, the U. S. Ambassador is never to speak on his own—he must only speak the message that the President of the United States tells him to speak.

We are Christ's Ambassadors to our community. Most of what the people around us will know about Christ, heaven, and church will be learned by watching our life and lifestyle. Our message must be the message that Jesus has commanded us to speak. Are you willing to live as a new creation today so that the world around you will understand more of what heaven will be like from watching your life?

Pray that you and the members of your FAITH Team will live today as ambassadors. Pray that you will not be afraid to speak truth to a school that desperately needs to hear truth.

Day Five:
Read Galatians 2:11-21
Turning Back To Your Old Life
It was easy for Peter to slip back into his old lifestyle of following the law and hoping that God would be impressed by his good behavior. But Paul caught him in the act and held him accountable for his hypocrisy! Paul reminded Peter that we cannot impress God through our good works. We follow God's leadership because of our great love for Him and our desire to be dead to our old way of life before we knew Christ. We live our life by faith, not by legalism. Like Peter, we will also battle against falling back into our old lifestyles. The old way of life may seem comfortable, but it will lead us away from an intimate relationship with Jesus. We must continue, even after we are saved, to turn from sin and self and trust Christ only.

Look at your life: If you went back to your old way of life, is there anyone around you bold enough to confront you in love and help you get back on track? Write the name of that person here._____ The next time you see that friend, tell him or her that you are counting on them to help you always walk with God. If you do not have anyone like that in your life, find someone this week who can help you stay consistent in your walk with Christ.

Pray for yourself and the members of your FAITH Team. Pray that you will not go back to your old lifestyles. Pray also that you will be bold enough to lovingly confront a friend if he or she wanders away from an intimate relationship with Christ.

Day Six:
Read Luke 5:1-11
A Public Letting Go
The fishermen were willing to obey Jesus, but not necessarily follow Him. When Jesus asked them to quit cleaning their nets and put their boats out into the water, they were willing to obey Him. When Jesus asked them to put their freshly-cleaned nets back into the water again, even though they were ready to go to their home and get some rest, they obeyed. Both of these acts of obedience were not necessarily acts of submission to Jesus as Lord. But when Jesus called them to follow Him, they had to make the choice to give up everything and everyone to follow Jesus. It was a private call to each of the four fishermen to publicly let go of their old life and lifestyle.

What is Jesus' private call to you today? Are you willing to write in this space his private call to a public "letting go" of some of your old life?

_____

_____

Pray that you and your FAITH Team will not be afraid to ask people in private to surrender their life publicly to Jesus. Pray for some people you have visited in the past weeks that have not yet made their decisions public. Plan to call or visit them again for a follow-up.

Day Seven:
Read John 7:37-44

It Doesn't Get Any More Public Than This

On the final day of a crowded festival, thousands of people heard Jesus shout, "If anyone is thirsty, let him come to me and drink." Talk about a public invitation, that one was *very* public! The people of Jerusalem were divided as to what to do with Jesus. Some followed Him, some ignored Him, and some believed wrong information and rejected Him.

 One of the great challenges you will have in your Christian life is the challenge of correcting wrong information some people believe about Jesus so they can hear your message and respond to God's great love for them.

 Students around you may assume that following God is no big deal, or that Jesus is for older people, or God is someone so private that they do not have to share Him or live Him. But, Jesus makes the call clear, public, and loving. Your call must be the same—clear, public, and loving.

 List some things that some of your peers believe about God that are wrong.

_____

_____

 Pray for yourself and your FAITH Team. Pray that you will not fail to call people publicly to follow Christ. Pray that you will make the invitation clear and inviting so your friends will respond to Christ.

The Weekly Sunday School Leadership Team Meeting

Use this space to record ways your FAITH Team impacts the work of your Sunday School department or class. Use the information to report during weekly Sunday School leadership team meetings. Identify actions that need to be taken through Sunday School as a result of prayer concerns, needs identified, visits made by the Team, and decisions made by the students being visited.

Highlight needs and reports affecting your class, department, or age group.

_____

_____

Pray now for teachers and department directors.

What are ways the department or class can seek to impact students with the truth that we must turn from sin and turn to Christ?

_____

_____

How does preparation for Sunday need to help students consider the truths of the gospel?

_____

_____

For Further Reading

Read pages 53-56 of *Evangelism Through the Sunday School: A Journey of FAITH* by Bobby Welch. How do the testimonies encourage you at this important time in FAITH training?

For the Team Leader

This weekly feature suggests actions the Team Leader can take to support Team members, prepare for Team Time, and consider ways to improve visits. This work becomes part of the Team Leader's Home Study Assignments. Add any actions suggested by your church's FAITH strategy.

Support Team Members
❑ Contact Team members during the week. Remind them you are praying for them. Discuss prayer concerns and answers to prayer.
❑ Record specific needs and concerns of Team members in the space provided.

Prepare to Lead Team Time
❑ Review Home Study Assignments of Team members.
❑ Review your "Team Time" responsibilities for Session 8.

Prepare to Lead Visits
❑ Review the FAITH Visit Outline.
❑ Be prepared to explain the significance of God's forgiveness being available to all but not automatic.

Connecting to Sunday School
❑ Share information from the weekly Sunday School leadership meeting.

ΠΟΤΕS

REVIEWING THE FAITH VISIT OULINE:

HEAVEN AND THE INVITATION

THE BELL RANG FOR THE DAY and Lyle and his friend, Nicholi, walked toward Lyle's truck. As he opened the door, Nicholi noticed Lyle's Bible laying on the front seat. He asked, "Why's your Bible in your truck?"

Lyle replied, "I try to read it every day—usually when I'm waiting for all the traffic to clear out of the school parking lot or when I get here a little early before school."

"Do you really believe all the things you read in that book?" Nicholi asked.

Lyle had been praying for an opportunity to talk to Nicholi about Jesus before they graduated from high school. He wondered, *Could this be the opportunity I have been looking for?*

"Yes," he answered. "There are some things I don't understand, but I hope to someday."

Nicholi replied, "I really haven't read much of the Bible—just parts of it. Some of the things I read, though, were scary to me."

Lyle responded, "Which parts are you talking about?"

"All those things about the end of time. You know—the things in the last part of the Bible. I started reading that part and I got scared and I haven't read any more."

Lyle thought, *Here's my chance!* and he began the FAITH presentation. Before he knew it, he was at "H is for heaven."

Nicholi had listened intently so far, but now Lyle had a problem—he had left all his copies of the *A Step of Faith (Student Edition)* leaflets at home. How could he finish his conversation with his friend?

TEAM TIME

The team leader leads this time. Learners are primarily responsible for reciting the assigned portion of the FAITH Visit Outline and for discussing any Home Study Assignments.

Keep in mind how Learners also look to leaders as role models, motivators, mentors, and friends. Team Time activities can continue in the car, as the Team travels to and from visits.

Check It

FAITH Visit Outline
- ❏ Listen while each Learner recites all of *Preparation*; all of the outline points for the letters F (FORGIVENESS), A (AVAILABLE), and I (IMPOSSIBLE); key words for the letters T (TURN) and H (HEAVEN); and key words for the *Invitation*.

Practice
- ❏ Give opportunity for Learners to practice reciting the portion of the FAITH Visit Outline they have learned up to this point.

Session 6 Debriefing (F is for Forgiveness)
- ❏ God's forgiveness is available to everyone. Even the most hardened of criminals or the most unloving person is the target of God's love and forgiveness. John 3:16 reminds us of the scope of God's love and forgiveness ("God so loved the world . . . that whoever"). This same verse introduces us to the fact that God's forgiveness is not automatic ("whoever believes in Him").

  This passage also focuses on the consequences of not accepting God's forgiveness ("perishing"). It is important to remember that many people you visit will not understand that God's forgiveness is available to them but it is not automatic.

Help for Strengthening A Visit
- ❏ Many students you seek to visit will indicate they don't have much time for a lengthy visit. Some persons may not allow your Team to enter the house because of time or personal constraints.

  Your primary job is to seek to build relationships with students and to introduce them to the idea of enrolling in your Sunday School class. Look for opportunities to ask the Key Question, hear responses, and share the FAITH gospel presentation. But also look for opportunities to build a relationship with the student through Sunday School enrollment.

  God may be using you to plant a seed. He also may be using you and your Team members to nurture relationships on His behalf. He also may be using you to prepare the harvest. Be sensitive to opportunities God is providing for you in the midst of visits.

Notes

_____
_____
_____
_____

Actions I Need to Take with Learners During the Week

_____
_____
_____
_____

A Quick Review

God cannot allow sin into heaven because of who He is and because of who we
are. If it weren't for His great love and mercy, we would be forever separated and
estranged from God because of our sin. Only Jesus' blood sacrifice made it possible
for us, and others we will visit who have not yet accepted His forgiveness, to enter
His presence as if we had no sin.

Our responses are many—praise, gratitude, worship. The response God requires
and most desires is repentance, a change of heart, and a life redirected in obedience
to Him. To choose to trust Christ reflects this dramatic, life-changing moment—
the beginning of one's journey in faith.

The Person God Uses

**The person God uses is forgiven and is learning to forgive and be forgiven by
others, as Christ commanded.**

We understand the need to ask God for His forgiveness. We learn many lessons
about our need to forgive others when they fault or grieve us.

The psalmist felt the weight of his sin always before him (Ps. 51:1-10) and separating
him from a holy God. Jesus told us to be different—to forgive others (Matt. 6:12,14)
and to forgive in unlimited measure, from the heart (Matt. 18:21-35).

It is much easier for us to realize our need to ask God for forgiveness and to forget
the persons we have wronged. The person God uses asks God for forgiveness; the
person God uses asks forgiveness from others.

Have you experienced the healing that comes when you go to someone whom you
have wronged and ask for forgiveness? The words of Christ echo in Matthew 5:23-
24, reminding us that the most worthy worship and service is broken by an
unforgiving heart.

There is a barrier in our lives when we are not reconciled with one another. If there
is anyone whom you have faulted (intentionally or unintentionally) and from whom
you have not asked forgiveness and reconciliation in the name of Jesus, then you are
not in a position to be freely used of God to your potential.

Read Ephesians 4:32. Then read the context of the passage by reading Ephesians
4:25-32. Can you recall from recent months, or even years, some individuals who
might have something against you? What actions might you have intentionally
done for which you need reconciliation? What actions will you take to ask
forgiveness from and to reconcile with this person(s)?

Dear Father: Give me the strength and courage to follow up on my desire to ask forgiveness from those I have wronged. Help me also to forgive others as You have forgiven me.

A Little Bit of Heaven on Earth

There are two dimensions of heaven on which we focus in this part of the gospel presentation. Heaven is *here*. Heaven also is *hereafter*. The phrase "heaven is here" describes the (_____ __ ____) available for every believer. Words such as *eternal*, *full*, and *abundant* are used to describe this quality of life. Although Jesus promised and provides the quality of life that gives us a hint of the complete joys and satisfaction of heaven, there is a general lack of understanding or awareness of the present dimension of spiritual life now for the believer.

Facts such as the following help remind us of the reality of the abundant life available to those who believe:

- *We have been set free and are no longer condemned because of Christ's redeeming actions (Rom. 8:1-2).*
- *We are made heirs of God and made able to share in His glory (Rom. 8:17).*
- *The Holy Spirit bears fruit in the life of the believer (Gal. 5:22-25).*
- *The Holy Spirit is the pledge of the believer's participation in heaven (2 Cor. 5:5).*
- *We are made as new creations and are reconciled to God (2 Cor. 5:17-18).*
- *We are made alive in Him and brought close to Him (Eph. 2:4-13).*
- *We are able to grow in relationship to Him, and know His power and fellowship (Phil. 2:10).*
- *We are given hope (Heb. 6:17-20).*

You, too, can share personal experiences describing assurance of your salvation and ways your life has changed.

Eternity in God's Presence

The phrase "Heaven is Hereafter" refers as much to the (____ ____ ___ ____) and (____ ___ _____ ___ ____) as to the (_____ ___ ____ ____) when there is no interference with His glory or temptation which could lure us away from His presence. For the believer, there is great joy and anticipation when we consider heaven in the hereafter.

You will probably visit many people who have been influenced by misconceptions about heaven. As this session focuses on the letter *H* in the FAITH gospel presentation, here are some of the (_____ ___ _____ ___ _____ _____):

- *Heaven is not a real or literal place.*
- *When a person dies and goes to heaven, he becomes an angel with wings.*
- *All people will go to heaven when they die.*
- *Heaven is a paradise existence here on earth achieved by only a few persons.*
- *Before a person can get into heaven, he must wait in a place (purgatory) to be purged of his or her sins.*
- *Heaven is a place of (sensuous) pleasure.*

Certainly this is not an exhaustive list, but it does alert us to the fact that not everyone we visit will have the same concept of heaven as we do. As a matter of fact, many students likely will not have thought of heaven much since, in their perspective, heaven is far off. On the other hand, recent opinion polls have indicated that most people believe in heaven and expect to go there when they die.

While Jesus was painfully enduring the cross, He made the following declaration to one of the crucified thieves who repented and believed: "I tell you the truth, today you will be with me in paradise" (Luke 23:43, NIV).

The Bible gives us many understandings of the magnificence and significance of heaven, including the following:

- *Heaven is a literal place (John 14:2-3).*
- *Heaven is the dwelling place of God (Matt. 6:9).*
- *Heaven is where Jesus is in bodily form (Acts 7:55-56).*
- *Heaven is eternal (2 Cor. 5:1).*
- *Jesus spoke of heavenly life as eternal time of joy, celebration, and fellowship with God (Matt. 26:29).*
- *Heaven is the place of God's throne and eternal presence (Rev. 22:3).*
- *Heaven is the future home of believers (2 Cor. 5:1-2).*
- *Presently all who have died in the Lord are there (2 Cor. 5:8).*
- *Heaven (the kingdom of God) is without the presence of sin (Gal. 5:19-21).*
- *Multitudes of angels are in heaven praising God and attending to Him (Rev. 5:11).*
- *There is no darkness in heaven (Rev. 22:5).*
- *Pain, suffering, and sorrow are not known in heaven (Rev. 21:4).*
- *Heaven is the place where the believer's inheritance is kept with care until the revelation of the Messiah (1 Pet. 1:4).*

For several reasons it is important to emphasize HEAVEN in the gospel presentation. Particularly important is the fact that believers will (_____ _____) in the (_____) of God. Remember, those who reject God's gift of salvation and die in their sins choose eternity away from His presence, fellowship, and care.

Explain HOW Clearly

The letter *H* also stands for HOW. Review your *Student FAITH Journal* to recall details for using *A Step of Faith (Student Edition)*: (1) The cover picture dramatically helps students realize their personal sin , how Jesus died for them and how he (or she), too, can have salvation and forgiveness; (2) using your hand again to share another meaning of FAITH (Forsaking All I Trust Him) presents yet another visual image of turning and trusting, as well as helping you make transition to the Inquiry question in the *Invitation*; (3) Romans 10:9 focuses the conversation on what the student must do to be saved.

A Step of Faith (Student Edition) can help you assess someone's understanding of the gospel, explain how to be saved, and guide a new believer to make significant commitments. It is especially meaningful for the student being visited.

However, as you are learning, not all visits go by the script. Don't lose an opportunity to ask someone to accept Christ as Savior and Lord by thinking you must have the leaflet to do so.

WHAT WOULD YOU DO?

Suppose that, in a daily-life encounter, you find an opportunity to share FAITH. The person gives a *works* response to the Key Question and permission for you to share how the Bible answers this question. You've moved through the gospel presentation, and the person seems under conviction by the Holy Spirit. You don't have a copy of *A Step of Faith (Student Edition)*. What should you do?

You can review the same HOW subpoints in the letter H (HEAVEN) by saying something like the following:

_____ (*student's name*), you may be asking yourself: How can a person have God's forgiveness, heaven and eternal life, and Jesus as personal Savior and Lord? We've talked about how H stands for HEAVEN; it also can stand for HOW. (*Extend your hand.*)

_____ (*student's name*), look at your own hand. Remember how we just spelled out meanings of the word FAITH on our hands? Another meaning of FAITH can be *Forsaking All I Trust Him*. And *Him* is Jesus.

_____ (*student's name*), if you would turn from your own way of trying to make life work and, in a way, reach out with your own hand of faith to Jesus you could find this same forgiveness, heaven and eternal life, and Jesus as personal Savior.

You can know for certain that you are on the right road, and you can receive God's forgiveness, eternal life, and heaven. Remember what we said earlier: "If you confess with your mouth the Lord Jesus and believe in your heart that God has raised Him from the dead, you will be saved."

_____ (*student's name*), understanding what we've shared, would you like to receive this forgiveness by trusting in Christ as your personal Savior and Lord?

If the student says *yes*, lead him to pray a simple prayer for salvation. One of the most important concepts of how a person receives salvation is to turn from sin to trust Christ only. Help the student understand the necessity of realizing he or she is a sinner, asking God for forgiveness, repenting from sin, and acknowledging Jesus' death and resurrection as the only way to be saved. The brief prayer should reflect these understandings.

You can begin to help the student understand significant commitments for growth, though follow-up will be important. Since you do not have *A Step of Faith (Student Edition)* leaflet, you do not have a place to record information; it is especially important to recall and record details so meaningful follow-up can be done.

Visitation Time
DO IT
As You Go . . .

Are Team members becoming increasingly comfortable with making adjustments as the visit proceeds? While your Team should plan in advance what is to happen and what responsibilities the various Team members will assume, the best visit is one in which visitors adjust to the needs of the situation.

Team Leader, as you make changes in the FAITH Visit Outline, be sure to explain why. Affirm your Team Learners as they show increasing confidence and ease in sharing their testimonies and in using the FAITH Visit Outline.

Pray for sensitivity to the situations Teams will be encountering in these visits. Always be open to enrolling a student in Sunday School.

Celebration Time
SHARE IT
As you return to share . . .

Ask a Team Learner to take the lead in sharing your Team's reports.
• Reports and testimonies
• Session 8 Evaluation Card
• Participation Card
• Visitation forms updated with results of visits

The Daily Journey

Day One:
Read Ephesians 2:1-10
All Expenses Paid
Imagine for a minute, that someone offered to pay your way anywhere in the world you wanted to go. You would spend some time choosing where you wanted to go, what you would do when you got there, and thinking about how much fun you were going to have. But the real fun would come when you actually went on the trip. For the rest of your life, you would be thankful to the person who paid for your trip because he or she provided a way for you to do something you might never have been able to afford yourself.

Heaven is like that. As a Christian, you will spend eternity in heaven. You will hang out with other Christians, be part of incredible worship times, and live life the way it was intended to be lived. All of this because Jesus paid the price for your trip!

That is what Ephesians 2 is referring to—an incredible event for which we can never take the credit. Jesus deserves the credit, thanks, and gratitude of our lives for His payment for our sins. Live each day in gratitude for what He did for you and work in Him to see as many of your friends as possible take the trip with you.

What are some of the things you are looking forward to in heaven? _____

Pray for the lost students around you in class that don't have your hope of heaven. Pray that you and the members of your FAITH Team will not become complacent as you share Jesus with people each week.

Day Two:
Read Matthew 13:44-51
Buried Treasure

It must have been hard for Jesus to try to describe what heaven would be like to people who have no point of reference for eternity. He did make it clear, though, that heaven is worth more than anything this life has to offer. It is worth any sacrifice we might be called on to make for the kingdom of God. Heaven is worth any temporary inconvenience we might have to endure in this life, because it is going to be awesome!

But as awesome as heaven is going to be, hell is going to be equally as horrible. Hell is often described as a burning lake, a place of torment, or a place of continual suffering. The testimony we share is important because we are the people God will work through so others can come to Christ. What a great week to be used of God to change someone's eternal destiny!

List several people or things in your life that you consider valuable. _____
_____

Are they more important to you than your relationship with Christ?

Pray for students around you who need to hear the gospel clearly. Pray that you and your FAITH Team can clearly communicate the joy of heaven and the reality of hell.

Day Three:
Read Romans 10:1-13
What Is Better Than Sharing Christ?

What an incredible privilege to be used by God to let people know how they can have a personal relationship with the God who created our entire world! Guiding people to their Creator who loves them more than anything else in the world— what could possibly be better than that?

A new car? Nope, it will eventually rust and break down.
Popularity? Nope. People will eventually forget.
Anything this world has to offer? Nope, it all fades away.

Our greatest privilege as Christians is to let people know how to connect to Jesus Christ. And they will know Him only when we tell them.

Honestly evaluate the last two weeks of your life. What has been the most important thing to you as you look at the amount of time, energy and attention you expended? _____

Pray that you and your FAITH Team will not lose the awe of God as you serve Him.

Day Four:
Read Romans 10:14-15
Beautiful Feet

It's fun to take good news to someone, any good news. You're excited about telling them because you know how much fun it will be to watch their reaction. You're happy because you get to watch someone else be happy! Whenever that person remembers that news, they will also remember that you were the one who let them know about it.

Gabe is one of those "good news" guys. One night during a Wednesday night meeting we were asking students to name the person who brought them to church for the first time. Out of 75 students, 9 or 10 of them said Gabe had brought them to church for the first time, and they eventually gave their hearts to Christ because of His influence. Those students will always be grateful for a friend who thought enough of them to make sure they heard what Christ could do in their lives. Make sure your feet become "beautiful" to someone this week as you let him or her know how to have eternal life.

Write the names of some people you know who still need to hear the gospel.

_____

Pray for their salvation today.

Pray also that you and your FAITH Team would share Jesus in your daily lives, not just when you are together as a team.

Day Five:
Read Luke 18:15-17
Raising A Baby

Imagine for a moment that you have been given the responsibility of caring for a newborn baby. Not knowing any better, you might take it to the grocery store, find the baby food aisle, and start explaining which food was appropriate for his or her age. You could read to baby the instructions about how to mix formula, which bottles to use, which diapers would be best and so on. But if you left the baby there alone to try and feed itself while you went on with your own life, it would starve to death surrounded by thousands of dollars worth of baby food— because it simply isn't capable of feeding itself yet. It needs you to mix the formula, bring it to the correct temperature, and put it into its mouth.

New Christians are the same way. Even if they are physically mature, new Christians are spiritual infants. They need someone to take the simple truths of the Scriptures and spoon-feed them so they can be spiritually nourished. We all need spiritual nourishment, but an infant needs it more than anyone else. An infant needs care, attention, and patience. Remember that God did not grow you to where you are in one day. When he places a new Christian in your life, He is allowing you the honor of helping one of His newborn children grow up in their spiritual walk. Take the responsibility gladly!.

What is one part of raising a child that looks like the most work? _____
Compare that in some way to helping raise a new Christian in the faith.

_____

Pray for all the new Christians you and other FAITH Team members have seen come to know Christ this semester. Pray that you and your spiritual peers will not walk away from these spiritual babies God has placed into your life.

Day Six:
Read Ecclesiastes 4:9-12

Two Are Better Than One

Today's devotion is a test! Which would be easier, lifting a heavy object by yourself or having a couple of people help you? If you answered having people help you, you are right! Second question: Which would be the most productive, doing research by yourself or combining the research of several people? If you answered using the group method, you are exactly right.

That's one reason why small group Bible studies are important. God gives each person a different way of looking at life. When we combine our experiences and research about Who God is, we get a more complete picture of how we can relate to Him and follow His directions. Pray that you will see this week's small group Bible study as a way of understanding God more.

Write down three things you have learned from your Sunday morning small group Bible study._____

_____

Pray for your Bible study teacher. Pray that you and your FAITH Team members will gain more insight about God this Sunday in your Bible study.

Day Seven:
Read Colossians 3:15-17

Peace in Sunday School

You have heard of all kinds of *peace* in your lifetime. *World peace* and *Greenpeace* are a couple of examples. But what about *heart peace*? That is really what most people are looking for. It's the kind of peace that comes from Jesus Christ Himself. It is the key to living in this world, and it is the key to effective small group Bible studies. Without peace and love, we judge other people in our group as better or worse than ourselves. With peace and love, we see the others the way God sees them—in perfect love. When we are confident of the love of the group, we are free to be used by God to share ideas and Scripture passages that will encourage the group, as well as to speak words of wisdom that will build up the group. Use your small group time this week to help others see themselves as God sees them. Build up the group in peace and love.

What is one way you can encourage others in your small group Bible study this Sunday?

Pray that you and your FAITH Team members create an environment in your Sunday School class where new Christians are happy because of the peace and love that are shown there.

The Weekly Sunday School Leadership Team Meeting

Use this space to record ways your FAITH Team impacts the work of your Sunday School department or class. Use the information to report during weekly Sunday School leadership team meetings. Identify actions that need to be taken through Sunday School as a result of prayer concerns, needs identified, visits made by the Team, and decisions made by the students being visited.

Highlight needs/reports affecting your class, department, or age group.

_____

_____

Pray now for teachers and department directors.

Highlight needs or reports affecting your class or department.

_____

_____

Pray now for this important meeting.

_____

What are ways the department and class can seek to impact students with the truth that, for believers, heaven is here?

_____

_____

. . . That heaven is hereafter?

_____

_____

How does preparation for Sunday need to help students consider explanation of the gospel and invitation for them to receive Christ?

_____

_____

For Further Reading

Review pages 116-120 of the Student FAITH Journal to study the process for using *My Step of Faith (Student Edition)* during the Invitation segment of the FAITH visit.

For the Team Leader

This weekly feature suggests actions the Team Leader can take to support Team members, prepare for Team Time, and consider ways to improve visits. This work becomes part of the Team Leader's Home Study Assignments. Add any actions suggested by your church's FAITH strategy.

Support Team Members
- ❑ Contact Team members during the week. Remind them you are praying for them. Discuss prayer concerns and answers to prayer.
- ❑ Record specific needs and concerns of Team members in the space provided.

Prepare to Lead Team Time
- ❑ Review Home Study Assignments of Team members.
- ❑ Review "Team Time" for Session 9.

Prepare to Lead Visits
- ❑ Review the FAITH Visit Outline.
- ❑ Be prepared to explain the significance of God's forgiveness being available for all—but not automatic.

Connecting to Sunday School
- ❑ Use information from the weekly Sunday School leadership meeting to share about FAITH.
- ❑ Encourage Sunday School teachers to periodically call on Team members to share reports from their FAITH experiences. Encourage your Team members to give periodic updates in your class.

FAITH Tip

Salvation and God's Grace

An understanding of the impact of God's grace on salvation is foundational to Christianity. Hershel Hobbs explained this truth in the following way.

". . . Salvation is by grace through faith in Jesus Christ. When man would not, could not be saved by the law, God provided salvation by grace through faith. By his sordid, sinful record, man proved that he would not obey God's law.

"If God knew from the beginning that this would be true, why did He wait so long to provide salvation through His Son? God knew it. But man had to learn by bitter experience that he was too weak and willful to be saved by law. . . . When man would not, could not save himself, he was ready for someone else to do it for him. So in Christ God did for man what neither he, no one else, nor anything else could do for him. That is the very essence of grace.

"C. Roy Angell once said that grace means that God gives us what we need, not what we deserve.

"Originally the Greek word rendered "grace" meant to make a gift, then to forgive a debt, then to forgive a wrong, and finally to forgive sin. So basically grace is a gift, as expressed in Romans 3:24. Literally, 'Being declared righteous as a gift by his grace through the full redemption, the one in Christ Jesus.'

"This truth is plainly stated in Ephesians 2:8-10. 'For by grace are ye saved through faith; and that not of [out of] yourselves: it is the gift of God: not of [out of] works, lest any man should boast. For we are his workmanship, created in Christ Jesus unto good works, which God hath before ordained that we should walk in them.'

"Note that salvation is not 'out of yourselves' or 'out of works' as the source. It is 'of God the gift.' It is by grace made possible in the individual through his faith. Good works are the fruit, not the root, of salvation."[1]

---

[1] Herschel H. Hobbs, *The Baptist Faith and Message* (Nashville: Convention Press, 1971), 50-51.

ΠΟ†ΕS

CONNECTING TO STUDENTS
THROUGH THE SUNDAY SCHOOL

LIBBA GILLUM

JACQUI AND JON WERE LOOKING forward to attending their first Sunday School Leadership Meeting. The meeting began with all workers in the same room. Announcements were made and assignments for future all-youth events were given. They were excited when they were both asked to be a part of a group to plan the next after-game youth event.

Then the large group broke up and Jacqui and Jon met with their teacher, Mrs. Fresno. They talked about what they were learning in FAITH and about prospects for their class. As they talked, Mrs. Fresno showed Jacqui and Jon the list of youth enrolled in their class.

Jacqui pointed to James Scott's name and said, "I didn't know James was on our Sunday School roll! I sit next to him in world history class. "

"His locker is next to mine, and I see him every day," Jon commented.

Mrs. Fresno explained that James had attended the church's Vacation Bible School when he was in fifth grade and he and his family had enrolled in Sunday School. She also explained that they had attended church only a couple of times since then and that she had visited James a few weeks ago.

"He is a little scared about coming to Sunday School now because he doesn't think he knows many people who come to our church. Do you think you two could change his mind about that?"

TEAM TIME

The team leader leads this time. Learners are primarily responsible for reciting the assigned portion of the FAITH Visit Outline and for discussing any Home Study Assignments.

Keep in mind how Learners also look to leaders as role models, motivators, mentors, and friends. Team Time activities can continue in the car, as the Team travels to and from visits.

Check It

FAITH Visit Outline

❑ Listen while each Learner recites the FAITH Visit Outline: all of *Preparation*; all of *Presentation*, adding T is for TURN to the gospel presentation, plus the key words for *Invitation*. Be aware of time limits if two Learners are sharing; someone may need to recite in the car going to and from visits.
Sign off each Learner's work in his or her Journal.
Practice other parts of the outline as time allows.

Other Home Study Assignments

❑ Emphasize the importance of involving the Sunday School class in FAITH, whether by prayer support, in training, or in follow-up. Discuss how, in this session, the Sunday School will be the focus of connecting to people.
Ask: Do class/department members who are not participating in FAITH still see themselves as a part of this ministry? In what ways? Are you sharing prayer needs and results of visits with fellow class members? Are they praying for you and for the students you and your Team will visit? Is your class, department, and church growing spiritually and numerically?

❑ Home Study Assignments and memorization are reaching their maximum. Make a special effort during the week to personally encourage Learners, especially those who may have fallen behind in memory work or home study.

Session 8 Debriefing (I is for Impossible)

❑ Some important theological truths are communicated in this part of the gospel presentation. Are Learners at ease and confident in sharing about God's love and His justice? About their own sinfulness?
Ask them to recall, from their personal experience—
• their need to be saved,
• their inability to save themselves, and
• God's saving initiative in their lives (their life-changing experience).
Doing so will help them continue to identify with the students they visit. All of us are sinners in need of God's grace. Some of us have been fortunate enough to receive and accept it, while others still need to know of God's forgiveness. Letting others know is a big part of what FAITH is all about.
If needed by your group, overview ways to respond to a works answer to the Key Question.

Help for Strengthening a Visit
- ❑ Have most Team members seen someone accept Christ during a home visit? If so, remind Team members of how such a visit should motivate them to continue in their efforts. If not, remind them that God is still working, even if they have not seen specific desired results.
  Call on the Assistant Team Leader (if you have one) to encourage other Team members; he or she may have had experiences in earlier FAITH training that can motivate others.
- ❑ As important as practice is, it is not the same as sharing the gospel in a home visit. Acknowledge that even as you encourage your Team to practice with one another and with other believers, as the opportunity allows.

Notes

_____
_____
_____
_____

Actions I Need to Take with Learners During the Week

_____
_____
_____
_____

A Quick Review

There are two dimensions of heaven on which we focus as part of the FAITH gospel presentation. Heaven is *here*, and heaven is *hereafter*.

Heaven *here* describes the quality of life—abundant life, as John 10:10 reminds us—which is available to every Christian. There also is great joy and anticipation when we consider heaven in the *hereafter*—as both the place where God lives and the place where we will live, as well as the kingdom God will rule when there is nothing to lure us away from His presence.

You are probably visiting many students who may have been influenced by misconceptions about heaven. The focus on the letter *H* in the gospel presentation helps Teams identify and address some misconceptions.

One of the most important concepts of how a person receives salvation is to "Turn from Sin" and to "Trust Christ Only." You will need to help another student understand the necessity of realizing he or she is a sinner, requesting forgiveness from God, repenting from sin, and remembering God has provided salvation. *A Step of Faith (Student Edition)* can help you in this process.

You have one of the greatest opportunities anyone can have when you carefully and prayerfully invite someone to accept Jesus as Savior. By making yourself available for God to use in this most important of encounters, you also experience the joy of seeing Him work to change someone's life.

The Person God Uses

The person God uses is a servant.

What is your attitude about being a servant? Are you willing and available to do whatever the Master says? The Scriptures teach many significant principles about servanthood. The primary concept we are to follow is to obey God and to love Him with all of our heart. We also learn that we are to be a servant in the same way Jesus modeled servanthood.

Philippians 2:5-11 describes the attitude and actions of Jesus as a servant. Jesus becomes our Example as well as our Mentor:

"Your attitude should be the same as that of Christ Jesus: Who, being in very nature God . . . made himself nothing, taking the very nature of a servant, . . . he humbled himself and became obedient to death—even death on a cross!" (Phil. 2:5-8, NIV).

Read the following words written by Richard Gillard. These words have been placed to music and have become a beautiful hymn. Think about ways Jesus showed us how to be a servant. Consider ways you can be a servant to God and to those we are to serve.

"We are trav-'lers on a journey, Fellow pilgrims on the road;
We are here to help each other Walk the mile and bear the load.
I will hold the Christ-light for you In the nighttime of your fear;
I will hold my hand out to you, Speak the peace you long to hear.
Let me be your servant, Let me be as Christ to you;
Pray that I may have the grace to Let you be my servant, too.
I will weep when you are weeping, When you laugh,
I'll laugh with you;
I will share your joy and sorrow, Till we've seen this journey thro'.
When we sing to God in heaven, We shall find such harmony,
Born of all we've known together Of Christ's love and agony."[1]

Keep in mind, ". . . servanthood is a holy place. It is the place where God and Christ desire each of us to live out our earthly existence. It is the place of great usefulness and great blessings for here and for eternity."[2]

Dear God: Use me as a servant who is obedient to You and who blesses others by following Your example.

The Role of Sunday School in Making Connections

Sunday School is designed to build relationships with people. Through ministry, assimilation, and discipleship, it is effective in connecting to and involving both new people and current members.

We focus on discipleship (Bible teaching), ministry (caring), worship (prayer), evangelism, and fellowship to better focus on people—both current members and those we have yet to reach and assimilate into the class. You already have discovered that FAITH Sunday School Evangelism Strategy helps your church focus on (_____)—both members and prospects.

You already know that FAITH is designed to help your Sunday School ministry identify opportunities to share the gospel, particularly to students who are prospective members of the class. FAITH also is designed to identify opportunities to help nonattending members and those with special needs find their way back to a group of caring and supportive individuals who are part of the class or department. The FAITH Team can help initiate relationship-building opportunities and activate class members to build relationships.

Your Team already has had opportunities to make ministry visits. You will continue to make such visits. Generally, your Team knows to make such a visit by information provided on your (_____ _____ _____ ____.) Occasionally, a FAITH Team will learn of a member's need at the last minute and determine to visit without having a specific assignment to do so.

Frequently and ideally, however, the need or situation surfaces each week in Sunday School leadership team meetings. This meeting provides the connection that unites FAITH training to effective Sunday School ministry.

One of the main features of the weekly meeting agenda is to identify situations reflecting personal need and to request a specific age-group FAITH Team to make a visit. You already know that no other group is more likely to know of such a need than the class or department. In some cases, a class member or FAITH Team member will know of a special need in the life of a class member before the leadership does. If this occurs, then an assigned ministry visit can be replaced by an assignment to visit this class member, especially if the need is of a more serious nature.

Then, the next week at the leadership team meeting, a report can be shared to indicate the results of the FAITH Team's visit. Additional follow-up or ministry can be planned and implemented.

On most occasions you will want to be aware, before leaving the church, of the recent (_____ __ _____)pattern of the member. Several consecutive weeks of absence could indicate a physical need. Or absences could indicate another kind of need, including a spiritual one. In some instances, you may discover a need that calls for immediate attention. Visiting a member after two or three unexplained absences (such as being on vacation) can keep that student from becoming a chronic nonattender.

Attitude Is Everything

The attitude of FAITH Team members is extremely important in making ministry visits. (_____) and an ability to (_____) are vital.

You are going in the leadership of the Holy Spirit. You are going as a minister in the name of Christ. You will be going to some students who are hurting, some who are depressed, others who may be angry, still others whose busy lifestyles have caused them to brush aside an earlier commitment to discipleship.

Some are under the direct attack of Satan, perhaps even moving into a sinful lifestyle. Others have lost sensitivity to the leadership of God in their lives. No matter what the situation, you will find that a ministry visit has the opportunity to accomplish several significant outcomes:

- *To let students know your Sunday School class (and church) cares for them—or otherwise demonstrate personal interest;*
- *To develop or strengthen friendships with class members;*
- *To gain firsthand knowledge, and thus identify additional ministry needs class members might address;*
- *To provide assistance or comfort during a time of crisis;*
- *To discover possible reasons for nonattendance and identify ways to make connections between the student and the class or church;*
- *To provide resources or some other gift to the student on behalf of the class or church; and*

• *To discuss ways to grow as a Christian and make a commitment to initiate or strengthen discipleship opportunities.*

How to Make a Sunday School Ministry Visit

In general, as you learned from Student FAITH training, Sunday School ministry visits are usually made to three main types of member situations: to (_____) (members who have been absent two weeks or more without a known reason such as vacation); to (_____), or chronic absentees (people who are on roll but do not attend); and to (_____ ____ _____ ____) (individuals who have experienced or are undergoing some life need).

Again as a review, individuals being visited are members of a specific Sunday School class or department. Your weekly FAITH assignment indicates the nature of such a visit, and that determination most often grows out of weekly Sunday School leadership team meetings in which many FAITH Team members participate.

Ministry visits require a strong sensitivity to the leadership of the Holy Spirit and a growing awareness of personal needs. Every situation has the potential of being uniquely different since every ministry need is unique. FAITH Team members who are good listeners, who encourage the student, who ask for opportunities to pray for the class member, and who assure him or her that the class and Team will not forget the need are likely to see other good results from ministry visits.

Although there is no script or visitation outline to follow, the FAITH visit outline used throughout training can help you accomplish your goals. In every Sunday School ministry visit seek to take the following actions:

• (_____)

Introduce your Team or become reacquainted.—In visiting an absentee or a member with a special need, everyone should know each other.

Frequently, in visiting a nonattender, it is possible that the Team and the class member do not know each other. The individual may no longer live at the address indicated on the card. Or you may find that the family is attending or considering joining another church. In such a case, record accurate information on the visitation assignment card. One of the benefits of FAITH ministry visits is to keep class rolls up-to-date.

• (_____)

Discuss common or evident interests, such as school, sports, and so forth.—Doing so puts the Team and the member at ease.

• (_____)

Focus on types of church involvement and participation.—This is where the Team Leader shares the purpose of the visit. Discuss the fact that class members have missed seeing the student in Bible study or worship. If applicable, acknowledge the ministry need that has come to the FAITH Team's attention.

Listen for clues about the student's spiritual condition.—This step is particularly important in visiting a nonattender, as a spiritual need may be at the heart of nonattendance. Be sensitive in listening for reasons the person no longer is attending. Share appropriate comments (but not confidential or personal information) during Celebration Time to help other Teams who encounter similar situations.

Share a Sunday School testimony.—Once the reason for not attending Sunday School has been identified, tactfully seek to address it. One way is by calling for a Sunday School testimony from a Team member. (Make sure the Team member knows in advance.) Whoever shares should describe general benefits of Sunday School and a current personal experience, all of which might encourage a member to return to the class. Leaving a copy of current Bible study material or *essential connection (ec)* also can help the student consider resuming attendance.

Discuss ways the FAITH Team and Sunday School class might make connections to the member and his family.

Invite the student to be part of specific class and student opportunities.—Take along any printed church information that describes such activities. Offer to meet the student at a specific time and place prior to the event.

• (_____)

In all ministry visits, especially those with nonattenders, be sensitive to the possibility that the student is unsaved.—Be sensitive to the leadership of the Holy Spirit; you may have been given a divine appointment. If the student is not a Christian and the opportunity presents itself, dialogue with him or her about benefits of conversion. Follow the same order of the evangelistic testimony and subsequent points in the FAITH Visit Outline.

If the student being visited is a Christian, ask permission for a Team member to practice.

Invite family members not enrolled in Sunday School to enroll.

Make sure the Team knows of prayer concerns of the member. Conclude the visit with prayer.

After the visit, update information on the FAITH Visit Assignment Card. Share appropriate information as part of Celebration Time.

The goal of a ministry visit is not merely to get a student back into Sunday School, although it certainly is a desired outcome because of the personal growth that occurs through the class. It is important that the student being visited does not think this is your main goal.

Instead, your purpose as a Team is to be there for students, to represent your class as a group of caring believers, to show support for members, and to emphasize how welcome they will be if they choose to return.

Preparing for a Ministry Visit

Since every visit is unique, it is difficult to identify every scenario that can be anticipated. On the other hand, you can do some things to be better prepared for the variety of ministry visit opportunities.

1. Work on (_____ _____) needed by a Christian minister.
   • Compassion—This characteristic means sharing the pain, the hurt, the plight of another person and wanting to do something to change the outcome, lessen the pain, or meet the need.
   • A desire to help and a willingness to be involved—Identifying another person's point of hurt or area of need is one thing; taking the risk of becoming involved to alleviate the pain or meet the need is entirely different.

- Listening skills—Listening includes hearing what the student is saying, as well as understanding what he or she is not saying.
- Sensitivity—By listening and observing, a person can become sensitive to another person's needs, moods, likes, and dislikes.
- Accepting others even when disapproving their actions—To be effective, try to relate to people as they are. That does not mean approving what they do; it simply means acknowledging the reality of their lifestyle. Your goal is to lead student(s) to become what Christ would have them become.
- Confidentiality—During a visit, personal information may be revealed. A person may say more than he or she intended. You also may learn some things intuitively. Whatever the case, the person being visited needs assurance that appropriate information will be kept in confidence. If there is any question about reporting certain information, be certain to ask for his or her permission. Then be careful how and with whom the need is shared.
- Emotional stability—Help Team members be in control of their emotions and avoid extremes in emotion. Inappropriate displays of emotion might upset the student being visited or make him or her uncomfortable. On the other hand, learn to laugh and to cry with the person.
- Spiritual maturity—Study the Word; pray regularly; apply God's Word by working in the church; and show concern for others. In other words, the spiritually mature are in a constant spiritual growth pattern. Second Peter 3:18 reminds us,"But grow in grace and in knowledge of our Lord and Savior Jesus Christ" (NIV)[3].

2. (_____ _____) of an effective cultivator.
- Build trust—You must be genuinely sincere. The skeptical mind will quickly detect pretense. You must be open, credible, responsible.
- Demonstrate a servant spirit.—You are a servant of Christ, and you are learning to serve others in the name of the Savior.
- Be a Christian conversationalist.—Grow in your ability to ask questions that probe the student's interest without being too personal. Conversation related to his or her family, sports, hobbies, and other interests is most productive.
- Be available—On many occasions, a FAITH visit will merely open the door for future relationship-building opportunities. Make yourself available for the student to contact you at home, at work, or at school.
- Follow up with meaningful expressions of care.—Unless you lead your Team and Sunday School class members to take the steps to actually respond to the needs, your commitments will be meaningless. Be sure to demonstrate Christian integrity so that the words you say and the actions you take are consistent.[4]

3. (____ ___ _____) a person is not attending. Identify ways class members can respond to these concerns and connect with him or her.
Following are some general concerns that may contribute to a student's becoming inactive in the class or other church ministries:
- Need for transportation
- Extended illness
- Family problems
- Lack of interest
- Lack of concern or friendship shown by class members and leaders

- Lack of class ministry during time of need
- Poor teaching or dislike of the teacher
- Personality clash with another student
- Dislike of music (or other aspect of the worship)
- No one to care for a sick family member
- Development of sinful attitudes or lifestyle
- Individual is lost

Many of the same issues appearing in an absentee visit also surface in a nonattender visit, but are more pronounced. If you are a Team Leader, help your Team anticipate the reasons and the increased complexity of a visit to a nonattender.

4. (__ _____ __ _____ ____).
Often needs that have not been anticipated will surface in a home visit; they require sensitivity and prayerful handling. These examples represent needs many students have that keep them from participating fully in Sunday School:
- Member or family member in the hospital
- Don't feel they fit in
- Death in the family
- Diagnosis of a serious illness
- Parent's loss of job
- No school friends go to this church
- Emotional trauma (divorce, separation, and so forth)

Many people drop out of attending Bible study and worship because they do not feel they have a support group during life transitions and challenges. Although Sunday School is designed to minister to members and prospects, many classes merely focus on meeting the needs of students who are regular attenders.

Your FAITH Team can help build relationships with absentees, nonattenders, and members who are experiencing unique needs or crises. Your ministry as a FAITH Team will be rewarded as you help students focus on ways they can grow as Christians.

---

[1] Words © 1977 Scripture in Song. Admin. by MARANTHA MUSIC. Renewal 1986 Broadman Press (SESAC). All rights reserved. Distributed by GENEVOX MUSIC GROUP.

[2] Bobby Welch, *Evangelism Through the Sunday School: A Journey of FAITH* (Nashville: LifeWay Press, 1997), 125.

[3] "Qualities Needed for Personal Visitation," by Neil E. Jackson, Jr., *Going . . . One On One: A Comprehensive Guide for Making Personal Visits* (Nashville: Convention Press, 1994), 34-36.

[4] "Making a Visit to Cultivate a Prospect," *Going . . . One On One: A Comprehensive Guide for Making Personal Visits* (Nashville: Convention Press, 1994), 53-54.

Visitation Time
DO IT
As you go . . .

Go out in the attitude and spirit of Christ Jesus, humbling yourself and allowing someone else to see Christ in you.

How are you able to serve others through the visits and contacts you make this week? Are there ways you can meet someone's need? Lift someone's load? Hold out the "Christ light" to someone else? How are you allowing others to serve you during any times of need? Remember, your Sunday School class is there for you, too!

As the Team returns to the church from its visits, the Team Leader should guide in an evaluation of what happened and what follow-up should be done by the Team and/or the class. Discuss how the report should be presented during Celebration Time; be careful not to tell things of a personal or sensitive nature that surfaced during the visit(s).

Celebration Time
SHARE IT
As you return to share . . .

Highlight the results of ministry visits as you debrief your Team. Indicate the different types of Sunday School ministry visits and why certain topics were discussed in the different types of visits. What would Team members suggest as actions for follow-up?
- Other reports and testimonies
- Session 9 Evaluation Card
- Participation Card
- Visitation forms updated with results of visits

The Daily Journey

Day One:
Read John 11:17-36
Why Did He Cry?
Today's passage is an interesting one because it raises an interesting question: *Why did Jesus cry?* If He knew that Lazarus was going to be brought back to life in just moments, why cry? Why not just be happy? Mary and Martha did not understand what was about to happen, so it is understandable why they were so unhappy, but why was Jesus upset? If we want to know Jesus, we need to understand why He reacted to life on this earth the way He did. These issues are the kind of issues that are addressed when people get together for small-group Bible Study.

The Holy Spirit may reveal one piece of the puzzle to one person while giving another piece of the puzzle to the person sitting next to them. He may use different people's experiences to help passages become clear to everyone. That is why we need to be committed to spending time together in prayer and Bible study; and this is especially true for new Christians.

Why did Jesus cry over the death of Lazarus? Why not ask your Sunday School class this Sunday.

Reflect on John 11:1-36. Are you walking with people through hard times in their lives so Jesus can be praised?

Pray for the students that you and your FAITH Team will be making ministry visits to in the coming weeks. Pray that you will have a soft heart for the pain of others.

Day Two:
Read Hebrews 10:23-25
Keep Going!

I hate to run! I vowed that as soon as high school was over I would never run again, and I have done my best to keep that promise! I never enjoyed it, but my high school wrestling coach loved to see his wrestlers run, so I ran. We ran before practice, after practice, and sometimes in our sleep! At the time, I was sure it was just some kind of torture, but later on I realized it was a tool he used to get us ready to face our opponents.

One of the main things that kept me running was the encouragement of the wrestlers around me. We encouraged each other to keep going and not to quit when things got tough. Small groups are good for things like that. As Christians, we are supposed to encourage each other to do what is right and to not quit when it gets tough. You will be in different positions at different times of your life—sometimes you will be the encourager and sometimes you will be the one who needs to be encouraged, but you will always need the strength of a small group's support.

Write down the names of a few people who used to be active in your Sunday School, but have now dropped out. Ask God for a way to encourage them to get back involved in your small-group Bible study._____

Pray that you and your FAITH Team members will encourage others in your class to study the Bible and do what is right. Pray that you will have the courage and personal spiritual maturity to help lead your class to study the Bible more faithfully.

Day Three:
Read Acts 2:42-47
Four Purposes

Every group needs a purpose. Today's Scripture passage gives four purposes for your small group Bible study or Sunday School class:

- The first purpose is to listen and learn about Jesus. We find out who He is and how He wants to impact our lives. Every group needs the life that Jesus brings.
- The second purpose is to experience fellowship. Fellowship includes sharing spiritual truths with each other. It involves people talking about how God is working in their lives and how He has interacted with them recently.
- The third purpose is unconditional acceptance (food). Every small group needs doughnuts! Most people get along with the people they eat with. In Acts 2, the people accepted each other the way Christ had accepted them.
- The fourth purpose is prayer. Prayer provides power to the times you spend

together. It is said that Satan laughs at our feeble efforts, smiles at our never-ending plans, but trembles when we pray.

These four purposes are some of the reasons why we should never give up on our small groups. You should make sure your time together each week includes learning about Jesus, sharing spiritual truths, accepting each other unconditionally (doughnuts optional), and spending time in prayer.

Look over the four purposes again. Which one is the most difficult for you? _____Which one is the easiest?_____

Pray that you and your FAITH Team members will model to new believers in your Sunday School how to walk intimately with God.

Day Four:
Read Daniel 3
No Matter the Cost

Good friends are great treasures in life. Great Christian friends are invaluable because you can gain strength from each other as you live out your Christian values. You can give each other support when you make decisions that other people just don't understand. That's what the situation must have been for Shadrach, Meshach, and Abednego. These young men were able to stand together as friends and let the king know that God could get them out of any situation; but even if God decided not to save them, they would still do what they knew was right.

When these guys gave their lives to God, they gave all of themselves to God. Some Christians try to withhold part of themselves—they think they can live a double life and it's no big deal to God. But it *is* a big deal; it's sin and hypocrisy. Encourage your friends to stand for what is right. Gain strength from each other and encourage each other as you become living examples of a living God.

Think of one area where you have taken a stand for God at school. _____When you stood for what was right, no matter what others said, what did it feel like? Are you willing to continue to walk with God, no matter the consequences?

Pray that you will encourage the other members of your FAITH Team and your Sunday School class to stand for what is right at school.

Day Five:
Read 1 Samuel 16:1-7
Let God Look at the Heart

Samuel set out one day to identify the person who would be the next king of Israel. As soon as Samuel saw Eliab he was sure that Eliab was the person God had chosen to be the next king. But, God had a different plan. God was looking for a heart that would be devoted to Him. David was the one with that kind of heart not Eliab, so in accordance with God's Will, Samuel anointed David king.

As a FAITH Team you will visit some people whom you feel will never accept Christ or live for Christ. Others seem like they are already Christians, but they are not. God knows which hearts are ready and which are not. Listen to Him as you present truth to families and realize that you are there to do His work, His way. That work may include ministering to more than just the students in the family, but also to the entire family. Do not judge a situation by the outside appearance, God knows the heart of people and He has a plan for each of us. Our job is to be faithful to Him as He leads us.

Describe a time when you visited with a student and you judged the family before you even knew them. Be prepared to share with your group this week how God is working in you to be faithful to share Christ with the whole family, not just those your age.

Pray for the students who have accepted Christ recently. Pray that they would understand how to share the love of God with the rest of their family.

Day Six:
Read Hebrews 12:1-3
Hall of Famer
Hebrews 11 has been commonly called the Christian Hall of Fame. Many of the godly people listed in Hebrews 11 faced some incredibly tough situations. Their strong stand for God provides an example for others to follow. God can use you in the same way. You are surrounded by a great number of heroes of the faith that have gone before you and they are cheering you on to victory. The families that you will see this week and in the weeks to come need you to be strong and to stand firm. Remember that your strength is in the Creator of the universe. He can, and will, give you everything you need to continue in the faith. Touch a family this week for all of eternity and look forward to one day stepping into the Hall of Fame yourself.

Which person in the Bible is most like you? _____
Which person in the Bible do you want to be like? _____
Pray that you and your FAITH Team will be faithful to share with a family rather than just individuals. Ask God to show you how you can help some of the students who recently accepted Christ grow in their faith and share Jesus with their own family.

Day Seven:
Read Deuteronomy 6:4-6
Prepare to Share
Total intimidation = Sharing Jesus with a parent when you visit a youth. Sometimes things seem to get reversed. In this passage God is telling parents to follow His commands and to be sure and pass them on to their children. Your generation has a new and different challenge, though: Many of you are being used by God to let parents know that there is a God who loves them and desires a relationship with them. That can be overwhelming except for the fact that this passage also lets us know how these things will be accomplished. Our responsibility is to love God with all of our hearts, souls, and minds. If we do this, God will be able to use us to do some pretty incredible things. Are you willing to be used this week in the life of an adult or student? God will open the door if you are willing to be used by Him.

List one time when you should have shared Christ with an adult, but you "chickened out." Be prepared to share how God has used that experience in your life to prepare you to take advantage of the opportunities God gives you in the future.

Pray specifically for the parent of a student you know who does not know Christ.

The Weekly Sunday School Leadership Team Meeting

Use this space to record ways your FAITH Team impacts the work of your Sunday School department or class. Use the information to report during weekly Sunday School leadership team meetings. Identify actions that need to be taken through Sunday School as a result of prayer concerns, needs identified, visits made by the Team, and decisions made by the students being visited.

Highlight needs and reports affecting your class, department, or age group.

_____

_____

Pray now for teachers and department directors.

How does preparation for Sunday need to consider needs of individuals or families visited through FAITH?

_____

_____

How will the class begin to follow up on students who received a ministry visit?

_____

_____

What areas in your Sunday School do you need to start or strengthen based on input from ministry visits?

_____

_____

For Further Reading

Read pages 66-72 in *Evangelism Through the Sunday School: A Journey of FAITH* by Bobby Welch.

For the Team Leader

This weekly feature suggests actions the Team Leader can take to support Team members, prepare for Team Time, and consider ways to improve visits. This work becomes part of the Team Leader's Home Study Assignments. Add any actions suggested by your church's FAITH strategy.

Support Team Members
❑ Pray for and personally follow up on any Learner who may need personal encouragement.
❑ Contact Team members during the week to remind them you are praying for them and to discuss their participation in FAITH.
❑ Learners are memorizing the gospel presentation through T is for Turn. As you discuss this content with Team members, remind them that this is the heart of the gospel.

Prepare to Lead Team Time
❑ Overview "Team Time" for Session 10.
❑ Review the FAITH Visit Outline.

Prepare to Lead Visits
❑ Be prepared to explain the benefits and procedures of making Sunday School ministry visits.
❑ Be prepared to model a visit in which Team member(s) are asked to lead in a visit up to the point of T is for Turn.
❑ Be prepared to lead your Team to participate during Celebration Time.

Connecting to Sunday School
❑ Participate in weekly Sunday School leadership meetings.
❑ Share pertinent information and other FAITH visit results.

ПΟΤΕS

Connecting to the Entire Family

Misty had been sharing Jesus with Abby at school. She went through the FAITH presentation with her in study hall and made an appointment for her FAITH Team to visit Abby's home. When Misty, Quintin, and Mr. Sanders arrived at her house, Abby was sitting on the front porch. After brief introductions, Mr. Sanders led Abby through the FAITH presentation and she prayed the salvation prayer. They visited some more and talked about baptism and becoming a part of Youth Sunday School.

While they were talking, Mr. Sanders realized Abby's mom had been listening to the conversation through an open window. When the prayer ended, Abby's mom, Mrs. Monroe, came to the front door.

"Can I talk to you, Misty?" asked Mrs. Monroe as she headed toward the opposite end of the front porch.

Leaving Quintin and Mr. Sanders to finish their visit with Abby, Misty joined Mrs. Monroe on the steps and asked, "Is there a problem?"

"No," replied Abby's mom. "Abby and I have always been able to talk about anything. She has been telling me about the things you two have been talking about at school. I knew why you visited tonight and I sat so I could hear your conversation. The things you and your friends have been helping Abby understand are things I have questions about as well. Do you think it would be OK if you showed me the same things you have been showing Abby?"

TEAM TIME

The team leader leads this time. Learners are primarily responsible for reciting the assigned portion of the FAITH Visit Outline and for discussing any Home Study Assignments.

Keep in mind how Learners also look to leaders as role models, motivators, mentors, and friends. Team Time activities can continue in the car, as the Team travels to and from visits.

Check It

FAITH Visit Outline
❑ Listen while each Learner recites all of the *Preparation* and *Presentation* content and key words for *Invitation*.

Practice
❑ Give opportunity for Learners to practice reciting the portion of the FAITH Visit Outline they have learned up to this point.

Other Home Study Assignments
❑ This may be a good time to discuss the benefits of writing a weekly journal as part of the FAITH training. Discuss some of the truths or understandings gained through the weekly Bible studies. Dialogue about how the reflective questions have impacted Learners' training experience.

Session 9 Debriefing (T is for Turn)
❑ T is for Turn. This is the point in the gospel presentation where a person makes a significant choice—as to whether to receive salvation. To be forgiven, a person must turn from his sin and turn to Christ. He must trust Christ and Christ only.

The imagery of turning is reinforced with the simple question, "If you were driving down the road and someone asked you to turn, what would he or she be asking you to do?" (*change direction*). Most people can easily understand the idea of changing direction from one thing to another.

The Bible uses the word *repent* to depict the same thing. The Bible is clear about the need for a person to repent of sin and to live for Christ (change direction) by committing to and trusting Him. Team members will need to remember the significance of the concepts behind the letter *T* to help explain and emphasize the how of the gospel.

Help for Strengthening a Visit
The illustration of changing directions in a car is the only dialogue that is planned as part of the actual gospel presentation. It is important to ask the student to share his or her answer to the question. The response is predictable, but by asking the question you call attention to the gospel and increase his or her participation in the discussion.

You might be talking with a child, a younger youth, or someone who obviously does not drive. If so, adapt the question to something like, "If you were riding down the road and you asked the driver to turn, what would you be wanting the driver to do?"

It usually will be significant to use the word *repent* only after the question has helped you explain what the word means. Use of the turning analogy to emphasize faith in Christ also helps clarify the meaning of *repent*. For many unsaved or unchurched people, *repent* is associated with religious or churchy terms; without a relevant, contemporary explanation, this word might lose much of its significance.

❑ Remind Team members to listen during each visit for ministry opportunities, as well as for things the student might say to help you identify with his or her spiritual journey.

❑ Discuss how, as Team Leader, you communicate follow-up information to the appropriate age class or department when you encounter family members of different ages in home visits.

Notes

_____
_____
_____
_____

Actions I Need to Take with Learners During the Week

_____
_____
_____
_____

A Quick Review

As you recall, your FAITH visits include several main types:
- *prospect or evangelistic visits*, in which the Team may have potential to share the gospel;
- *follow-up visits*, in which the Team visits someone who has made a significant commitment, most often a decision to accept Christ as Savior, during the previous visit;
- *Opinion Poll visits*; and
- *Sunday School ministry visits*.

The last type of visit has the potential to—
- help your Sunday School keep in touch with members;
- meet specific and unique needs in their lives; and
- reactivate absentees before they become chronic nonattenders.

Information to be addressed through ministry visits often surfaces during weekly Sunday School leadership team meetings. Other details are recorded on weekly FAITH Visit Assignment cards, enabling Teams to make contacts using the most up-to-date information possible. Class members are praying and are sensitive to needs they can address.

While the different situations may vary significantly, the FAITH Visit Outline, especially the **Introduction** section, is a good framework for involving the Team and the Sunday School member in a meaningful visit. A capacity to listen with sensitivity, among other skills and personal characteristics, can make the difference in a good visit.

A "good visit" can reclaim someone for your church and Sunday School. A number of FAITH churches have experienced significant results and meaningful personal impact when visiting chronic absentees or inactive members. In some cases, a ministry visit may reveal for the first time a Sunday School member's need for God's forgiveness and salvation. Ministry visits are a significant part of the FAITH strategy.

The Person God Uses

The person God uses gives the glory to God.

Acts 2:43 declares that a simply remarkable thing took place in the early church: "Everyone was filled with awe, and many wonders and miraculous signs were done by the apostles" (NIV). The amazing thing is not that God was at work among His people, but that the believers were available to God so He could do marvelous things through them. They opened their spiritual eyes and saw God at work in their midst. They gave the glory to God for what only He could do (Acts 2:47).

A danger for churches is the tendency toward spiritual pride. We are honored to see God at work saving people and drawing them to Him, yet it becomes easy for us to take credit even for some of the work with which He allows us to be associated. Many believers pray diligently for God to do something wonderful and unique. Yet when God acts, it is so easy for us to forget Who did the work and to seek to take some of the credit.

Be careful to give glory to God for the work He has done and continues to do in people's lives—action that results in salvation. Remember to humbly walk in footsteps that follow the Master. Remember Who does the work of salvation. Remember that God alone deserves the glory!

Lord, forgive us for failing to recognize You at work in our midst. Forgive us for our spiritual pride. Let us be faithful in giving You the glory that is due You and You alone!

You committed to be part of the FAITH Sunday School Evangelism Strategy® training in order to focus on students in your Sunday School class or department. You have spent nearly two semesters in FAITH focusing on ways to minister to and share the gospel with students. In doing this, you have discovered many opportunities for visits with family members and persons who are not students. Although the principles and approaches have focused on making a visit to a student, you have experienced and heard about visits with persons of all ages. It is important to be sensitive to and to address the distinctive needs and issues of all age groups.

This session will help you overview some important considerations when visiting in a home with people of other ages—adults, preschoolers, and children. Look for ways you can help your Team adjust a visit when someone from that age group is present in the home. As you do, you may be making connections in different ways to help reach the entire family for Bible study or Christ.

What If a Preschooler Is in the Room?

As a general rule, Preschool Sunday School workers visit homes to contact parents and to make ministry visits with preschool members or prospects. However, your Team may find itself visiting a home in which a preschooler is present and active. What should you do?

Begin by being prepared for the dynamics of such a visit. Observe these and other guidelines developed with your church's Preschool ministry:

- *Be sensitive to the (_____ _____ ___ _____) of preschoolers.*— Preschoolers demand a schedule in which at least one parent must respond immediately to physical, social, and emotional needs. Often loud, unfamiliar voices cause strain and disruption for young preschoolers. Parents will appreciate Team members who are conscious of the timing and effects of visits during such important times as sleeping, eating, and bathing.

  There may be times when it is appropriate to consider scheduling the visit at another time, especially if doing so might allow adults in the home to give better attention to your message. Especially when young preschoolers are in the home, be sensitive to this potential need.

- *Sit near the preschooler.* —If the family gives permission for a visit now, (_____) the child with your presence. Some preschoolers may be shy or hesitant around strangers, while others will want to be the center of your attention.

  At least one Team member might offer to sit with and give attention to the preschooler as needed during a visit. Such involvement and help by a Team member is especially important if the student you are visiting is open to hearing the gospel presentation.

- *At the same time, never allow a Team member to be alone with a preschooler for any period of time.*

- *Be sensitive to (_____ _____ ___ _____).*—On occasion, a ministry visit will reveal situations in which preschoolers and their families are hurting or have special needs. Parents will appreciate someone who listens and provides care, comfort, and help in meeting needs. You may be able to make important connections to your Sunday School for parents and the preschooler.

- Build bridges for the preschooler's involvement in (Sunday School) by taking along a sample of appropriate materials.—Leaflets such as "Early Bible Steps" or "Preschool Bible Fun" are good to give to preschoolers because they are suitable for the age of the child. Also, offer to parents Bible study material and information that identifies (_____ _____) on security, safety, and teaching of preschoolers while they are at church.

  Preschoolers and their families quickly can sense the comfort and security provided by caring adults. Parents will be glad to know their child will be part of a church and Sunday School that cares about their safety and happiness.

- *In making connections, be open to opportunities to (_____ _____ _____ _____) to preschoolers.*—Every moment with a preschooler is a teachable moment. In talking about God, Jesus, the church, and the Bible with preschoolers, use simple Bible verses, phrases, or thoughts. Such Bible phrases and verses as "God loves you" or "Jesus loves you" help a preschooler feel secure and can build trust in others at church. Simple Bible stories—such as Jesus and the children or the birth of Jesus—will help preschoolers begin to build foundations of faith.

  As you build relationships with and introduce important Bible thoughts to preschoolers, you lay foundations for a future decision for Christ—one that the individual will understand and that will guide and direct his or her life.

- (___ _____) *with the preschooler.*—Remember, preschoolers are literal-minded. Avoid abstract or symbolic concepts—for example, "let Jesus live in your heart." Instead, use language that is clear and simple.

- *If an opportunity has not come up earlier, (___ _____ __ _____ __ _____ _____) in Sunday School.*

What If A Child (Grades 1-6) Is in the Home?

How should a FAITH Team best handle the presence of elementary-age children in the home when making a FAITH visit? Keep several important principles in mind:

• *Just as there are major differences between younger and older preschoolers, so are there (_____ _____ _____ _____).* —In particular, children are active in their physical, mental, and social development. They are beginning to move from almost exclusive concrete thinking to more abstract thinking.

• *Recognize that children are at a significant time in their (_____ _____).* —Many children are privileged to be raised in loving, caring homes that build strong foundations for their understanding of God's love. Other children are in homes that lack such support.

• *(____ ____) them.* —Children are not adults; but they can think, talk, and ask and answer questions. Children appreciate someone who talks with them and not merely at them. It helps if a Team member can talk with children on their level—for example, to ask questions about school activities, interests, and hobbies.

• *Children like to be with other children in fun, meaningful experiences.* —Tell the child about the type of activities he or she would engage in during (_____ _____). Provide a sample of material used on Sundays.

• *Help the child feel comfortable with you and with the idea of participating in Sunday School and church experiences.* —One way, if known, is to indicate some of the children who are in the department to which the child would be assigned. Seek to (_____ ___ _____ _____) in Sunday School.

• *Team members should become sensitive to (_____ _____) many children are facing.* —Such issues include, but are not limited to, having parents who are divorced and/or who have remarried; being in a single-parent home; facing challenges with schoolwork; exhibiting a low self-image; and being limited by physical disabilities.

• *It may be helpful for one Team member to focus attention on the child while other Team members relate to the student and/or other family members.* —It also is important to relate necessary information to Children's Sunday School leaders by writing appropriate details on the FAITH Visit Assignment Card.

• *Never leave a Team member (_____) with a child for any period of time.*

• *Even though the concepts shared in the FAITH gospel presentation are simple, many facts of the gospel are particularly abstract for a child.* —Remember that many children will be hearing these concepts for the first time and will not understand the personal significance of such truths as the availability of God's forgiveness, the need to turn from their sin to Christ, and the implications of heaven.

The Holy Spirit works in the tender lives of children, and children certainly can make the decision to accept Jesus as their Savior. However, be sensitive to the need many children have to think about and ask personal questions over a period of time about their relationship to and understandings of the gospel.

When Adults Are Present

When making a FAITH visit to a student, it is entirely possible that one or both parents may be present in the room as Team members talk with the student. Especially in situations where the family has not been exposed to church, parents may feel a need to sit in and hear what you have to say to their teenager. This can provide an excellent opportunity! Many times parents (and entire families) have made professions of faith and become members of a church because of their student's involvement in that church. As described in the case study with Abby's mom (at the beginning of this session) often a parent will overhear the gospel presentation and want to learn more. In many homes, several generations live together. Be aware of the many differences and needs adults represent.

- *Adults are distinctive from one another.*—Each person has a wonderfully unique personality and background. Many adults have learned to respond negatively to other people because of abuse or other hurtful factors. Other persons are going through extreme transitions of life. Most lead very busy and complicated lives. In general, adults are searching for meaning and purpose in life, no matter their marital, financial, or physical status. It is important that you treat each person as a (_____ ___ _____ _____), no matter how he or she responds to your Team's overtures.
- *Many adults are protective of their time, family matters, and home space.*—They are resistant to allowing a stranger to intrude on their time or space. Many persons feel strangers at the door are only there to sell some unwanted item or to get something from them. Sometimes our timing is not the best for them.
- *A related principle is to quickly and carefully gain the trust of adults.*—We must demonstrate respect. Building relationships starts with building trust.
- *All adults have a story to share.*—Their lives are invested with both positive and negative experiences. They want to be understood and loved no matter what their stories. Making a connection involves (_____ _____ ___ _____).
- *Many adults desperately desire meaningful relationships.*—But some tend to reject persons who seek to reach out to them. Others have been hurt in the past and fear that any new relationship will result in added pain. We must be willing for some people to reject us while patiently looking for ways to initiate and demonstrate a safe, caring relationship.
- *Not every adult you encounter will be ready to hear the message of the gospel.*— Many will need to watch you, as well as the integrity of your message, before they will begin investigating the potential impact of the gospel for their lives. We have been told that it takes a business an average of 13 contacts before a customer begins considering the potential of purchasing its product or service. In the same way, many adults need to (____ ___ __ ___ ____ __ _____) about the implications of such a powerful message before they commit their lives to Christ.
- *The Holy Spirit works in the lives of adults no matter their background, status, experience, successes, or failures.*—Even if you have difficulty relating to some adults when you go on a FAITH visit, remember that your job is simply to share the best way you know how. The Holy Spirit will do the rest! In many situations, when you reach the adult, you have an inroad to reaching the entire family.

---

[1] David Scott, *Good News for Youth: The Power to Change Lives* (Nashville: Convention Press, 1998), 9.

Visitation Time
DO IT
As you go . . .

Think about the long-term connections of relationship and time that your FAITH Team is building, as preschoolers and children feel love expressed to them in a home; as relationships of love and good experiences extend to the church; as the church extends its support to families. Remember the children who some day will meet Christ and begin to grow in Him.
 Remember the students in that home you visited and the untapped potential that teenager seemed to have. Does he or she need the support and love of peers, the encouragement to take risks and to grow, and the insights from God's Word?
 Remember adults who are still growing and seeking to find meaningful ways to leave their imprint on the world. What a joy when an adult has the life-changing experience only Christ can provide!

Celebration Time
SHARE IT
As you return to share . . .

Ask a Team member to take the lead in sharing reports.
• Reports and testimonies
• Session 10 Evaluation Card
• Participation Card
• Visitation forms updated with results of visits

The Daily Journey

Day One:
Read Acts 16:22-34
Tough Situation, Incredible Outcome
Most people would do anything to get out of a tough situation. In this Scripture, Paul and Silas had just been beaten for teaching about Jesus, and they found themselves in prison chains. Instead of complaining about the bad things that were happening to them because of their faith, they sang praise songs and prayed. It must have been an incredible sound because it captured the attention of the other prisoners. What captured the attention of the jailer was the fact that when Paul and Silas had the opportunity to escape, they hung around. It would have cost the jailer his life if they had escaped, so the fact that they chose to remain in the prison made a huge impact on him. He wanted to know how he could follow the same God that they followed! Following God means that sometimes difficult situations really make a difference in the lives of other people.
 Because of Paul and Silas' obedience, the guy who was to keep them in jail was the same one who took care of their wounds and gave them something to eat. Because of their faithfulness, that jailer and his entire family are enjoying

heaven today. God may use you this very week to change the course of an entire family's final destination. Look at every situation as that kind of opportunity. Difficult situations could be the front door to heaven for someone around you this week.

Describe what the outcome may have been if you had been in jail instead of Paul and Silas. What do you think is the difference between you and Paul?

Pray that you and your FAITH Team will not complain about difficult situations. Pray that you will rejoice that God has allowed you to grow. Watch for how God can use you in difficult situations this week.

Day Two:
Read 1 Timothy 4:6-13
You Set the Example

There may be a lot of people who think you are not old enough to make a significant impact for the cause of Jesus Christ. But God is not one of them! Through your faithful obedience, you can set an example and be a messenger for the church, even though you are young. Throughout history God has used students your age to impact the world around them. In Samuel's day, there were adult ministers living and working in the Temple, but it was Samuel who was chosen by God to deliver a message to Eli. There were thousands of soldiers listening to Goliath challenge the God of heaven, but it was the boy, David, that God used to beat a huge army. It can be the same with you. God wants to use you to impact your world and He's already working on situations and people around you. Listen for His voice, watch for His hand at work, and then be strong and courageous to follow Him wherever He leads you. You too can be a part of some incredible, history-making events. But first you must decide if you are willing to set the example and live a life of absolute integrity and commitment to following God's leadership.

Read 1 Timothy 4:12 again. In which area of this verse do you set a good example? _____ Which area is your weakness?_____

Pray for yourself and your FAITH Team today. Pray that you will set an example of godly speech, consistent life, open love, true faith, and absolute purity for your church.

Day Three:
Read Acts 16:11-15
What If God Has A Bigger Plan?

I heard a story one time about a group of people who went on an evangelistic visit and it seemed like they were getting nowhere. The more they explained about God, the less their prospect seemed to listen. Finally they asked him if he would be willing to respond to God's offer of forgiveness. He said *no*, but from another room of the house, his wife asked if she could take advantage of it. Her kids, who also wanted to give their hearts to Christ, followed her. This family was changed because a team was faithful to keep sharing the good news of Jesus' forgiveness, even though it seemed like they were going "nowhere." Because they were not pushy or rude about the father's apparent lack of concern, the rest of the family was able to hear all the truth they needed to commit their lives to God.

Today's Scripture introduces us to Lydia. We don't know anything about Lydia except that she heard the gospel from Paul when he went to a river to pray. She (and her whole household) was saved because Paul understood that God sometimes has a bigger plan.

Write a prayer to God explaining your willingness to follow His plan over yours in every life situation—school, work, church, home or play.

_____

_____

Pray for yourself and the members of your FAITH Team. Pray that you will not go into situations with a negative attitude. God is able to do much more than you think or understand. Pray that the friends you have at school who have parents or siblings who are lost would be bold in sharing with their families. Pray for your part in that mission.

Day Four:
Read 1 Timothy 5:1-2
Respect

Respect is the key word for this passage. You will continually go into situations where you have the right answer, and people may not recognize it as the truth. Treating them with respect will go a long way toward allowing the truth to settle in on them. Remember that it is the Spirit of God who is at work drawing them to the Father. Your job is to love them with a God-sized love and let them know that you know Jesus and how He has impacted your life. The rest is up to that person and God's Spirit.

A lack of respect will erect a barrier that will make people resistant to anything you have to say, whether it is truth or not. Jesus continually treated people with great respect. Every person you will visit is deeply loved by God, and your concern for their well-being will allow them to see that kind of love first hand.

List a time when you showed disrespect for another person and now you know that the person is not a Christian.

_____

Ask God to forgive you for your disrespect and then ask God for a way to approach that person for forgiveness.

Pray that you and your FAITH Team members will respect the parents and authorities in your life this week.

Day Five:
Read Judges 7
Led by the Spirit

Joni is not someone about whom everyone would automatically say, "she will be great sharing her faith." Joni is just a girl who is willing to be used by God and led by God. She struggled learning the FAITH outline and she struggled with fear every time she shared the outline. But, she was willing to let God use her. Joni led someone to Christ one day. Was it because her presentation was polished, or was it because she was willing to be used by God and led by Him?

Gideon was not the biggest man mentioned in the Bible and he was not from the strongest family. In fact, Gideon is known more for his weakness and fear than for his victory in battle. But Gideon was willing to be used by God and led by God. How about you?

What is the greatest barrier to your total obedience to God? _____ How can you learn to listen to God's voice and obey Him more?_____
_____

Pray for yourself and your FAITH Team. Pray that you will not be afraid to listen and obey God in your daily lives.

Day Six:
Read John 12:44-50
Light Words

Jesus came to be a light—no one who believes in Him will walk in darkness. What does that mean to you?

It is a different way of life for a Christian to live in the light of Jesus. Many people try to live "out of the darkness" instead of living in God's light. Their philosophy is, "I don't do anything really bad, I basically behave and do the right thing." But the question for a Christian is not whether or not they have avoided the bad stuff, it is, "Are you following Jesus fully today?" Jesus said that God instructed Him throughout the day, even telling Him "what to say and how to say it" (vv. 49-50). Are you willing to live today listening to God's instructions? Pray that you will be attentive to the leading of God. Make a commitment that you will not just try to avoid doing bad things, but that you will follow God and do whatever He leads you to do today.

Write down ten attitudes that you feel describe a person who lives in darkness.
_____
_____
_____

Now list ten attitudes that are examples of living in the light. _____
_____
_____

Pray for yourself and the other FAITH Team members. Pray that all of you will listen to the leading of the Holy Spirit today. Pray that God will lead you today to people who need to hear about Jesus. Also pray that you will be willing to share Jesus with them today.

Day Seven:
Read John 10:1-15
The Big Question of Prayer

Eating out one afternoon at a fast food restaurant, I saw a dog wandering around the garbage can. He was obviously a stray, and hungry from being away from home. I tried to call the dog and lure him into my car so I could take him home, but he would not come to me. Even after I called the name on his collar, he wouldn't get in my car. The dog just looked at me and walked away.

In John 10, Jesus teaches us to listen to Him. Christians will know the voice of God and will be instructed by Him because He is their shepherd. God's voice is not something we can describe or record on a CD; God's voice is something you hear inside you and His Spirit confirms that it is indeed God. Jesus said His sheep would know His voice (verse 4). The more you talk with God in prayer and the more you listen for Him, the more you will recognize His voice in daily life. Just like the lost dog that would not go with a stranger, (even when I knew his name), you will learn to respond to Jesus because you will recognize His voice and respond only to Him.

When is the best time for God to speak to you? _____ _____

When are you typically not listening for God's voice?_____

Pray that you and the members of your FAITH Team will listen for God's voice today. Ask God to teach you more about His leadership in your life over the next 24 hours.

The Weekly Sunday School Leadership Team Meeting

Use this space to record ways your FAITH Team impacts the work of your Sunday School department or class. Use the information to report during weekly Sunday School leadership team meetings. Identify actions that need to be taken through Sunday School as a result of prayer concerns, needs identified, visits made by the Team, and decisions made by the persons being visited.

Highlight needs or reports affecting your class, department, or age group.

_____

_____

Pray now for teachers and department directors.

How does the preparation for Sunday need to consider the varying needs of families represented by selected FAITH visits?

_____

_____

How does your teaching appropriately focus on life needs of various ages? How could it be more effective? What training needs might be identified and followed up on?

_____

_____

For Further Reading

Read the FAITH Tip: "Talking with Children About Salvation."

For the Team Leader

This weekly feature suggests actions the Team Leader can take to support Team members, prepare for Team Time, and consider ways to improve visits. This work becomes part of the Team Leader's Home Study Assignments. Add any actions suggested by your church's FAITH strategy.

Support Team Members
- ❏ Contact Team members during the week. Remind them you are praying for them. Discuss prayer concerns and answers to prayer.
- ❏ This week Learners are memorizing the FAITH presentation through the *Invitation*. As you discuss this content with Team members, remind them that this is when someone has the opportunity to make a life-changing decision.
- ❏ Encourage Learners to read all FAITHTips.
- ❏ Record specific needs and concerns of Team members in the space provided.

Prepare to Lead Team Time
- ❏ Review Home Study Assignments of Team members.
- ❏ Overview "Team Time" for Session 11.

Prepare to Lead Visits
- ❏ Review the FAITH Visit Outline.

Connecting to Sunday School
- ❏ Share about FAITH during this week's meeting.

FAITH*Tip*

Talking with Children About Salvation

From birth, God is at work in the lives of girls and boys. He desires for parents and other adults to nurture and to instruct children in such a way as to provide a foundation leading them toward faith in Jesus Christ. At some point, often during the first- through sixth-grade years, most children become aware of their sin.

When the opportunity presents itself to talk with children about salvation, these guidelines can help in sensitively assessing a child's readiness to accept Christ.

1. Counsel children individually. When possible, invite parents to be present.

2. Be conversational. Often when adults talk with children, the conversation sounds like a monologue. Talk with, not to, the child.

3. Ask open-ended questions. For example, ask, "Juan, why do you want to become a Christian?" or "Judy, why do you think a person needs to become a Christian?" Open-ended questions require the child to think and give you an answer other than *yes* or *no*. Often when adults ask a *yes* or *no* question, they unconsciously answer the question for children with their body language, such as a nod of the head to indicate *yes*. Toward the end of the conversation at the time of commitment, you will use some *yes* and *no* questions; but at that point the questions are simply to confirm what the child has already told you.

4. Give the child time to think. Adults are not comfortable with silence. When children are asked questions they often need time to think. Wait for the answers.

5. Listen carefully to the child's questions and answers. The insight you gain from the responses will guide you as you continue the conversation and help you know if the child understands the information. To become a Christian, a child must be able to comprehend that his personal sin separates him from a relationship with God, express sorrow over his sin, and willingly repent of his sin.

6. Use the Bible. The Bible gives authority to what you say. As you use your Bible, you model how to use it. Use five or six key verses, if possible, from the child's Bible.

7. Show sincere concern, but avoid becoming emotional. Children are easily influenced emotionally. They are eager to please adults. If you become teary-eyed, you will confuse them. Most children still associate tears with negative emotions.

8. Speak in your normal tone of voice. Adults have a special high-pitched voice they often use with children. Older children may be distracted or annoyed by the condescending tone.

9. Avoid talking about sin in such a way that you penetrate the child's privacy or elicit an unhealthy sense of guilt. Adults can easily make a child feel guilty. Just because a child agrees she has lied does not mean she can relate her sin to rebellion against God. God holds a person morally responsible or accountable when she is able to relate her actions to Him.

10. Be sincere. In 17 years of full-time children's ministry, I have found that when a child is truly ready to hear the plan of salvation, the Holy Spirit places in him a willingness to listen to the presentation.

Adapted from *Good News for Kids: The Power to Change Lives,* by Cindy Pitts.(Nashville: Convention Press, 1998), 28-30.

RECOGNIZING A DIVINE APPOINTMENT

LIBBA GILLUM

MRS. PHAM WORKS AS A SECRETARY at a local school. Johnny, a student who helps in the office during his free period, overheard Mrs. Pham talking on the phone to a church friend. When she hung up the phone, Johnny asked about her church—he wanted to know more about Sunday School and the Wednesday meeting for youth. Mrs. Pham promised to bring him some information about her church's youth activities.

On the following Monday, Mrs. Pham brought Johnny the information she had promised. Johnny looked though the colorful brochure and the calendar, but was most interested in the copy of *essential connection*. When he got home that day after school, he went to his room and began to read the articles in the *ec* magazine. He especially noticed the information about "How to Become a Christian" on the inside front cover of the magazine, wondering why he never heard any of that information before; he wished someone could explain it all to him.

His parents were working late, so Johnny fixed himself cheese nachos in the microwave for supper. As he prepared the cheese, he continued to read and think about the plan of salvation printed in the magazine. Just as he took the nachos from the microwave, he heard a knock on the door. When he opened it, he was greeted by three people from Mrs. Pham's church.

"Hi! my name is Amy Lou—and this is Danny and Randy. We're from Fourteenth Street Baptist Church and we are trying to better understand how we can help your neighborhood. Do you mind if we ask you a few questions?"

TEAM TIME

The team leader leads this time. Learners are primarily responsible for reciting the assigned portion of the FAITH visit outline and for discussing any Home Study Assignments.

Keep in mind how Learners also look to leaders as role models, motivators, mentors, and friends. Team Time activities can continue in the car, as the Team travels to and from visits.

Check It

FAITH Visit Outline

❑ Listen while each Learner recites all of the *Preparation* and *Presentation* content and key words for *Invitation*.

Practice

❑ Give opportunity for Learners to practice reciting the portion of the FAITH Visit Outline they have learned up to this point.

Other Home Study Assignments

❑ This may be a good time to discuss the benefits of writing a weekly journal as part of the FAITH training. Discuss some of the truths or understandings gained through "The Daily Journey."

Session 9 Debriefing (T is for Turn)

❑ This is the pivot on which the gospel opens. A person must turn from his sin and turn to Christ. He must trust Christ only. The imagery of turning is reinforced with the simple question, "If you were driving down the road and someone asked you to turn, what would he or she be asking you to do?" (change direction). Most people can easily understand the idea of changing direction from one thing to another.

The Bible uses the word *repent* to depict the same thing. The Bible is clear in the need for a person to repent of sin and to live for Christ (change direction) by committing to and trusting Him. Team members will need to remember the significance of the concepts behind the letter *T* to help explain and emphasize the *how* of the gospel.

Help for Strengthening a Visit

The illustration of changing directions in a car is the only dialogue that is planned as part of the actual gospel presentation. It is important to ask the student to share his or her answer to the question. The response is predictable, but by asking the question you call the student's attention to the gospel and increase his or her participation in the discussion.

You might be talking with a child, a younger youth, or someone who obviously does not drive. If so, adapt the question to something like, "If you were riding down the road and you asked the driver to turn, what would you be wanting the driver to do?"

It usually will be significant to use the word *repent* only after you have explained what it means during this segment of the FAITH presentation. It also helps to use the word *repent* by also using the word *turn* to frequently emphasize the importance of this step of faith in Christ. For many persons, *repent* is associated with religious or churchy terms and might lose much of its significance without having a relevant, contemporary explanation.

Notes

_____
_____
_____

_____

Actions I Need to Take with Learners During the Week

_____
_____
_____
_____

A Quick Review

Take the following brief quiz. It (and similar questions from previous sessions) will help prepare you for the written review in Session 16.

___ 1. True or False: Your Team is responsible only for persons who are or would be assigned to your own Sunday School department or class.

___ 2. Actions you can take with family members in the home include (Place a check mark beside all that apply in a FAITH visit)—

___ a. Ask to enroll the person(s) if not participating in Sunday School.

___ b. Engage the person in conversation and include the person(s) in the ministry or evangelism visit as appropriate to their age or situation.

___ c. Have a Team member work with the person one-on-one, particularly if with a young family member, while the other Team members focus on older member(s) of the family.

___ d. Gather information on the person(s) and be prepared to share it using the FAITH Visit Assignment Card for the appropriate Sunday School class/department.

Be Ready for Divine Appointments

You are leading other Team members to be prepared to minister and to share the gospel with Sunday School members and prospects. Your assigned visits usually will be in the homes of members or prospects. In addition, you are leading Team members to be prepared to conduct Opinion Poll visits. At this point you realize that most of the visits you make, though bathed in prayer by many people, are those for which you are prepared and are to places and people you are prepared to visit.

After you make several visits with your Team, you will begin to realize some encounters are more spontaneous than others. Although you cannot explain it, you may "just happen upon" some people who seem more responsive than usual to the ministry or evangelistic message of Team members. You may discover that some individuals are not necessarily those who have been assigned to the Team. This session will help focus on the challenges and opportunities for divine appointments you may experience as a Team.

Divine appointments can be defined as those encounters where it can only be explained that God has been at work directing the specific Team to intersect and engage a specific person at a given time.

It becomes apparent that God has been at work so the person is particularly prepared to hear and respond to the gospel or to the Team's ministry. This kind of encounter significantly reminds us yet again that it is God who makes just the right time, just the right person, and just the right thing(s) to say and do.

Every ministry and gospel presentation contact, in reality, is a divine appointment when God is in charge. When you begin to grasp this reality, you realize that even when one student is not at home or someone rejects the ministry of the gospel, you are intentionally (_____ ___ _____ __ _____ _____). God may have sent you to a house or to a neighborhood to encounter someone He has prepared and placed at that site to intersect with Team members who are prepared to be used by Him.

Principles for heightened preparation for divine appointments include the following:

1. (_____) is an integral part in divine appointments. We pray for God to use us. Moreover, we join other believers in praying for—
• your Team to be in the right place at the right time;
• nonbelievers to be prepared and receptive;
• God to be active in and to soften the hearts of individuals who need to be touched by the message of and ministry of the gospel.

When it becomes apparent that God has led your Team to a particular student who is convicted or convinced by the Holy Spirit, it is vital that Team members pray for each other and for the specific leadership of the Spirit in all that is said.

2. The (____ _____) is ultimately in control of every situation of the believer's life and places people in situations in which He can most appropriately use them for His glory. God uses all your experiences for His good. He may assign you to encounter someone who can relate to the gospel message only because you can relate to his particular situation. Many times a believer discovers that his previous experiences (trials, valleys, learning experiences) are used by God to help someone who needs the gospel better relate to the good news.

3. (_____ ___ ___ _____ __ ___) become more sensitive and usable for spontaneous situations. God may close some doors of planned visitation in order to place you at open doors of opportunity, in which you minister and/or share the gospel. God will let you know what to say and do at the appointed time. Remember Jesus' words: ". . . do not worry about what to say or how to say it. At that time you will be given what to say, for it will not be you speaking, but the Spirit of your Father speaking through you" (Matt. 10:19-20, NIV).

4. Often it takes an (_____ __ ____ _____ _____) to intersect our lives with the students who need God's message. God uses persons at every stage (FAITH Group Leaders, Sunday School leaders during weekly leadership meetings, church secretaries, and others who coordinate making visitation assignments) to link a specific Team with someone who needs to hear the gospel. God can choose to use a believer even when that person is not aware of the situations leading up to the encounter with another person. Recognize that every visit will be a good one because God is at work both in

the lives of the Team members as well as those who are being visited.

5. (_____ _____) is not the same as ours. On many occasions, you may be assigned to visit where no one is at home or where all the "doors" are closed for any effective visit. It is then that you encounter a person who is in need of and receptive to the ministry of the gospel. The world may call such occasions "chance encounters" or "coincidence"; Christians know them as divine appointments.

Ways to Prepare the Team

1. (_____ _____ __ __ ___ _____) in all aspects of training and personal encounters.
2. Emphasize and (____ __ ___ __ _____) for Team members, for the students assigned to be visited, for situations that block some encounters and open up others.
3. (___ ___ _____ ___ ___). Look for open and closed doors to the gospel. Try to view individuals as Jesus sees them.
4. (___ ___ _____ ___ ___). Listen for questions and comments that might indicate the movement of God's Spirit in the student's life. Listen for the still, small voice of God as He teaches and uses you.
5. (___ ____ __ _ _ ___) and go be part of it.[1]
6. (___ ___ ____ ___) and in touch with God's leadership. Although God can use anyone, He seeks persons who are obedient and submissive to Him. "A tender and sensitive heart will be ready to respond to God at the slightest prompting."[2]
7. Realize that divine appointments may be to (____ _ ____) so that someone will begin considering the gospel for his or her life, to (_____ _ _____ _____) that opens the gospel for someone, and to (____ __ _____) with a person at just the right time.
8. Understand that (____ _____ ____ _____ _____) in your way to obscure your sensitivity to and availability for divine appointments. However, never forget that "the one who is in you is greater than the one who is in the world" (1 John 4:4, NIV).

Divine appointments can take place as a result of or during a planned visit. They can take the place of a planned visit (for example, you try to make a visit and find no one at home; upon leaving, you encounter someone with whom you begin talking, only to discover he has been looking for someone to explain how to have assurance of God's forgiveness.)

Such encounters can take place going to or returning from a planned visit. Often these are spontaneous encounters, and usually away from the home setting. Although such a visit could be in a home as part of the planned visit where the entire visitation outline is initiated, you could find yourself in a store or restaurant, on the side of a street, in a parking lot, in a yard, or by a car. Be particularly sensitive to the leadership of the Holy Spirit in anticipation of and in response to divine appointment encounters.

What Would You Do?
Tom and his FAITH Team members, Carlos and Cindi, attempted three visits. No one was at home, and time was becoming a factor. Carlos had yet to share the entire gospel presentation during a visit, and Tom was certainly hoping for Carlos to have the experience.

On the way back to the church, Tom decided to pull into a fast-food restaurant to get some cold drinks. *At least,* Tom thought, *we can practice on each other and give Carlos the opportunity to share the gospel with us.* After placing their orders and finding a table in the nearly-empty restaurant, a young couple came in and sat near them.

Carlos thought the guy looked familiar. He struck up a conversation with him and soon realized that he had recently waited on him in the mall. Carlos told the couple that the Team was visiting for their church; Cindi and Tom moved closer and entered into the conversations. The young man responded that he and his girlfriend wanted to get married but did not have any connection with a church. He shared that she was pregnant and had been alienated from her family who lived in another state.

Tom looked at his watch and realized it was time to return to the church. Without realizing what was happening, Cindi shared her Sunday School testimony. A few customers came into the restaurant, and Tom thought the conversations would die down. Yet he began to pray for God's leadership. Cindi also was praying. No one seemed to know what to do.

Maximize the Potential

Consider these guidelines to help your Team members anticipate and respond to significant opportunities.

1. (_____) the student(s) and (_____ _ _____). Keep in mind the kinds of things you ordinarily would talk about during the *Introduction* of a FAITH visit.
2. (_____ ____ _____) and briefly explain what you are doing (visiting Sunday School members and prospects on behalf of your church).
3. Learn to (_____ _____ _____ _____) to discover a student's spiritual journey in a spontaneous situation.
4. (_____ ___ _____) and ways to identify or associate with the student.
5. (__ ___ ___ _____ _ _____ __ _____) evangelistic testimony, to ask the Key Question, and to share the FAITH gospel presentation.
6. Humbly (_____ ____ ___ __ __ _ _____ ____) and that you may have the privilege of being His instrument in leading a student to faith in Christ.
7. Look for ways to (_____ __) on needs, concerns, and decisions.

[1]Henry T. Blackaby and Claude V. King, *Experiencing God* (Broadman & Holman Publishers, 1994),
[2]Ibid., 122.

The Story Continues

Although there was more noise in the restaurant than when the conversations began, Carlos asked the Key Question and then asked for permission to share what the Bible has to say. The man's response was, "I never thought I'd say this, but now more than ever, I really want to know. Please tell us." Carlos took the few minutes to share. Tom and Cindi realized that the Holy Spirit was the One in charge as both the young man and his girlfriend listened carefully and committed their lives to Christ. All this happened because they were killing time before Celebration Time. Tom realized that one of their challenges would be to identify ways to begin follow-up.

What would be appropriate ways to ensure follow-up in this situation?

Visitation Time
DO IT
As you go . . .

The weather is messy; you have a ton of homework. Recent visitation assignments have not been very promising. Last week's maps and directions were confusing, and the Team got lost in an unfamiliar part of town. You're tired and have to be in class early tomorrow. It would be a lot easier not to go on FAITH visits this week.

By going out to visit even when it would be easier not to, you show your obedience to God and a desire to serve. You also position yourself more firmly against the devil as you "put on the full armor of God."

Recognize that, in God, every visit is a good visit. During times like these, you may find yourself refreshed and revived by a divinely orchestrated appointment. Don't allow yourself to miss out!

Celebration Time
SHARE IT
As you return to share . . .

- Reports and testimonies
- Session 10 Evaluation Card
- Participation Card
- Visitation forms updated with results of visits

The Daily Journey

Day One:
Read Acts 16:14-33
Look for God Anyway

You never know what to expect from Paul and Silas. They were led by God to go to a town called Philippi, and while they were there they shared Jesus with as many people as they could. In the process they healed a girl who was possessed by demons. That seems like a good thing to do, doesn't it? It was good in God's eyes, but not in the eyes of the townspeople. They threw Paul and Silas in jail. But, surprise—all along, God had a plan! God knew that there was a man who worked in the jail that really needed to know Jesus. So, God allowed Paul and Silas to get locked up so they could tell the jailer how to know Jesus.

Those two men didn't complain and moan about being put in jail, rather they looked for opportunities to share Christ where they were. How about you? When interruptions happen in your day do you complain, or do you look for opportunities to share Christ? Are you willing to share Christ if God moves you to a different place to sit in class, or puts you with a different team, or moves you to a new town? God is always moving people who are willing to share Christ toward people who are ready to receive Christ. Are you willing to be used by God if He decides to move you?

Look back over the past week. List any divine appointments that you may see now, but at the time you did not notice.

Pray for yourself and your FAITH Team. Pray that you will be faithful to share Christ when God brings people into your life unexpectedly.

Day Two:
Read John 4:4-42
Following God's Voice
Kristen second-guessed God on this one—"Go to McDonald's?" she said aloud. Sitting in her car she thought, *I'm not even hungry*. But everything within her said, "Go to McDonald's," so she went. She sat down and waited for the reason that God had sent her. She didn't have to wait long before one of the employees struck up a conversation with her and she had an opportunity to share Christ with him. But, he didn't receive Christ that night, and as Kristen drove home she was confused about why God had sent her there. She was excited that she had been faithful and useful to God.

The next Sunday there was a new girl visiting Kristen's Sunday School class. Kristen sat down with her and talked, only to find out that she worked at McDonald's. She said she was at church because, "Somebody came in late one night and talked to one of the guys at work about Jesus, and that guy later shared a little with her." Later that day, Kristen's new friend became a believer.

Are you willing to listen and obey God's voice? If you are willing to listen, God will direct you toward some divine appointments. It may be on a FAITH visit, at school, work, or even at home—but God will direct a willing witness toward a person who needs to know Christ.

Write here a brief description of a FAITH visit or other moment when you knew later you definitely had a divine appointment._____
_____
_____

Pray that you and your FAITH Team will be watching for divine appointments—especially in the next 24 hours. Pray that you and the other members of your team with be faithful to share when God brings people into your lives.

Day Three:
Read Mark 10:46-52
Divine Appointments from the Other Side

Most of the time when we think about divine appointments, we think of them from our perspective, right? This description of Jesus' ministry is from the other perspective, the person who needs Jesus. God is always leading willing witnesses toward people who need Christ, but God is also leading the person needing Christ toward a willing witness. God really is in control!

You may not encounter a blind man this week screaming your name, but you will encounter some people that God has moved out of their routine right into your path. Watch for people in your day who are looking for God, and they don't even know who to ask or what to ask for. Divine appointments happen all the time on FAITH visits, but they also happen in daily life—watch out for them!

Write a brief reflection on Mark 10:46-52. Write your thoughts and what God is teaching you from this passage.

Pray this week for a divine appointment. Pray also for divine appointments for the other FAITH Team members.

Day Four:
Read Acts 8:26-35
Total Obedience

I have to admit that if I had been Philip and the Holy Spirit had told me to run to some guy that I had never met and start talking to Him about God, I would have had some good excuses why I shouldn't go. There might even have been the temptation to pretend I wasn't sure it was God speaking. I might have taken so much time to respond to God that the man would have driven by before I arrived. But Phillip did not seem to worry about things like that. Because of Philip's obedience, he was used by God to introduce an Ethiopian officer to the true living God. It was not up to Phillip to arrange a special meeting and try to impress the official in order to get close to him. God had done all that already. Phillip's job was to answer the questions God had already put in this man's heart and mind. God is still doing the same kind of thing today—you may see it happen this week at school or on one of your FAITH visits. These are divine appointments, arranged by God to allow you to be used by Him to touch someone's life. Look for them, listen to Him, and see how He can use you this very week.

Day Five:
Read Ephesians 1
The Eyes of Your Heart

Do you ever look at someone and wonder what he or she is thinking? If you could climb into another person's body and look at life through his or her eyes, you would understand completely how they see life. If you could hear their thoughts you would know whom they liked and who got on their nerves. You would know why they react to certain situations the way they do. It would all make sense.

Paul's prayer for us is that the eyes of our hearts would be open to understand God, to know the exciting things that God has in store for us and understand His great power—to see life as God sees life. If we see things the way God sees them, we will have an incredible amount of confidence in every situation because we know that God has the power to care for us.

What part of God do you understand least? What aspect of God do you think you understand? Be prepared to talk about your answers.

Pray that the eyes of your heart will be opened today to His incredible riches and ultimate power. Pray that you and your FAITH Team will not try to see life and situations of life only through your own eyes. Pray that you will see life as God sees life.

Day Six:
Read Ephesians 2
Created with a Purpose

Each of us wants to feel that we are special for one reason or another. This passage lets you know three very important things. One: God created you, you are His workmanship. Everything about you is special because it is unique to you. Two: You were created with a purpose in mind—to do good works. Not works that will save you (Jesus did that!) but works that show people that God is real. Good works that show people how much God really does love them. Three: There are things that God planned long ago for you to accomplish with your life. Some of them you will get to do today, some tomorrow, and more in the future. Look for the good works He has set aside for you today.

Write in your own words what Ephesians 2:19-22 means to you._____
_____
_____
_____

Pray that you and your FAITH Team will not forget what it is like to be separate from God, so that you will not become complacent in sharing Christ with people who are now separated from God.

Day Seven:
Read Ephesians 3
This is Deep!

This is one of the most incredible passages in the Bible about the *awesomeness* of God's love. Paul encourages us to let our roots grow deep into the soil of God's marvelous love. This is done through Bible study, prayer, and following the direction of the Holy Spirit. It is a process that takes time, but you are guaranteed to grow as a Christian if you continue doing these things. You can begin to get a glimpse of the size of His love, but it is actually too vast for us to ever understand completely.

Stay in the Word, drink in the truth of the Scripture, and listen to the voice of God as He speaks to you. Keep filling up—a little more each day—with His wisdom. Continue to seek to understand how much God really loves you. If you ever begin to understand a small portion of His love, you will always be eager to share His love with others.

Write down a time when you needed to know the depth of God's love for you.
_____

Pray for a few moments the prayer of Paul in Ephesians 3:14-19. Each time you read the prayer to God, put another FAITH Team member's name into the Scripture so that you are praying Paul's prayer for them.

The Weekly Sunday School Leadership Meeting

Use this space to record ways your FAITH Team impacts the work of your Sunday School department or class. Use the information to report during weekly Sunday School leadership meetings. Identify actions that need to be taken through the Sunday School as a result of prayer concerns, needs identified, visits made by the Team, and decisions made by the persons being visited.

Highlight needs and reports affecting your class, department, or age group.

_____

Pray now for teachers and department directors.

How does preparation for Sunday need to anticipate divine appointments that may be encountered during Sunday School? By class members during the week? By FAITH Team members as they make visits?

_____

How will the class begin to follow up on students that FAITH Team members discover as a result of divine appointments?

_____

What are ways to involve members in praying for and celebrating in God's leadership during divine appointments?

_____
_____

For Further Reading

Read *Evangelism Through the Sunday School: A Journey of FAITH* by Bobby Welch, pages 48-50.
Read the FAITH Tip, "My Most Discouraging Night."

For the Team Leader

This weekly feature suggests actions the Team Leader can take to support Team members, prepare for Team Time, and consider ways to improve visits. This work becomes part of the Team Leader's Home Study Assignments. Add any actions suggested by your church's FAITH strategy.

Support Team Members
❑ Pray for and personally follow up on any Learner who needs encouragement.
❑ Contact Team members during the week to remind them you are praying for them and to discuss their participation in FAITH.
❑ This week Learners are memorizing the FAITH presentation through the Invitation. As you discuss this content with Team members, remind them that this is when someone has the opportunity to make a life-changing decision for himself or herself.
❑ Encourage Learners to read the FAITH Tip.

Prepare to lead Team Time
❑ Overview "Team Time" for Session 11.

Prepare to Lead Visits
❑ Review the FAITH Visit Outline.
❑ Be prepared to explain the benefits and procedures for making ministry visits.
❑ Be prepared to model a visit in which Team member(s) are asked to lead in a visit up to the point of the letter *H* (HEAVEN).
❑ Be prepared to lead your Team to participate during Celebration Time.

Connecting to Sunday School
❑ Share information about FAITH during this week's meeting.

FAITH*Tip*

My Most Discouraging Night

It was a dark and stormy Monday night in Fort Lauderdale when I was sent out with a pastor and his wife to demonstrate the use of a gospel questionnaire. Since I was teaching the clinic on evangelism, they naturally sent me to the hardest location during this spring break, the infamous Fort Lauderdale strip.

That night, a U.S. Navy carrier was in port, so the beachfront was filled not only with drunken college students but also with drunken sailors. Surrounded by thousands of crazy, jostling people, I scarcely could find anyone interested in answering the questionnaire, much less in hearing the gospel. Just when I was feeling as low as I thought I could feel, it began to rain!

The rain actually encouraged me. Now I had an excuse to head back to the car, drive slowly back to the church, and not be ashamed about being the first team to report back. As I trudged through the rain, seemingly surrounded by people who didn't care about the gospel, the pastor's wife spoke up for the first time all evening. "Are we going back already?" Guilt stabbed me in the heart; I became defensive. "Sure," I replied. "We're not doing any good here. If we have some extra time, I'll help you review your homework." She persisted. "Would you mind checking to see how many of those questionnaires we completed?"

A fresh wave of depression swept over me. Just that afternoon in class, I had made the rather authoritative statement that on the average, for every ten people who were asked, at least one would want to hear the gospel. Furthermore, I had cheerfully said that God was in charge of reaping a harvest; our only charge was to not give up. Now my credibility was on the line.

"One in 10 is an average. I've talked to as many as 25 people in an evening with no response. Other times, the first person I talk to wants to hear the gospel. It's not a mechanical process of percentages. But, for the record, we have nine completed questionnaires."

"Just for me," she said, "could you ask one more person?"

She would not let it go! Determined to prove my point, I looked around for the most carnal person (other than myself, at that moment) that I could find. There: A guy was hulking in an alley near the exit to a night club. I vividly remember his long, shaggy hair, multiple tattoos, earrings, and his biker T-shirt and dirty jeans. I thought, I'll show her that the expert on evangelism knows when to quit!

Within five minutes the guy was in tears! He literally begged me to share the good news of Jesus Christ. Out of all the people I've encountered in a street-witnessing situation, he was the most obviously prepared to hear the gospel.

"I can't believe you people had the guts to walk up to me," he said. "Nobody does that. A buddy of mine conned me into going to a Baptist church yesterday. I sat on the back pew and was overcome with emotion as I heard what Jesus did for me. During the invitation I clung to the pew in front of me until my knuckles turned white. All day long I've been praying to God to give me another chance because I knew I was headed straight to hell."

What a strange-looking group we must have been! The biker was crying, I was dumfounded, the pastor was in shock, and the pastor's wife was dancing a jig—figuratively speaking, anyway. In all the intervening years, whenever I am tempted to give up, I remember that humbling-yet-happy experience on the Fort Lauderdale strip. [1]

---

[1] David Self, *Good News for Adults: The Power to Change Lives* (Nashville: Convention Press, 1998. 37-39.

ΠOTES

MAKING CONNECTIONS THROUGH PRACTICE

LIBBA GILLUM

"I CAN'T BELIEVE I FROZE," Keri told Mr. Schroeder.

Keri had been trying to find a way to share Jesus with a certain friend for weeks. In fact, it was her desire to share with this friend that got Keri interested in FAITH training to begin with. She had been trying to bring it up in their conversations, but it just hadn't happened. Today had been different, though.

In the middle of a phone conversation, the subject of life after death came up and Keri asked her friend the key question. She was so proud! This was something she had looked forward to. "She gave me a classic works answer: 'If I do more good things than bad things, I think I should be able to get into heaven,'" Keri continued. "I told her there was a word I use to remember how the Bible answers that question and then I couldn't remember the word!"

It appeared to Mr. Schroeder that Keri had gotten so excited about finally getting to ask her friend the key question that she could not think of anything else.

"All I could tell her was I would like to come by and share with her this evening," explained Keri. "I would really like for our FAITH Team to go and see her."

"That will be fine with me," replied Mr. Schroeder. "But you'd better get ready. I think you should be the one who leads this visit. Would you like to practice on me?"

TEAM TIME

The Team Leader leads this important time, checking off memory work, reviewing previous sessions and completed assignments, answering questions, and providing guidance to strengthen home visits.

Check It

❑ Entire presentation, including Invitation, practiced and evaluated? Check it!

Team Leader: In the adjacent box, check off each word as the Learner recites it correctly. In the space provided for sign-off, indicate your approval by signing your name.

FAITH Visit Outline

❑ **PREPARATION**
❑ **Introduction**
❑ **Interests**
❑ **Involvement**
   ❑ **Church Experience/Background**
      ❑ Ask about the student's church background.
      ❑ Listen for clues about the student's spiritual involvement.
   ❑ **Sunday School Testimony**
      ❑ Tell general benefits of Sunday School.
      ❑ Tell a current personal experience.
   ❑ **Evangelistic Testimony**
      ❑ Tell a little of your pre-conversion experience.
      ❑ Say: "I had a life-changing experience."
      ❑ Tell recent benefits of your conversion.
❑ **Inquiry**
   ❑ **Key Question:** In your personal opinion, what do you understand it takes for a person to go to heaven?
   ❑ **Possible answers:** *Faith, works, unclear, no opinion*
   ❑ **Transition Statement:** I'd like to share with you how the Bible answers this question, if it is all right. There is a word that can be used to answer this question: FAITH *(spell out on fingers).*

❑ **PRESENTATION**
❑ **F (Forgiveness)**
We cannot have eternal life and heaven without God's forgiveness.
"In Him [meaning Jesus] *we have redemption through His blood, the forgiveness of sins"* (Eph. 1:7a, NKJV).

❑ **A (Available)**
Forgiveness is available. It is—AVAILABLE FOR ALL.
"For God so loved the world that He gave His only begotten Son, that whoever believes in Him should not perish but have everlasting life" (John 3:16, NKJV).

BUT NOT AUTOMATIC
"Not everyone who says to Me, 'Lord, Lord,' shall enter the kingdom of heaven" (Matt. 7:21a, NKJV).

❑ **I (Impossible)**
It is impossible for God to allow sin into heaven.
GOD IS—
• LOVE
"*For God so loved the world that He gave His only begotten Son, that whoever believes in Him should not perish but have everlasting life*" (John 3:16, NKJV).
• JUST
"*For judgment is without mercy*" (Jas. 2:13a, NKJV).

MAN IS SINFUL
"*For all have sinned and fall short of the glory of God*" (Rom. 3:23, NKJV).

Question: But how can a sinful person enter heaven, where God allows no sin?

❑ **T (Turn)**
Question: If you were driving down the road and someone asked you to turn, what would he or she be asking you to do? (*change direction*)
Turn means repent.
TURN *from* something—sin and self
"*But unless you repent you will all likewise perish*" (Luke 13:3b, NKJV).

TURN *to* Someone; trust Christ only
(The Bible tells us that) "*Christ died for our sins according to the Scriptures, and that He was buried, and that He rose again the third day according to the Scriptures*" (1 Cor. 15:3b-4, NKJV).

"*If you confess with your mouth the Lord Jesus and believe in your heart that God has raised Him from the dead, you will be saved*" (Rom. 10:9, NKJV).

❑ **H (Heaven)**
Heaven is eternal life.

HERE
"*I have come that they may have life, and that they may have it more abundantly*" (John 10:10b, NKJV).

HEREAFTER
"*And if I go and prepare a place for you, I will come again and receive you to Myself; that where I am, there you may be also*" (John 14:3, NKJV).

HOW
How can a person have God's forgiveness, heaven and eternal life, and Jesus as personal Savior and Lord?
Explain based on leaflet picture, F.A.I.T.H. (Forsaking All I Trust Him), Romans 10:9.

❑ **INVITATION**
INQUIRE
Understanding what we have shared, would you like to receive this forgiveness by trusting in Christ as your personal Savior and Lord?

INVITE
- Pray to accept Christ.
- Pray for commitment/recommitment.
- Invite to join Sunday School.

INSURE
Use *A Step of Faith (Student Edition)* to insure decision.
- Personal Acceptance
- Sunday School Enrollment
- Public Confession
_____ *Team Leader sign-off*

Visitation Time
DO IT
As you go . . .

Be prepared to take the lead in a visit. As the situation allows, move into the gospel presentation. The Team Leader will be ready to handle the Invitation, if appropriate. One way to transition is to say, "_____ (your Team Leader's Name), what do you think about this? He or she will be ready to pick up the conversation from this point. Your Team Leader always will be ready to resume the FAITH Visit Outline at any point you feel you cannot continue.

As always, discuss plans in the car enroute to the visit. There should be no surprises; your purpose and goals are too important. Pray for God to lead you and help your team to be sensitive to opportunities for sharing the gospel.

Celebration Time
SHARE IT
As you return to share . . .

Share highlights of your visits so everyone can pray and follow up appropriately.
- Reports and testimonies
- Participation card
- Visitation forms updated with results of visits

The Daily Journey

Day One:
Read Ephesians 4

Watch Your Words

The challenge for the day is this, "Don't let any unwholesome talk come out of your mouths, but only what is helpful for building others up according to their needs, that it may benefit all who listen." You can be a person that people want to be around just by being positive in the things you say. Most people have enough criticism in their lives, and they don't need anyone else pointing out their weaknesses or failures. People love to be around people who love them because they will usually build them up rather than tear them down.

Being positive to people might be compared to a billionaire giving away hundred dollar bills. It doesn't cost him much to do it, and it's more fun than being greedy. Practice using a little positive speech today and see if you don't have a lot of fun. The people around you will really appreciate it too.

Who is someone that needs to hear something positive from you today?

Pray that you and your FAITH Team will watch your words today and not say anything that does not build others up. Memorize Ephesians 4:29 and share the verse with someone in the next 24 hours.

Day Two:
Read Ephesians 5

Carpe Diem!

"Be careful then how you live, not as unwise but as wise, making the most of every opportunity, because the days are evil." (vv. 15-16) One thing I have noticed about great Christians through the years is they do not have an "I'll do it tomorrow" mentality. They seem to understand that they are in a lot of situations every day that only happen once, so they obey God fully in that situation. If God wants to change their plans for a divine appointment, they are ready to follow Him. They never see God's plan as an inconvenience—instead it is a great opportunity to see Him at work. They are wise with their days, committed to fully obeying God each day wherever He leads. Today is filled with many opportunities, and we should make the most of every one. *Carpe diem*! Seize the day!

Write a short description of what your life would be like if you took Ephesians 5:1 seriously._____

Pray that you and your FAITH Team members will not get caught up in the thoughts and actions of the world this week. Pray that you will not waste a moment of your time out of the will of God today.

Day Three:
Read Ephesians 6

His Strength, Not Ours

"Finally, be strong in the Lord and in His mighty power" (v. 10). I hang out with several karate guys that are great people. They love the Lord and spend the majority of their time serving Him. They are also great fighters. One of them is a six-time world champion kick boxer. The other guy is 6'5" and weighs around 250 pounds. I always feel really safe when I am with these guys, not because of my strength, but because of theirs.

Ephesians 6 reminds us that our real strength and power comes from and through our Lord Jesus Christ. Our confidence comes from the fact that He can handle any situation that might come up. In fact, He knows it is going to happen long before it happens. When we rely on His strength, wisdom and power, we can feel complete confidence in the fact that He will do what is best for us. Today, be strong in the Lord and in His mighty power. Live confidently as a son or daughter of the one who created everything you see. Do not live in constant fear of the world, live confident knowing that God is stronger than any problem you will ever face.

Write what you think Ephesians 6:10-18 is saying to you today. What part of the armor of God is most difficult for you to "put on" each day?_____

_____

_____

Pray that you and your FAITH Team will put on the full armor of God for battle today.

Day Four:
Read 1 John 1:1-4
The Power of A Testimony

Leslie assumed that no one was interested in knowing how she decided to accept Christ. She also was sure she could never memorize all the FAITH outline verses. But now she feels differently—she realizes there are many students who are interested because they have wondered how they could know Christ personally. She also discovered that the Scripture memorization was not that hard.

John started his letter by stating that he was telling the truth; he had seen and experienced the Word of Life. John had incredible joy telling people how they could know Jesus like he knew Jesus. FAITH is much like 1 John 1:3. As we participate in the FAITH process, we tell people about the life change in us since we met Jesus—and offer them the chance to walk with us on this incredible journey.

Some Christians fall into the trap of thinking Jesus is about church, morals, and not going to hell. The reality is that knowing Jesus brings you incredible joy, peace, security, love, and much more on this earth. We are not offering people church, morals, and a way out of hell; we are offering people a relationship with the God Who spoke and made the universe. We are giving people the opportunity to know the God Who has changed our lives. How has God changed you lately?_____

_____

When you tell people about Jesus, what emotions run through your mind? Awe, joy, wonder, _____

Pray for your FAITH Team members today. Pray that each of you will remember that sharing Christ is not about church, morals, and skipping hell; but it is about a personal relationship with Jesus that changes their lives *here* and *hereafter*.

Day Five:
Read 1 John 1:5-10
Walk in the Light

It's amazing that we can read a Scripture passage like this and sometimes lose the profound but simple truth that God is pure light—no darkness at all. God is not unjust, moody, or unstable. God doesn't have bad days or lose his temper. He is not sinful like a person; He is total purity. As followers of God, we should always walk in the light.

Sometimes we catch ourselves simply trying to avoid bad things, but avoiding the darkness does not necessarily mean living in the light. Being a Christian means you live in God's presence and under His leadership in the light.

What if you have done something against God's Will? According to this Scripture you have two choices: You can either keep on living in the darkness and be out of fellowship with God, or you can confess your sin and allow God to forgive you. It's your choice!

Think about the way you live your Christian life. Are you living your life trying to avoid the really bad stuff, but not completely following Jesus? What needs to happen in your life if you are going to live totally in the light?

_____

Pray for yourself and your FAITH Team. Pray that you will live in the light of God's leadership this week. Pray that you will not become arrogant in your Christian life. Pray also that each team member will actually live a pure life, not just claim to.

Day Six:
Read 1 John 2:1-14
I Know Him

It was just after 3:00 p.m. and Joey was parked on the side of the road, watching his friends drive by and wave at him. He was talking with a very nice man in a uniform who was asking Joey some questions about the speed limit on the street beside the school. Joey knew the speed limit, but he had chosen to ignore it. Because he ignored the speed limit, the policeman was wondering if Joey even knew the limit.

God is not a policeman—He is a loving Father. But people around you watch your daily life, and if you choose to ignore God's commands, they wonder if you know Him! Verses 5 and 6 issue a clear challenge to Christians (who claim to live in Christ) to live as Jesus lived. John is not encouraging us to put on sandals, grow long hair, and ride a donkey around town, but he is encouraging Christians to seriously look at the actions of their lives and evaluate if they are living in a love relationship with Jesus. Or if they are faking a relationship with God to look good to their friends and parents. We should live in purity and integrity because we love Jesus and we wouldn't want anything in our life to hurt our relationship with Him.

What attitudes, habits or relationships are in your daily life that may cause people around you to wonder about your relationship with God? Have you been ignoring those attitudes, habits, or relationships hoping to get away with them and still keep your intimate relationship with God?

Pray for yourself and your FAITH Team's consistent daily walk with God. Pray that God's love will be complete in you as you follow His direction today.

Day Seven:
Read 1 John 2:15-29
Stuff or Jesus?

Juan wanted a car more than anything! To him, a car meant freedom. He also knew his friends loved looking at and talking about cars, so a car would mean respect. Juan had a job, but he was not earning enough money to buy the car he really wanted—he wasn't working enough hours. So, Juan told his boss he could start working on Sundays. Within three months he had enough to buy the car, but Juan kept working on Sundays to pay for gas and insurance. Juan had his car, but he lost his intimate relationship with Jesus.

Verses 15-17 of 1 John issue us a difficult challenge: we must love God first. If you love anything in the world more than God, that thing will push out your love for God. God knows our needs and He is fully capable to meet our needs. But when we try to meet our needs our way, we show God that we love the stuff of this world more than we love Him. Have you allowed any relationship or possession to push away your love for Jesus?

Read verse 28 again. Write what this verse means to you._____
_____

Pray that you and the members of your FAITH Team will not become distracted by possessions and allow your relationships with God to grow cold.

Review Assignments

You have learned the entire FAITH Visit Outline. You are learning to take the lead in visits. There is no new memory work.

Practice will be important parts of Team Time and Teaching Time. Continue to work through your Home Study Assignments.

Making Connections in Daily Life

"Our FAITH Team has asked the key question more times than your Team has," Chantil challenged Troy.

"That's OK—we've made more visits than you have," returned Troy.

"Well, we've enrolled more people in Sunday School than your Team has."

"Maybe, but I'll bet we had more students decide to accept Christ than your Team."

"Prove it!" responded Chantil.

Troy pointed to his FAITH participation card and began to total each row. Chantil did the same. They determined there was the same number recorded in the "Profession" row. After comparing their cards, they realized their teams were tied. As they continued to look at each other's cards, they realized there was at least one mark in each column of their participation cards except in the "Life Witness" section.

Wanting an explanation, Chantil turned to her Team Leader and asked, "Mrs. Robison, can you tell me about this last section on the card? I've never done any of these kinds of visits before."

TEAM TIME

The team leader leads this time. Learners are primarily responsible for reciting the assigned portion of the FAITH Visit Outline and for discussing any Home Study Assignments.

Keep in mind how Learners also look to leaders as role models, motivators, mentors, and friends. Team Time activities can continue in the car, as the Team travels to and from visits.

Check It

FAITH Visit Outline
- ❏ Listen while each Learner recites the FAITH Visit Outline. Since there is no new memory work, it may be best to ask Learners to recite the segment they have the most difficulty sharing during a visit.

Session 11 Debriefing (Recognizing A Divine Appointment)
- ❏ Since Session 12 was a practice session with no new material, debrief Session 11 (Recognizing A Divine Appointment) now.
- ❏ Discuss ways Team members are finding *A Step of Faith (Student Edition)* helpful in prompting discussion in a visit. If time permits, allow Team members to practice the *Invitation* using the leaflet.

Help for Strengthening A Visit
- ❏ Discuss some of the difficulties the Team has encountered in leading someone to hear and consider the FAITH gospel presentation. Evaluate ways the Team responded to selected experiences, and identify appropriate ways to improve responses. Indicate that, while most visits go smoothly, next week's session will help all Team members better handle challenges in a visit.

  Difficulties arise when things happen or something is said that keeps you from sharing the gospel and leading someone who is ready to respond to make a commitment to Christ.

  Principles for dealing with difficulties relate primarily to building relationships with the person, dealing with questions and objections, and working through the obstacles and distractions that take place.
- ❏ As you talk with Team members during the week, share ways you are seeking to take advantage of the daily-life witnessing opportunities you have. Also talk with them about opportunities they have to share the gospel during the week with persons they encounter.

Notes

_____

_____

_____

_____

Actions I Need to Take with Learners During the Week

_____

_____

_____

A Quick Review

Tom's FAITH Team ("What Would You Do?" case study, Session 11) exercised sensitivity and openness to God's leadership during a seemingly nonproductive visitation time. A "chance" fast-food encounter opened up opportunities to which the Team was able to respond.

Your Team, like Tom's, can learn how to make connections in the most unlikely situations. You do so as you become more sensitive to those settings non-Christians might characterize as chance encounters but which Christians know to be God's direct intervention. A growing dependence on the Holy Spirit's leading and a greater availability to Him will be the most important things you can learn.

Being ready for God to do a great work—and joining Him in it—is one of the joys of participating in FAITH. Through such experiences we are reminded again that it is God who brings together the right people, the right timing, and the right words. As we continue to pray and make ourselves available to God, such experiences will become a regular part of our Celebration Time reports.

The Person God Uses

The person God uses is consistent.
One of the biggest challenges faced by Christians is that many believers say one thing and do something else. Many nonbelievers are resistant to the gospel because of us; they do not see enough examples of Christians who are consistent in doing what they say they believe. We understand that no person is perfect except Christ; on the other hand, we are called to live holy lives.

The person God uses is growing in head knowledge of what Christ has done for him or her. The person God uses is growing in a personal relationship with Christ.

Are you learning to place your trust in Christ through the joys as well as the trials of life? Are you demonstrating a growing understanding that Christ wants to direct all areas of your life and to show you the abundant life that results in knowing and serving Him? Are you learning to talk with other believers about what Christ means to you? Can others tell that you are maturing in your relationship with Him?

FAITH Is a Both/And Approach

We tend to go through periods of change in how we emphasize or encourage Christians to do evangelism. Basically, there are two main views:

Confrontational describes any evangelism method or strategy designed to train a person in how to share the message of the gospel with another person.

The *lifestyle* approach emphasizes developing a relationship before a verbal witness is attempted. The problem became an "either/or" approach to evangelism. Personal training and equipping in how to witness were perceived as too confrontational, as compared to the relational approach of living the results of salvation so that an unsaved person (hopefully) would ask the Christian to share the gospel with him or her.

While both approaches have merits, each is incomplete alone. Lifestyle evangelism becomes a lifestyle without evangelism if a person does not know what to share and how to share it. One-on-one evangelism becomes impersonal unless connections are made to the individual before, during a presentation, and after the gospel is shared.

A biblical model for evangelism takes an appropriate balance in a both/and approach: BOTH (_____ _____) and demonstrating a lifestyle that draws people to faith AND (_____ _ _____ _____), demonstrate the biblical model of evangelism. The FAITH strategy emphasizes the both/and approach to evangelism.

It is important to remember that although FAITH training occurs on a specific day of the week, we are to be witnesses every day. We are to intentionally share the gospel both as a lifestyle and with words that communicate to others. (_____) is the key word, meaning a Christian is at all times open and alert to opportunities to witness.

Once a Christian discovers that he or she can share the gospel with another person without fear, he realizes there are many opportunities to share. Many people have the kind of personality that enhances spontaneous conversations with individuals they have just met. Others are shy and reserved and feel more comfortable talking with individuals with whom they have developed a relationship. But, the more you participate in FAITH visits, the more comfortable you will feel in sharing with persons in spontaneous situations.

During FAITH Basic, your Team members have been introduced to the fact they can share the gospel with persons they encounter during situations such as the following:

- In the school cafeteria
- At parks, beaches, and other recreational facilities
- At work
- At family gatherings
- During telephone surveys/opinion polls
- At sporting events
- At school events
- At the mall or other student hangouts
- In waiting rooms or offices (doctor, hospital, nursing home, hospice, and so forth)
- Through written communication (mail to family and friends)
- Through casual contacts with service personnel (waiters, mechanics, clerks, and so forth)
- At drug or alcohol rehabilitation centers

As you know, there are many other opportunities in which a Christian has the opportunity to share both a verbal and a lifestyle witness.

Encourage your Team members to identify and take advantage of sharing the gospel in daily-life experiences. As you talk with Team members during the week, share ways you are seeking to take advantage of opportunities you have; also talk with them about opportunities they have to share the gospel during the week.

Most persons are well aware of IQ as measuring Intelligence Quotient, an attempt to measure a person's mental capacities. Consider a "WAQ" as a "Witness Awareness Quotient." Although not intended in any way to be scientific, a Witness Awareness Quotient can help you identify areas in which you already are strong and ways you can grow in sharing both a verbal and a lifestyle witness.

Such a tool can help raise the awareness of opportunities and encourage a person in his or her commitment as a Christian.

My Witnessing Opportunities

The following list can help you determine your witnessing opportunities. As you respond, consider the encounters and opportunities you have apart from weekly FAITH visits with your Team. This exercise is designed to help you determine the extent to which the FAITH strategy is influencing your daily life.

How many people do you know or regularly come in contact with during a given week? How many of that number are unsaved?

Encourage Learners to read the FAITHTip, "Identifying Your Outreach Networks." Part of that FAITH Tip is the assignment to complete "Your Network Potential." In preparation for completing the Witness Awareness Quotient and as a reminder of what Learners have experienced, write your own responses in the space below.

YOUR NETWORK POTENTIAL

Calculating your network potential: Take a typical day or work week. Estimate the number of people with whom you had some kind of contact that day. Total the numbers.

____ Family members
____ People at work or school
____ People talked to on phone or by computer
____ People met casually during day (gas station, restaurant, and so forth)
____ People met during recreational activities
____ Others

____ **TOTAL**

Multiply your total for one day times five (typical work week)
____ My weekly networking potential

Although there is likely an adjustment in the number in some categories from week to week or month to month, write an estimated number that realistically reflects your situation. In each category write the number of individuals you encounter who are unsaved.

Immediate family	Number of Unsaved ____
Relatives	Number of Unsaved ____
Friends	Number of Unsaved ____
Work associates	Number of Unsaved ____
Acquaintances	Number of Unsaved ____
Strangers	Number of Unsaved ____

Total Number of Unsaved: ____

VERBAL WITNESS OPPORTUNITIES

Place a checkmark in each Yes *space beside those opportunities in which you attempted to share a verbal witness during the past week; if more than once, put multiple checkmarks. Check* No *if you have not attempted to take advantage of such verbal witnessing opportunities.*

A verbal witness can be defined as "taking advantage of an opportunity to share the message of the gospel expressed in words."

1. Who?
Immediate family	Yes _____	No _____
Relative	Yes _____	No _____
Friend	Yes _____	No _____
Work associate	Yes _____	No _____
Acquaintance	Yes _____	No _____
Stranger	Yes _____	No _____

2. Where?
In my home	Yes _____	No _____
In a neighbor's house	Yes _____	No _____
In a friend's house	Yes _____	No _____
In a relative's house	Yes _____	No _____
In the workplace	Yes _____	No _____
In a store	Yes _____	No _____
In a public place (such as a sports complex)	Yes _____	No _____
In a private place (such as a counseling room)	Yes _____	No _____

3. How?
In person	Yes _____	No _____
Over the phone	Yes _____	No _____
By mail	Yes _____	No _____

Add the total of *Yes* responses. Add the total of *No* responses. The total should add to 17. Write your total of Verbal Witness Opportunities here.

Verbal Witness: Yes _____   *No* _____

LIFESTYLE WITNESS OPPORTUNITIES

Place a checkmark in the Yes *space beside each opportunity in which you offered a lifestyle witness during the past week; if more than once, put multiple checkmarks. Check* No *if you had no lifestyle witness attempts.*

A lifestyle witness could be defined as "taking advantage of an opportunity to share the message of the gospel expressed in actions."

1. Who?
Immediate family	Yes _____	No _____
Relative	Yes _____	No _____
Friend	Yes _____	No _____
Work associate	Yes _____	No _____
Acquaintance	Yes _____	No _____
Stranger	Yes _____	No _____

2. Where?

In my home	Yes _____	No _____
In a neighbor's home	Yes _____	No _____
In a friend's home	Yes _____	No _____
In a relative's home	Yes _____	No _____
In the workplace	Yes _____	No _____
In a shop	Yes _____	No _____
In a public place (such as a sports complex, airport)	Yes _____	No _____
In a private place (such as a counseling room)	Yes _____	No _____

3. How?

Enroll the person in Sunday School	Yes _____	No _____
Visit in the home or at work	Yes _____	No _____
Write a letter, card, or email message	Yes _____	No _____
Present gift (flowers, resource, meal)	Yes _____	No _____
Provide service (transportation, repairs, lawn maintenance)	Yes _____	No _____

Add the total of *Yes* responses. Add the total of *No* responses. The total should add to 19. Write your total of Lifestyle Witness Opportunities here.

Lifestyle: Yes _____   No _____

REWRITE YOUR TOTALS HERE:
Number of Unsaved: _____
Verbal: Yes _____   No _____
Lifestyle: Yes _____   No _____ = _____
Total *Yes* Responses _____
Total *No* Responses _____

This simple Witness Awareness Quotient can call attention to the fact you can strengthen your lifestyle and verbal witnessing opportunities.

The higher the number of unsaved, the more potential you have for sharing a witness. The more *Yes* responses you have, the more you are taking advantage of these witnessing opportunities.

If your *No* responses are greater than your *Yes* responses, then you can consciously strengthen your awareness of opportunities to share the gospel. If your *Yes* responses are greater than the *No* responses, then you can model comfortably for others the significance of sharing FAITH during daily-life opportunities.

Do not see your numerical results as being a definitive response. Do not perceive the test as a pass-fail experience or results for an active witness as indicating a "Super Witness." Always look for opportunities where you can share your faith.

Maximize Your Opportunities

Witnessing opportunities are (_____). You will have more opportunities to share the gospel when you are in one-on-one settings than you ever will when you are with your FAITH Team.

One reason for providing FAITH Sunday School Evangelism Strategy® training is to give you a heightened confidence to share as you make connections to unsaved people throughout your busy schedule. Many FAITH trainees have declared that, for them, FAITH has taken the fear out of witnessing.

Remember you also are helping Team members identify an awareness of sharing the gospel throughout the week by completing the FAITH Participation Card each week. The (____ _____) category on the Participation Card and the FAITH Report Board call attention to the need to take advantage of the natural opportunities we are given each day to share the gospel.

We need to maximize our intentional approach to sharing the gospel. "The first-century Christians . . . were so convinced of the difference Jesus made that they came to see their former existence outside of Christ as a sort of living death (Ephesians 2:1; 4:17-19; Colossians 2:13).

We must unapologetically share the good news with those who are in need of hearing and seeing it lived out. We must stop waiting for them to come to us so we can refer them to someone else.

Pray that your sensitivity to daily opportunities to witness will increase. Pray for Team members as they learn to share their faith during FAITH visits as well as during the daily opportunities given them.

Visitation Time
DO IT
As you go . . .

Be aware that every witness you share can have a rippling effect: to other family members, friends, acquaintances, even total strangers. That rippling effect may be even greater in daily-life settings in which you share your faith; for example, a non-Christian often has a large number of unsaved friends.

The network of people who might be reached by one contact is known only to God. He has allowed you to join Him in His work.

Celebration Time
SHARE IT
As you return to share . . .

Ask a Team member to share your Team's reports.
- Reports and testimonies
- Session 13 Evaluation Card
- Participation Card
- Visitation forms updated with results of visits

The Daily Journey

Day One:
Read 1 John 3

They Don't Understand

You know what you were before you met Christ, right? Do you remember how much God has changed you? God has made you unique, special, and different from many of your friends. Sometimes they may have trouble understanding you. You listen to different music, you don't watch the same movies, you talk differently, you go to church, you pray . . . you are different!

First John 3:1 helps us know why the people around you misunderstand you—they don't understand God. If your friends at school don't understand God, they will never understand you because your life is committed to serving God and others. People may make fun of you or criticize you for living in purity. Just remember, Jesus was misunderstood, too!

Write down the names of people around you who have made fun of you in some way for living in purity as a Christian._____

_____

Spend a few minutes praying for each of them by name.

Pray that you and your FAITH Team will not stop loving people and serving God, just because someone makes fun of you for living as a Christian.

Day Two:
Read 1 John 4

Love Them?

Dawn and Glen were both active in the youth ministry of their church, but at the moment were not speaking to each other. Glen was loud and obnoxious. and Dawn just didn't like being around him. In fact, she secretly wished he would go to another church. When their pastor encouraged Dawn to approach Glen about being on a FAITH Team the next semester she thought, *no way!* Dawn had no interest in being around Glen at school, work, or church and especially not for FAITH training.

Glen probably needs to learn some manners, but Dawn needs to read 1 John 4:20. Our love for each other shows the world that we love God. If God loves Glen, Dawn should try to also. Think about the people in your church—are there adults or youth that you will not talk to or want to be with? Take some time today to pray for your attitude toward them. If they are your Christian brother or sister, you need to show the love of God to them in your daily life. Jesus calls us to love them as He loves them.

Write down the names of three people to whom you do not speak at church because you really don't get along with them. _____

_____

After you have written down their names, spend some time praying for them.

Pray that you and your FAITH team will live your daily lives loving other people instead of isolating them or putting other people down.

Day Three:
Read 1 John 5
You Know Who You Are, Right?
You have eternal life. You will live with God forever in heaven because you have accepted Jesus as your Savior and Lord. It gives you amazing confidence and allows you to take risks with people. When you doubt your salvation, you will not be bold in sharing your testimony with other people. But when you are confident in God's love, you can be confident with other people.

Millions of people are not confident in God's love. Daily they wonder if God loves them and if they can overcome the struggles of life. You are different; you know that you can overcome the world because of God's power and love within you. Now the challenge for you is to continue to allow the Spirit of God to flow out of you to encourage other people to know God, like you know Him. To live in joy and love so that people around you will see God is real in your life. FAITH is not about one day a week. FAITH is about seeing your life transformed and the lives of people around you transformed through the daily presence of God in your life and your daily witness of God to their life. Walk in confident love today.

Read 1 John 5:3-5 again. Write in this space what you think these verses mean in your life._____
_____

Pray that you and your FAITH Team will continue to boldly share Jesus with the people you meet daily. Pray that FAITH will become a lifestyle and not just a weekly event in your life.

Day Four:
Read Acts 3:11-26
God Did It, Not You
With crowds of people around them and everyone in awe of what they had done, it would have been very easy for Peter and John to take their eyes off of God and put the attention squarely on themselves. The temptation certainly was there—after all, these things weren't happening to all of the other disciples.

After seeing the power of God heal the lame man at the Gate called Beautiful, Peter and John were on "cloud nine." Their words to the downtrodden man were simple and direct, "Silver or gold I do not have, but what I have I give you. In the name of Jesus Christ of Nazareth, walk!" Simple words that brought joy and life back to this man. The words also revealed something else about these two disciples: they were ordinary men serving an extraordinary God! Although they were financially poor, they were rich in God's Spirit.

Later, in verse 12, Peter asked a penetrating question of the people crowding around him, "Why do you stare at us as if by our own power or godliness we had made this man walk?" Basically saying, *Why are you looking at us like we did something incredible? God did it, not us!* Again, we see the two disciples shift attention away from themselves and back to Jesus.

Do you ever feel like you are unworthy for God to use? Do you ever find yourself guilty of wanting the spotlight when it is all about God, anyway? How can you avoid that in your life?

Pray for God to give you and your FAITH Team a healthy perspective on people and yourself. Ask God to help you live a life of humility and sacrifice, totally dependent upon God.

Day Five:
Read Acts 4:1-20

How Do You Know?

When is it time to speak up and when is it time to shut up? As messengers of the Gospel, we know that we must tell what we know, but what are we supposed to do when the audience is less than thrilled to hear about Jesus?

 Peter often faced this dilemma in his ministry. Though he was an ordinary man, (untrained and unpolished), Peter courageously took a stand for Christ even though it sometimes cost him much. He was not rude and arrogant; he was filled with mercy and love, bridled by courage. When confronted with the order to never again speak or teach in Jesus' name, Peter's reply was "We cannot help speaking about what we have seen and heard."

 How do you respond in difficult witnessing situations? Do you "clam up" in fear? What should be your guideline for knowing when to talk about Jesus and when not to talk about Jesus? Are humility, love, and mercy evident in your attitude as you tell others about Jesus?

 Think about how you decide when and how to share Jesus with other people. When is the right time?

 Pray for yourself, members of your FAITH Team, and believers all over the world in these difficult days. Pray that you will choose to refuse to keep quiet about your faith in Jesus.

Day Six:
Read 1 Corinthians 1:20-25

Much Too Simple

Christianity has been called everything from a bloody religion to a simple man's escape from real life. Many people view the message of the cross as absolutely foolish, too simple, and too easy. Paul addressed this directly when he said that God was pleased through the foolishness of what was preached to save those who believe. The Jews wanted their emotions satisfied through signs and wonders. The Greeks just wanted an intellectual approach to God. But God was interested in everyone knowing Him, not just knowing what He does or what He thinks.

 For many people, the cross is an incomprehensible thing. We must ask people to see the wisdom of God through personal faith. Paul's words should challenge us again, "For the foolishness of God is wiser than man's wisdom, and the weakness of God is stronger than man's strength" (v. 25).

 Have you ever had someone reject your witness as foolish or silly? How did you respond? Do you have to stop using your brain to really believe in Christ?

 Pray today for your FAITH Team—that each person will become committed to the wisdom that comes from the foolishness of the cross. Pray for those who struggle to accept the simplicity of the Gospel.

Day Seven:
Read Galatians 1:6-10

How Many Ways Are There?

How many ways are there to God? What about all the other religions that claim to be true? Isn't sincerity the ultimate deciding factor for what religion is right? Who can really know truth anyway?

The correct answers are: *One, they are wrong, nope, and Christians.*

Paul laid it on the line for us: Any gospel that is different from the one found in God's Word is no gospel at all. Good news is not good news if it is false! False teachings and misguided claims result in confusion. The answer to life's big questions is found in holding tightly to the message of Christ, and His life, death, and resurrection. You must spend time alone with God each day studying His Word so you will know the truth and you can lovingly correct those who believe a lie.

List three people that you know believe something about God that is not true._____

Pray right now that they will soon accept the truth about God. Pray for all people to understand the Truth as the Holy Spirit speaks to their hearts.

Seek today to be a loving defender of truth as found in God's Word.

The Weekly Sunday School Leadership Team Meeting

Use this space to record ways your FAITH Team impacts the work of your Sunday School department or class. Use the information to report during weekly Sunday School leadership team meetings. Identify actions that need to be taken through Sunday School as a result of prayer concerns, needs identified, visits made by the Team, and decisions made by the persons being visited.

Highlight needs and reports affecting your class, department, or age group.

_____

_____

Pray now for the important leadership meeting.

What are ways the department or class can follow up on life-witness opportunities shared by class members?

_____

_____

What actions can be taken to encourage members and leaders to share both a lifestyle witness, as well as a verbal witness, during the week?

_____

_____

How does preparation for Sunday need to consider persons who might attend because they received a witness by members during the week?

_____

_____

For Further Reading

Read the FAITHTip, "The Ripple Effects of FAITH."
Read pages 97 and 155 of *Evangelism Through the Sunday School: A Journey of FAITH* by Bobby Welch.

For the Team Leader

This weekly feature suggests actions the Team Leader can take to support Team members, prepare for Team Time, and consider ways to improve visits. This work becomes part of the Team Leader's Home Study Assignments. Add any actions suggested by your church's FAITH strategy.

Support Team Members
❏ Contact Team members during the week. Remind them you are praying for them. Discuss prayer concerns and answers to prayer.
❏ As you talk with Learners this week, discuss opportunities they have for witnessing during the week. Encourage them as they seek to be a witness to persons they encounter.
❏ Record specific needs and concerns of Team members in the space provided.

Prepare to Lead Team Time
❏ Review Home Study Assignments of Team members.
❏ Overview "Team Time" for Session 14.

Prepare to Lead Visits
❏ Review the FAITH Visit Outline.

Connecting to Sunday School
❏ Share about FAITH during this week's Sunday School leadership meeting.

FAITH*Tip*

The Ripple Effects of FAITH

During the last months of 1997, Tony Antolino hit bottom. Suicidal, the heroin-addicted gang member made a call to a friend in Daytona Beach, Florida. This call saved not only his life, but also his soul.

The person he turned to was Laura Parks. A new Christian who had made a profession of faith only months earlier, Laura had become involved in a College and Career Sunday School class at First Baptist Church, Daytona Beach, and was eager to share her newfound faith.

"I just wanted the Jesus in me to be the Jesus in other people," she explained, "but I didn't know how. So, I did the FAITH thing." After counseling and encouraging Antolino, Parks led her friend to Christ over the telephone and launched him on a new course for life.

"Back in New York, all my friends thought I'd be the first one to die. Now I'm the first one with eternal life," Antolino testified during a January 20, 1997 FAITH enlistment banquet at The Ocean Center in Daytona Beach, Florida, drawing a standing ovation from the more than 1,000 attendees.

Parks and Antolino are living examples of the "ripple effect" of the FAITH Sunday School Evangelism Strategy. Antolino accepted Christ after Parks shared with him over the phone. She became a Christian partly through the witnessing efforts of her sister, Patricia, and friend Anthony Orzo, both of who were going through FAITH training.

A year earlier, Orzo was an alcoholic who spent his events partying at local nightclubs. After accepting Christ through Parks' witness, he became actively involved at First Baptist, ministering to kids through the church's bus ministry. A short time later, he went on his first mission trip, sharing his faith with youth in Brazil.

Another First Baptist Daytona Beach member shared her testimony during the banquet. Following her conversion, Karen Adams of Port Orange, Florida, said God "lit a fire in me that was almost overwhelming." Raised as a Roman Catholic, she became involved in a Lutheran church before meeting her husband, Mack, a retired Baptist missionary, over the Internet. Largely through his witness, she accepted Christ about a year before sharing the testimony; the couple became members of First Baptist Church, Daytona Beach.

Eager to share her faith with others, Adams enrolled in FAITH training at her church. On the fifth week of training, she and her two-member witnessing Team were going through their visitation assignment cards when she discovered one listing the name and address of her oldest son, 25-year-old Kyle.

"I couldn't believe it. I knew he had visited our church, but he had refused to fill out a visitor card," Adams said in an interview after the banquet. "He didn't want anyone visiting him. We have no idea how that card got there."

Though she hadn't yet shared the plan of salvation using the FAITH gospel presentation, she asked if she could present it to her son. "For the next half hour, I talked to my son on my fingers," Adams said, using them to share the five-point FAITH presentation.

"When I asked him if he wanted to pray to receive Christ as Savior, he said *yes*. The feelings I had that night I cannot describe. To me, that was the greatest moment a mother could ask for. FAITH has really been a gift to me."

The Sunday School Leader, September 1998, 17. © LifeWay Christian Resources of the Southern Baptist Convention. Adapted from a Baptist Press release.

NOTES

DEALING WITH DIFFICULT VISITS

LIBBA GILLUM

THE SCENE: *Dave Puwitzski's home on a Tuesday evening during a FAITH visit.*

Sylvia asked, "Dave, if you were driving a car and you were told you had just passed your exit, what would your passenger be saying?

"They'd be saying he is just like his daddy," jumped in Mrs. Puwitzski, Dave's mom. "I am always having to tell his dad where to turn and he still gets lost!"

"Well, Dave, when that happens and your mom tells your dad he has missed the exit, what is she asking your dad to do?" Sylvia continued.

"Just the other day, we were on our way to see some friends and his dad got us lost; I thought he would never stop and ask for directions," interrupted Mrs. Puwitzski.

"Well, Dave, what would your mom be asking?" Sylvia persisted.

Dave quickly answered, "To turn around." He then gave his mom a look of victory for getting to answer the question before she did.

"That's exactly right," said Sylvia. "The Bible uses the word *repent* when . . . ."

"Turn! That reminds me—it's time for me turn on my favorite TV show. I never miss it." Mrs. Puwitzski said as she turned on the TV.

"As I was saying, the Bible uses the word *repent* when talking about turning. That means we turn from one thing . . . ."

From the back of the house, Dave's dad bellowed, "I'm going to the store. Who wants to go for a ride?"

TEAM TIME

The team leader leads this time. Learners are primarily responsible for reciting the assigned portion of the FAITH Visit Outline and for discussing any Home Study Assignments.

Keep in mind how Learners also look to leaders as role models, motivators, mentors, and friends. Team Time activities can continue in the car, as the Team travels to and from visits.

Check It

FAITH Visit Outline
❑ Listen while each Learner recites as much of the FAITH Visit Outline as time allows. Make sure each student has a turn. It may be best to ask Learners to recite the segment they have the most difficulty sharing during a visit.

Practice
❑ As time permits, allow for additional practice on any part of the visit presentation, sequence, and materials (*Student Baptism* tract, for example).

Session 13 Debriefing (Making Connections in Daily Life)
❑ Review:
The FAITH Sunday School Evangelism Strategy® is designed to help equip the Sunday School member and leader to share the gospel and minister to prospects and members. A strength of this evangelism training is that participants learn a simple and direct approach to talking with people about the message of the gospel when visiting with a Team of three.
Another benefit is that a student who learns to share the gospel becomes more aware of witnessing opportunities during encounters throughout the week. Remind Team members that, as they continue training, they will become more aware of opportunities to share both a verbal and a lifestyle witness with students whose lives they intersect.

Help for Strengthening A Visit
❑ Discuss some of the difficulties Teams have encountered in leading someone to hear and consider the FAITH gospel presentation. Call attention to the fact that this session formally introduces Learners to ways to deal with difficulties and distractions. At the same time, Team Leaders and other Student FAITH participants will be learning still other ways to help their Teams respond appropriately.
❑ As time allows, consider sharing a copy of the Witness Awareness Quotient for Team members to use at their convenience. Or discuss some things you learned as a result of your responses to the questions.
Briefly help Team members see the impact of increasing their awareness of witnessing opportunities. It is one way to focus attention on strengthening both lifestyle and verbal opportunities to witness.

Notes

_____

_____

_____

_____

Actions I Need to Take with Learners During the Week

_____

_____

_____

_____

A Quick Review

Many Christians have daily encounters with the unchurched and the unsaved. Until we begin to be more sensitive to everyone we encounter as potentially in need of the gospel, many of these relationships and opportunities may go unnoticed.

The FAITH strategy already is helping us respond with a positive verbal witness, and you can probably share instances in which someone seemed to be waiting for such a witness. As FAITH becomes increasingly integrated into your life, you will find yourself more aware of daily-life encounters.

What casual comments might indicate a need? What surface conversation might lead to a more serious one? What cultivation of a friendship might result in a verbal witness? What relationships have been established for the first time? You will find yourself becoming more aware than ever before of the meaning of events and words.

Because you are trained and available to God, the potential increases.

The Person God Uses

The person God uses depends on the Holy Spirit.

The Holy Spirit is the Spirit of God sent forth to do His work. The Holy Spirit's role is to—

- reveal God's will;
- guide persons in understanding and doing God's will;
- convict people of sin and enable lost sinners to turn to Christ in faith; and
- take up His abode in the believer's life.

The Holy Spirit is the Comforter, the One who walks alongside the believer through all situations. The Holy Spirit provides and cultivates a spiritual gift for each believer.[1]

Jesus said, " 'If you love me, you will obey what I command. And I will ask the Father, and he will give you another Counselor to be with you forever—the Spirit of truth' " (John 14:15-17a, NIV).

The Holy Spirit indwells every believer. "One may be filled with the Holy Spirit but not filled with His power. To be filled with the Holy Spirit, one must be submissive and available to the indwelling Spirit. It is not how much of the Holy Spirit the Christian has, but how much of the Christian the Holy Spirit has."[2]

How much of your life does the Spirit of God control? In what ways do you depend on the Holy Spirit to guide your thoughts and actions? To work in leading unsaved people to recognize their need for God's grace? To use you in sharing the good news of God's salvation through Jesus' death and resurrection?

Pray that God will help you learn the joys and results of depending totally on His Holy Spirit.

All Visits Don't Go "By the Script"

Throughout your FAITH training, you have viewed video segments of model FAITH visits. Nearly everything in these visits goes "by the script." The student hears the gospel presentation, recognizes his or her need, and prays to receive Christ.

By now you have realized that obstacles often arise during a visit—problems that can keep a person from hearing, considering, or accepting the gospel presentation. Generally, (_____) are those kinds of interruptions related to the (___) of the visit—the dog barking, people in and out during the visit, the TV staying on, and so forth. We use the word (_____) to describe problems that come up related to the (___) of the visit—"I don't believe the Bible" or "I don't understand what it means to repent."

In most cases, the simplicity of the gospel presentation answers many questions students might have at the beginning. Most visits go smoothly and without major problems. However, for those times when obstacles do arise, this session will help focus on ways to deal with difficulties and distractions. You will learn to handle problems so that, by building relationships, you still have an opportunity to present the gospel.

During each FAITH training course, a Team Leader continues to develop skill in dealing with difficulties; no one ever "graduates" from this subject. Many people who attempt to witness are rendered ineffective because they are not equipped to relate to the difficulties they encounter.

Although the problems you encounter will be varied, the principles used to deal with them are few.

When they do occur, problems can be encountered during all three parts of a FAITH visit: *Preparation*, *Presentation*, and *Invitation*. Potential problems in a FAITH visit can crop up as—

1. A (____). For example, "Why wouldn't a loving God allow everyone into heaven?"
2. An (____). For example, "I don't think I've ever done anything that bad."
3. A (_____). For example, "Are you saying, that for me to turn from my sin I have to . . . ?"
4. A (_____ _____). For example, "I don't think much about organized religion. I've had some bad experiences in the past."
5. A (_____) that interrupts the flow and the discussion of a visit. For example, the TV stays on during the visit, phone calls interrupt, or the dog barks.

Here's another way to think about potential difficulties: Comments you may encounter generally can be categorized as *philosophical* (growing out of issues related to the gospel message)—for example, "I don't see why it is necessary to have a life-changing experience" or *practical* (based in someone's personal experiences or preferences)—for example, "I want to receive Christ, but I want to do it later." In your Team's response it is important to know where students are coming from, to acknowledge that perspective, and to try to address their concern appropriately.

 Session 14 of Student FAITH introduced you to some principles for dealing with difficulties (especially those categorized as distractions). This session will help you focus on actions to take—especially when encountering other, more complex difficulties—in each part of the visit.

Minimize Difficulties: Make Connections to Get Acquainted

The same guidelines that get any visit off to a good start can help your Team avoid difficulties. The *Preparation* portion of the visit is significant as you build or strengthen bridges. Consider the following guidelines.

1. Clearly and cordially (_____) yourself and your Team. Do everything you can to put the student at ease. Remember, you are asking someone to take his or her time to allow your Team to enter their home.

 Many people feel awkward permitting strangers inside their homes. Your sensitivity to this reality can help you make connections in many challenging situations. Many students will be glad to discover that you are from the same group they would identify with in the church. They may welcome you as they discover you share lots of the same interests.

2. Spend (__) getting to know the student and helping him or her feel comfortable with you and your Team members. Often, it is good to bring up information you have about them that would help begin or strengthen the conversation. Some details may have been provided on the FAITH Visit Assignment Card—for example, the student visited the church or was referred by someone he knows.

 Do not rush this get-acquainted time. It is vital in connecting with trust and friendship. At the same time, recognize you have a limited amount of time, so do not spend so much time getting acquainted that you never get to the gospel presentation (if appropriate).

3. Be a good (_____). Many times a person subtly shares information that can help identify a ministry need or a spiritual condition.

 If your Team comes across as more interested in sharing a presentation than in building a relationship, you are more likely to meet resistance. Sometimes you must be willing to listen to someone's story—even when it includes criticism, questions, denial, or resistance—before he or she will feel comfortable trusting you with the truth of the gospel.

4. (_____ _____) to build relationships. The Sunday School testimony is one of the most simple, yet significant, features of the FAITH Sunday School Evangelism Strategy®. Many students will be surprised to discover that your Sunday School class has something to offer and that your class is important to you personally.

 The evangelistic testimony is intended to briefly whet the appetite of the student and determine whether there is interest in a similar life-changing experience. As you help Team members with their evangelistic testimonies, you enable them to share naturally and meaningfully from their experience. Your Team is seeking to make connections of relationship that ultimately allow you to share the gospel, if appropriate.

Minimize Difficulties: Transition from the Key Question

A student who realizes you really care for him or her will be more receptive to hearing the good news you have to share.

 1. Know how to make transition between the Key Question and the way(s) a student responds to the question. Generally, a response will indicate that the student—

 • *Already believes in and has accepted Christ.*—If so, celebrate the person's faith response. Ask for some events that led to this experience. Also, look for opportunities to ask whether a Team member could practice the gospel presentation. Look for opportunities to enroll the student in Bible study if he or she is not already participating.

 • *Has yet to realize he cannot save himself.*—What we call a *works* response usually will reflect the person's belief that one goes to heaven primarily as a result of "good, clean" living. Some people believe that, ultimately, all will be saved. When such a response occurs, help the student understand that many people respond this way.

   Then, rather than telling the student the answer is wrong or dealing with a side issue, ask permission to share how the Bible answers the Key Question. In many situations, the Holy Spirit has used the gospel presentation to convict the student of wrong thinking and the need for Christ.

 • *Is giving mixed responses.*—The prospect sometimes gives a combination of answers—for example, "I believe the Bible—and that you have to live a good life to go to heaven." Gently probe to clarify what is meant.

   Someone who gives an unclear answer usually will gravitate toward a *works* answer when asked to clarify his response. If and when a works answer surfaces, restate it to find out whether it reflects the student's belief. If a works answer is established, ask for permission to share how the Bible answers this question.

 • *Seems to have no definite opinion.*—When this occurs, consider suggesting an answer (other than a faith response) and see whether the student agrees with it. If he or she does not agree with your suggested answer, rephrase it.

   If the person fails to agree with any works answer you supply, help him to understand that a no-opinion response concerning heaven really is not an option; *at some point everyone must come to a decision regarding whether to accept Jesus.* Ask for the privilege to share how the Bible answers the Key Question.

 2. Sometimes at this point in a FAITH visit (*Key Question/Transition*) people will resist hearing what the Bible has to say. Some will wonder how long it will take you to share the answer. Others have personal needs that make it difficult for them to listen to you.

 You can overcome many difficulties by being sensitive to the barriers students will try to place for not hearing the answer. Remember, the answer to the Key Question often comes in the presentation of the gospel. Be sensitive to the leadership of the Holy Spirit.

During the Presentation

Be aware of ways to minimize the potential of difficulties that could arise in sharing the gospel presentation. If during the FAITH presentation itself a difficulty arises, attempt to follow these guidelines while recognizing that each situation is unique:

1. If a student asks a question while you are sharing the FAITH gospel presentation, generally it is best to (___) answering until you are ready for the Inquiry question in the *Invitation*. Frequently, if you are allowed to share the gospel presentation in its entirety, the questions the student might have asked at the beginning of the visit are answered. Usually, you will have the opportunity to completely share the brief gospel presentation.

2. (_____ ____) if the question comes at the point at which you are sharing and if it clarifies your response. You also can supplement the presentation with information about the message of the gospel.

For example, if the question "What does it mean to repent?" comes when you are addressing T is for TURN, it is best to clarify at that time.

3. If a question is asked that you cannot answer, simply (___ __) and ask for permission to continue.

4. (__ _____ __ ____ ____) reflected by a seemingly negative comment. Someone who says, "We can't listen to this right now" may be indicating a serious personal need or situation for which the family needs help. Actually, there may be greater openness to the gospel than ever before.

Minimize Difficulties: At the Point of Invitation

Be aware of ways to deal with difficulties that could arise after sharing the gospel presentation and as you are inquiring about further commitment.

1. Some students who answered the Key Question by saying their good works will enable them to enter heaven may give a different answer to the *Invitation* Inquiry question. In such a case, tactfully remind them of an earlier *works* answer, and (___) the importance of trusting in Jesus and Jesus only for forgiveness. Also, reemphasize the *T* (TURN) part of the FAITH gospel presentation.

2. If you have asked permission to delay your answer to the student's question, do (_____) the question again when you are ready to answer it. Doing so lets the person know you have not forgotten about it.

3. On occasion, a student may make a comment, interrupt you, or share a response because of something he or she misunderstands. This misunderstanding may grow out of some personal background or experience or from something you said.

Be glad for this type of interruption or response. It gives you an opportunity to (____ __ _ _____).

4. Some people will object to something you said during the *Presentation*. Many times you can overcome objections by saying something like, "I used to feel the same way; let me share what helped me change my mind." If this response does not match your experience, choose an answer that mirrors your experiences and helps you relate to the other person.

Another response would be to listen to the objection and to (___) it in a way you can answer. Continue by clarifying the gospel presentation.

5. Some students may try to get off the subject of spiritual commitment by talking about such things as church participation, family heritage, or even a negative situation (perhaps something that happened to them).

You may merely need to be a (____ _____) during this situation; let the student vent his or her negative emotions. Remember the importance of making connections to help the student be open to hearing and responding to the gospel. Also remember that you reflect Christ and His church in how you act—as well as what you say.

6. Some students will indicate a lack of belief or trust in something that is important to you or something that is the basis of your message, including—
• the Bible,
• heaven, hell, or life after death, or
• other aspects related to the gospel presentation.

Even though you may be able to briefly share some historical evidences of the truth or doctrine, remember that you are not to debate or argue.

A strong yet positive way to answer such a response is to share your (_____ _____). One appropriate response to make is (for example) "What if (the Bible, heaven, hell, or life after death, and so forth) is true?" and proceed by sharing.

Perhaps the following story recounted by Billy Graham will be helpful.

"In Wellington, on New Zealand's North Island, I spoke at the university. Among many other things, I spoke on the reality of Hell . . . . After the meeting (late) at night, there came one of the students, and he was angry— *very* angry.

" 'What do you mean coming over here from America and talking about Hell? I don't believe in Hell, and you have no right to come over here and talk about it!'

"'Let me ask you a question,' I responded. 'Suppose you went to Auckland to catch a plane for Sydney. And suppose they told you there was a 10 percent chance the plane would not make it but was going to crash. Would you get on?'

"'No,' he replied, 'I wouldn't.'

" 'Well, what if there were only a 5 percent chance the plane wasn't going to make it? Would you get on then?'

" 'No, of course not.'

" 'Now suppose there's only a 10 percent—or even just a 5 percent chance—that Jesus was right and there is a Hell. Do you think there's at least a 5 percent chance that He might have been right?'

" 'Well, yes, I suppose there is.'

" 'Then is it worth taking the risk and ignoring those odds?'

" 'No. No it isn't,' he admitted.' "[3]

Principles for Dealing with Difficulties and Distractions

Based off what already has been presented, a few significant principles emerge for dealing with the varied situations you will encounter. Remember, as you approach a FAITH visit expecting God to work, you will be relying on Him to help your Team resolve difficulties.

Following are what we might call some ABC's of handling difficulties. As you think of each key word, perhaps in new situations you encounter, you also may easily recall a possible solution.

Much of what we are discussing becomes easier and more natural with prayer and with practice as you continue to make evangelistic and ministry visits. Review this content as needed throughout FAITH training.

Avoid being the difficulty.

Make sure the actions or attitudes of your Team are not the source of someone's problem. A Team member who is more interested in getting to and through the gospel presentation while overlooking the needs of a person may lose the privilege of sharing the gospel with that individual.

Be a good listener in dealing with negative reactions.

In a situation in which someone has had a negative experience, especially with the church, you likely need to let the student vent his or her emotions. Those emotions may be strong and deep-seated. At the same time you are exercising patience, especially rely on the work of the Holy Spirit to bring grace into the situation.

Clear up misunderstandings.

Be grateful for opportunities the student gives you to clear up any misunderstandings. This is especially important as misconceptions relate to the gospel presentation. Perhaps the student simply has not heard all of what you said. He or she may have misunderstood a point. Unless the point can be handled later, clear up the misunderstanding at the time. If not clarified at the time, the misunderstood concept may influence a person's entire understanding of the gospel.

De-fuse objections.

To be able to continue with the presentation after an objection is voiced may require a capacity to listen carefully and to relate personally to the comment or the experience. Avoid becoming defensive. Seek to maintain the relationship and to continue the communication.

For example, after an objection you are better able to continue by saying something like: "I used to feel the same way about _____; this is what helped me change my mind." (Be honest!) Another way to deal with objections is to restate the person's statement in such a way that you can respond.

Expect the Holy Spirit to work in difficulties.

Be aware that Satan will do everything possible to distract and confuse in any situation. At the same time, you can approach every visit with confidence, knowing that the Holy Spirit is at work and that He is using you and your Team as His instruments. He already may be working in the lives of people you are visiting.

Knowing that God is at work, you can be assured that He can make any difficulty a positive experience. Go in an attitude of prayer and dependence.

Function as a Team to cover distractions.
To deal effectively with the distractions posed by TV or stereos playing, the telephone ringing, children coming in and out, and so forth requires teamwork. While one person shares the gospel, the other two Team members can allow the student to hear it by talking to a sibling, petting the cat, or whatever could prove to be distracting. Team members should do whatever is necessary to provide opportunity for the student to hear and respond to the gospel presentation.

God uses you in different ways.
God uses you and your Team in different ways in visits. In some cases, you may till the soil, while in other visits you may plant a seed. Occasionally you will nurture a young seedling. In some memorable visits, your Team will be there to harvest fruit.
 You will not see the results of every visit, and you won't see professions of faith in every visit. Your responsibility is to go and to share, leaving the results to God and to further opportunities for cultivation.

Handle responses to the Key Question appropriately.
Understand the type of answer the prospect gives to the Key Question, and respond appropriately. Your Team frequently will encounter answers that indicate dependence on his own efforts to achieve heaven. Sometimes the answer reflects uncertainty. Be grateful for such a response; it allows you a God-given opportunity to share the gospel.
 A student's response may represent a combination of answers. In this case, try to restate the response or probe for more information. In some cases, it will be important to clarify, perhaps by putting an answer in your own words and seeing whether it reflects his or her opinion.

Improve your debating skills elsewhere.
Dealing with difficulties is not about improving your debating skills; it is about handling situations in such a way that you still have an opportunity to present the gospel. Remember, your goal is to gain a hearing for the gospel. Many questions someone might have had at the beginning of the visit ultimately are answered by the FAITH presentation.
 You have a limited amount of time; make the best use of this time by moving to the main point of your visit—discovering whether that student has received God's forgiveness in Christ and, if appropriate, sharing the gospel.
 Even if questions or difficulties cannot be resolved in one visit, one very positive result can be to enroll the student (and maybe the family) in Sunday School—or to follow up with that possibility in mind. Over time, with caring Christian friends and exposure to God's Word, difficulties may become opportunities!
 In all situations, seek to make solid connections so additional cultivation and relationship-building can take place.

---

[1]Herschel Hobbs, *The Baptist Faith and Message* (Nashville: Convention Press, rev., 1996), 40-41.
[2]Ibid., 41.
[3]Billy Graham, *Just As I Am: The Autobiography of Billy Graham* (Billy Graham Evangelistic Association, 1997) 331-332.

Visitation Time

DO IT

As you go . . .

Think about: Are your Learners ready to take the lead in a visit? Have you built a strong relationship with the Learners on your Team? Are they growing in their faith and in their capacity to share their faith? Are they learning to recognize when the FAITH Visit Outline needs to be adjusted in visits? Are they helping establish relationships between the community and your Sunday School?

How far have Team members come since Session 1? Have you taken the time to affirm them for their progress and to thank the Lord for this mentoring experience?

What changes in your Sunday School class or department might be attributed to FAITH? How are Sunday School and church members growing in their faith?

Hopefully, you are continuing to grow in your faith, too!

Celebration Time

SHARE IT

As you return to share . . .

- Reports and testimonies
- Session 14 Evaluation Card
- Participation Card
- Visitation forms updated with results of visits

The Daily Journey

Day One:
Read Acts 9:1-19

Life Change

The last thing Saul expected that particular day was a roadside chat with Jesus! Still running on full throttle in his persecution of the Church, Saul was determined to wipe out the scourge of Christianity. When he least expected it, Jesus broke into his life.

When Jesus has a face-to-face encounter with us, He always requires a response. He asked Saul "Why are you persecuting me?" Saul was not just persecuting the Church, he was persecuting Jesus Himself. Saul was immediately faced with a decision—would he follow Jesus at that point or would he stiffen his neck in pride and walk away even more determined to harm the Church? His decision was obvious because he had experienced a real, personal, and intimate encounter with Jesus. Saul, the Christian killer became Paul, the champion of the Church!

How is your personal relationship with Christ right now? Are you experiencing a face-to-face relationship with Jesus, or are you relying upon others to just tell you about it?

Write down the names of three people who could be effective champions for God, if only they would turn their lives over to Him. Pray that you will be bold in sharing Christ with them and pray that God will convict their hearts of their need for Him._____

_____

 Pray that you will always remember what it was like to meet Christ and experience forgiveness and life change. Pray that the members of your FAITH Team will continue to meet with Jesus daily.

Day Two:
Read Acts 10:9-36
God Loves Everyone. Do We?

Is anyone disqualified from being a part of God's family due to race, nationality, or background? Is there some guideline that God follows when it comes to those who may believe?

 Peter said, "I now realize how true it is that God does not show favoritism, but accepts men from every nation who fear him and do what is right" (v. 35). Having shocked the Jewish world by opening up the message of Christ to Gentiles, Peter made one thing crystal clear: Jesus offers eternal life to any man, woman, boy, or girl who will "fear Him" (faith relationship) and "do what is right"(live with a heart to honor the Lord).

 This truth challenges us to take a good long look at how we treat people. Are we committed to win the world, or simply those who happen to be just like us? Do we agree with Peter that God shows no favoritism, but offers eternal life to all?

 Reflect on your FAITH visits. Have you ever assumed, before even entering a home, that the people who lived there would not be interested in following Jesus? What do you think caused you to feel that way?_____

_____

 Some visits are more difficult only because of our own biases and prejudice. Pray that you and your FAITH Team would allow God to love people through you, no matter who they are and what your past prejudices may be.

Day Three:
Read John 14:1-14
But What about Jesus?

The heart of our message is Jesus Christ. On witnessing occasions, we may find ourselves debating or arguing over issues that are not really important. There is nothing wrong with theological debate, as long as the center of the theology is correct. The problem is that we may win an argument but lose an opportunity to share the incredible story of Jesus Christ and what He can do in a person's life.

 In this passage of Scripture, Jesus was trying to explain to the disciples the way, the truth, and the life. But the disciples were still trying to figure out Who Jesus really was. If the disciples were still struggling with Jesus after three years, we should have compassion on people today who are struggling with Who Jesus will be to them. Make sure, in your discussions with people, that you are directing them to Jesus and not dealing with other biblical issues. The real issue is what a person decides to believe about Jesus in his or her own life.

 What are some of the spiritual discussions you have had while on a FAITH visit or with friends at school that didn't help them know Jesus any better? Write down a few examples of times when you have allowed someone to get you off track in the past. _____

_____

Be prepared to share one of these stories with your FAITH Team this week. Pray that you and your FAITH Team will continue to prioritize sharing Jesus with students rather than trying to argue them into the kingdom of God.

Day Four:
Read 2 Timothy 4:1-5
The Answer to the Question

Imagine discovering a cure for cancer and not telling anybody! Go one step farther and imagine being in a room full of cancer patients and not telling them about it! Obviously, if we had that knowledge, we would do everything we could to get the word out, right? Living around people who don't know God is like living around cancer patients in need of a cure. The greatest need of a person without God is to know about Jesus. They cannot experience real life or heaven without Him.

When God opens a door for us to share Christ, we have an obligation to walk through that door. We are called to be ready "in season, and out of season" to give an answer for the hope that is in us. That means we should be ready to share about Christ on FAITH visits and at school, work, play, and at home. We should always be on the lookout for opportunities to share the message of Jesus with people we meet.

As you go through the day, look for open doors to share your faith. Don't allow yourself to become intimidated so that you miss a chance to share Jesus or ask a friend to follow Him. When God gives you an opportunity, take it!

Do you remember how you felt when you shared Christ with someone and he or she rejected Jesus? How did it feel to know you have the answer to their greatest need and they rejected Him?_____

_____

Pray that you and your FAITH Team will not stop sharing Christ just because some students reject Him.

Day Five:
Luke 4:1-13
Answering Big Questions with the Big Book

Perhaps the strongest words in the Bible are the three words, "It is written. . ." Jesus knew the value of coming back to the authority of God's Word when He faced the devil. Throughout His dealings with the enemy and his tempting words, Jesus simply referred him back to the Word of God.

Our authority as a believer is founded upon God's Word. One of your best tools as a witness for Christ is to use His words to speak to the heart of a lost person. A prepared witness often takes his listener straight to the truth of the Bible. When someone tells us he or she does not believe the Bible is true, we don't stop using the Bible—we continue to share Scripture with them and allow the Spirit of God to convict their hearts with the Truth. Do not surrender using the Bible in any witnessing situation—quote it, read it, reference it, and learn it.

Are you memorizing portions of Scripture in order to be a more effective and faithful witness for Christ? Write down a goal for this month. How many passages of Scripture would you like to memorize? _____

Pray for a greater love for the Bible so that you and your FAITH Team will be better equipped to share and be faithful followers of Jesus.

Day Six:
Read 2 Corinthians 7:8-10
Easy Does It!

We live in an age of ease and comfort where there is a remote control for everything. Our philosophy is, "The easier, the better!" Unfortunately, that thinking often carries over to the spiritual realm of life. "Easy believerism" has permeated our world. Many people think they can believe in Jesus and gain entrance into heaven without any changes in their lives. That would make Jesus our servant rather than us becoming His servant! And that's not what Jesus taught—He called us to repentance, to turn away from our sin.

Sometimes it is easier to simply ask friends to come to church or to pray a certain prayer to be saved, but by doing that we skip over or downplay the importance of *repentance*. We simply cannot dismiss the vital importance of turning our lives totally over to God.

Why is it so hard for us to talk about repentance? Is it too personal? But, is salvation possible without repentance? _____

Pray for your FAITH team today that you will each live your lives in repentance so you may share with others when God gives you the opportunity.

Day Seven:
Read 1 Corinthians 13
Genuine Love

Perhaps nothing is more important in relational evangelism than the need for love. When you love someone, you want the best for them, and the best thing anyone can have is a personal relationship with Jesus. We show our love for others when we share Jesus with them. We also show our apathy for people when we fail to share Jesus with them.

Many times it becomes a struggle for FAITH Teams to keep the love for God and the love for people the main motivation for sharing. We don't visit students and tell them about Christ so we can boast about our "success" at Celebration Time or to show our team we have learned the FAITH outline. We share the good news so people may know the incredible love of God and so they may experience heaven *here* and *hereafter* because of that love relationship.

Do your words reflect love and compassion? Do you view a witnessing opportunity as a chance to reflect the love of Jesus, or is it just another church activity?

How you can reflect the love of God to someone this week on a FAITH visit?

_____

_____

Pray that you and your FAITH Team will not see students as spiritual conquests, but that you will genuinely love people as God loves them.

The Weekly Sunday School Leadership Team Meeting

Use this space to record ways your FAITH Team impacts the work of your Sunday School department or class. Use the information to report during weekly Sunday School leadership team meetings. Identify actions that need to be taken through Sunday School as a result of prayer concerns, needs identified, visits made by the Team, and decisions made by the persons being visited.

Highlight needs and reports affecting your class or department.

_____

_____

Pray now for teachers and department directors.

What are ways the department or class can learn from difficulties encountered during FAITH visits?

_____

_____

How does preparation for Sunday need to consider persons who raised questions and difficulties during a FAITH visit? How do their questions challenge you to look at your teaching, assimilation, and outreach efforts?

_____

_____

For Further Reading

Read pages 140-43 of *Evangelism Through the Sunday School: A Journey of FAITH* by Bobby Welch. What church-devouring monsters have been represented by some FAITH visits this semester?

For the Team Leader

This weekly feature suggests actions the Team Leader can take to support Team members, prepare for Team Time, and consider ways to improve visits. This work becomes part of the Team Leader's Home Study Assignments. Add any actions suggested by your church's FAITH strategy.

SUPPORT TEAM MEMBERS
❏ Contact Team members during the week. Remind them you are praying for them. Discuss prayer concerns and answers to prayer.
❏ Record specific needs and concerns of Team members in the space provided.

PREPARE TO LEAD TEAM TIME
❏ Review Home Study Assignments of Team members.
❏ Be prepared to remind Team members to draft a "What FAITH Has Meant to Me" testimony, due Session 16.

PREPARE TO LEAD VISITS
❏ Review the FAITH Visit Outline.

CONNECTING TO SUNDAY SCHOOL
❏ Share about FAITH during this week's Sunday School leadership meeting. Add other information appropriate to your class/department/FAITH Team's experiences.

STRENGTHENING THE
FAITH STRATEGY

"WE'VE JUST ABOUT MADE IT through another semester of FAITH," stated Keri.

"You know what that means," replied Jeff. "We get a few weeks off."

"To be honest, during the last break I kinda missed the visitations. I got a little rusty on the FAITH presentation and had to brush up on my memorization."

Both Jeff and Keri admitted that they missed the weekly times with their Teams and they remembered some of their visits over the past semester.

—The time Jeff was chased by the dog;

—The night the hamster got loose in the house during the visit;

—When Chantil's mom accepted Jesus;

—Listening to the exciting reports of everyone during Celebration Time;

—Seeing James, who was visited by several Teams, become a regular attender of Sunday School.

"Wonder what we could do to keep this going?" asked Jeff.

197

TEAM TIME

The team leader leads this time. Learners are primarily responsible for reciting the assigned portion of the FAITH Visit Outline and for discussing any Home Study Assignments.

Keep in mind how Learners also look to leaders as role models, motivators, mentors, and friends. Team Time activities can continue in the car, as the Team travels to and from visits.

Check It

FAITH Visit Outline

❏ Listen while each Learner recites as much of the FAITH Visit Outline as time allows. It may be best to ask Learners to recite the segment they seem to have the most difficulty sharing during a visit.

Practice

❏ As time permits, allow for any additional practice that is needed on the visit presentation and sequence.

Session 14 Debriefing (Handling Difficulties in a Visit)

❏ Briefly talk about distractions Team members have encountered in earlier visits.
❏ While reminding Team members that most visits go very smoothly, help them begin to recognize principles and actions for handling difficulties. As you model ways to handle difficult situations during visits, be sure to explain what you did and why.

   It is important to deal appropriately with difficulties that could take place at any time during the visit. Difficulties are those things that happen or are said during the visit that could keep you from sharing the gospel and leading a person who is ready to respond to make a commitment to Christ.

   Principles for dealing with difficulties relate primarily to building a relationship with the student, dealing with any questions and objections, and working through the obstacles and distractions that take place.

Other Home Study Assignments

❏ Remind the group of the assignment, due next week, to write a testimony indicating what FAITH has meant personally.

Help for Strengthening A Visit

❏ Remind Team members to listen during each visit for ministry opportunities and for ways to follow up appropriately.
❏ If you have shared the Witness Awareness Quotient with Team members, reemphasize as follows:

   The greater the number of unsaved identified, the greater the potential for sharing a witness. The greater the number of *Yes* responses, the more someone is taking advantage of witnessing opportunities.

   If *No* responses are higher than *Yes* responses, then someone can consciously strengthen awareness of opportunities for sharing the gospel. If *Yes* responses are higher, then a witness can comfortably model for others the significance of sharing FAITH during daily-life opportunities.

Notes

_____

_____

_____

_____

Actions I Need to Take with Learners During the Week

_____

_____

_____

_____

A Quick Review

In all evangelistic visits, your goal is to make connections that ultimately provide
an opportunity to share the gospel. Your Team's attitude and approach should be
part of what attracts students to Christ; they should never be barriers to the gospel
message or to the person of Christ and His church.

When difficulties present themselves, realize that cultivation may be needed or the
person may not be ready. Initially you may be planting a seed, ministering to a
person's need, or cultivating the work of others. Some difficulties may reflect the
convicting power of the Holy Spirit already at work in someone's life.

Your purpose is not to establish the rightness of your position, but to lovingly find
out whether a person has need of God's forgiveness and salvation. You respond to
that need with words, as well as by example and respect. Rather than being
judgmental, always be ready to share the hope that is in you. Difficulties may be
opportunities in disguise.

The Person God Uses

The person God uses is a disciple and one who disciples others.

Jesus said, "Follow me, and I will make you fishers of men" (Matt. 4:19, NKJV).
The word _disciple_ comes from the same root word as _learner_. A disciple is someone
who follows his Master; a disciple is one who learns from the Master. God uses
Christians who give themselves completely to follow and serve the risen Christ.

Jesus requires a high level of commitment from those who follow Him. As
Dietrich Bonhoeffer wrote, "When Christ calls a man, he bids him come and die."[1]
There were times when many people wanted to follow Jesus because of His
popularity and His miracles; then, when Jesus declared the commitment that was
required, many abandoned Him.

Jesus demonstrated that He teaches His followers to disciple others. Your job as a
Christian is to train others to follow Christ. Indeed, we have the teachings of
Scripture to study and the perfect model of Christ to imitate. Without question, we
are to train others to learn from Christ by what we say as well as by what we do.
Great Commission work is about going, teaching them to observe, baptizing—and
remembering that He is with us always. As you seek to be obedient, look for
opportunities to continue training students to be disciples of Christ.

Imagine . . .What Can Happen

The FAITH Sunday School Evangelism Strategy® is designed to be an intentional multiplier concept: One student who has been trained to share his or her faith trains two more persons. Those two individuals are equipped and encouraged to train two more students from their Sunday School department or class—the strategy is designed to be continuous. Imagine the benefits for a church of having every Sunday School member equipped and functioning as a Great Commission Christian.

Read through the following scenarios. Imagine every member of your Sunday School class receiving a ministry visit at least once every few months. Imagine every prospect receiving a personal visit by a Team of members, each of whom is prepared to share a simple but direct gospel presentation. Imagine students who are excited about witnessing and training others to do so. FAITH is designed to help accomplish all of these outcomes and more.

The FAITH Sunday School Evangelism Strategy® depends on constant cultivation of Sunday School leaders and members who have not been trained. More and more benefits are realized as additional students become actively involved in FAITH.

Some students have been able to be involved in FAITH as prayer partners, and that is important. Some have been involved by providing names and information about prospects who need to be visited, and that is essential. Others have assisted by helping prepare visitation packets, updating information in Sunday School records about prospects who are visited, and providing meals or child care for those being trained; the FAITH process needs all of these involvements. All of these responsibilities are vital for the success of this strategy.

But imagine what would happen if even one person who has received training chooses not to reenlist and commit to train two additional persons. Think about the impact—

• in your (____) if you were not to reenlist. Write it here.

_____

_____

• in your (_____ _____ ____). Write it here.

_____

_____

• in the lives of (____ ____ _____). Write it here.

_____

_____

Now do some math and consider the possible outcomes for your FAITH strategy and your church.

Do the Math . . . and Consider

If one Team Leader were to drop out of Student FAITH training, the following results take place.

1—	One Team Leader drops out of the next semester of Student FAITH.
Plus 2 —	The number of Learners who cannot be trained by this leader during the next semester.
Equals 3 —	The Student FAITH strategy would have 3 fewer students than would have been involved in making ministry and evangelism visits after 16 weeks of Student FAITH training.
Times 3 —	Each of these 3, in turn, would have trained a new Team.
Minus 9 —	The Student FAITH strategy would have 9 fewer students than would have been involved after 32 weeks of Student FAITH training.
Times 3 —	Each of these 9, in turn, would have trained a new Team.
Equals 27 —	The strategy would have 27 fewer students than would have been making ministry and evangelistic visits after 1 1/2 years.
Times 3 —	Each of these 27, in turn, would have trained a new Team.
Equals 81 —	The strategy would have 81 fewer students than would have been making ministry and evangelistic visits in less than 2 years.
Times 3 —	Each of these 81, in turn, would have trained a new Team.
Equals 243 —	If one Team Leader drops out of Student FAITH, in less than 2 1/2 years the strategy potentially could have 243 fewer people involved in making ministry and evangelistic visits.

Do you begin to get the picture of the impact if only one Team Leader chooses to drop out of active participation in FAITH training? This could be called "Satan's math." Satan can deceive us into thinking we are too busy to do the basics of Great Commission work. He can deceive us in thinking our "one" doesn't matter. Begin to think about the number of people who would not hear or respond to the ministry of the gospel because of the one person who does not commit to stay in training and train two more members.

Soon the Official Kickoff Begins

During this session Team Learners are being introduced to reenlistment in FAITH. This session officially begins the period of time when your church begins making transition to the next semester of FAITH. Some Learners are beginning to realistically consider how God may be leading them to train two other people from their class or department. Others are considering reenlistment to repeat training as an Assistant Team Leader.

If you are a Team Leader, you are concerned about enlisting two people for your own future Team. You also are involved in helping your present Team members identify persons who might be on their Team, particularly if they will be Team Leaders.

Consider the following actions you can take as you and other Team members consider reenlistment in the FAITH strategy.

1. Help team members consider (_____) who might be interested or would benefit by participating in FAITH training. Some Sunday School class members have shown an interest or expressed excitement by hearing testimonies of FAITH participants. Some students have become convicted by their lack of commitment or participation in the FAITH emphasis. Others have expressed a desire to participate someday in training.

On many occasions, those who have been reached by FAITH visits may be among the first to consider their own participation in learning how to share their faith; they have realized firsthand the benefits of this ministry.

God may have placed on your heart the name of someone who should be contacted as a participant in this significant strategy. Don't say no for any of your friends or Sunday School class members. You may be reluctant to ask someone to be on your Team because you think he or she is too busy, would not be interested in FAITH, or would have another excuse. If you fail to ask the student after prayerfully considering God's leadership, then, in effect, you have said *no* for him or her. Many people make this mistake!

2. Encourage Team members to preenroll in the next semester of training. You will need to be prepared to review the ways a student can participate in FAITH training.

3. As always, it is best to make a (_____ _____) to the individual(s) you are seeking to preenlist as Team Learners. It becomes a very important model for you to take your current Team members as you seek to preenlist your future Team members. As a current Team, you can work together in assisting the other Team members in preenlisting their future Team Learners.

4. Although preenlistment is not the official enrollment for the next 16 weeks of training, you already are getting a good indication of potential participation. Encourage students (__ _____ _____) their participation. One of your most meaningful responsibilities is to help Team members understand their realistic role in the next semester of Student FAITH. Some may be ready to take the responsibility of serving as a Team Leader. They need your encouragement. Some Team members will do well serving as an assistant on a Team.

5. Be a (_____ _____) by reenrolling in Student FAITH training as an Assistant Team Leader. You will be needed in the next semester even more than you are in this current semester if your church's FAITH strategy is to grow. Your church needs individuals who are trained to model the training. Your church needs people to model reenlistment.

6. The time to actually enroll in the next semester of FAITH is always important. Although you can preenlist a potential Team member at any time, it is best to officially enroll a student on a FAITH Team approximately (_____ _____) before the first session of the next training course. You will be working in conjunction with your church's publicity and prayer efforts.

7. Plan to participate in (_____ ___ _____) efforts planned by your church. Encourage class members to participate with you in the following actions:

- Participate in the Kickoff Banquet.
- Be ready to share a testimony of what Student FAITH has meant to you.
- Volunteer to serve on a FAITH planning committee to help publicize and begin the next semester of FAITH.
- Be positive and encouraging in your remarks about Student FAITH training.

With such a simple step as reenlistment, you are turning "Satan's math" into Great Commission math, as the disciple becomes more involved in making disciples of others. It is what Jesus had in mind when He gave us the Great Commission, and FAITH is a strategy to help us help our church do Great Commission work. Imagine what might happen!

---

[1] Dietrich Bonhoeffer, *The Cost of Discipleship* (New York: MacMillan Publishing Co., 1949), 99.

Visitation Time
DO IT
As you go . . .

Realize that by going, you are obeying the Great Commission. You are indicating the availability and obedience God desires and needs. Recognize that not everyone you visit will have the same understandings and motivations as you do. But you can approach your visits knowing that as you go, three by three, you are helping reach your Judea and Samaria for Christ.

Celebration Time
SHARE IT
As you return to share . . .

Know that you have reason to celebrate and rejoice together in the efforts made. If you do not have this realization, think about reasons to celebrate as you read the testimonies this week.
 Ask a Team member to share your Team's reports.
- Reports and testimonies
- Session 15 Evaluation Card
- Participation Card
- Visitation forms updated with results of visits

The Daily Journey

Day One:
Read Jeremiah 1:4-9
But I Am Only A Child!
Jeremiah was much like many of us—he alternated between self-confidence and doubt, and this young man often felt inadequate for the tasks God gave him. The truth was that by himself, he was not able or capable to complete the tasks God gave him. But, with God working through him he *was* able!

God reminded Jeremiah to quit doubting when He said "Do not say 'I am only a child.'" Jeremiah's job was to love, trust, and obey God fully; then God would take care of the tasks. You may doubt and wonder about what kind of impact you could have in the world since you are so busy and so young. But keep in mind, your first job (like Jeremiah) is to love, trust, and obey God fully. God is at work right now in your life. He will continue to be your strength as you yield yourself to Him.

Will you commit to a life that is yielded to God day-by-day? Will you look at this FAITH journey as a beginning point rather than an ending? Write a short prayer to thank God for what He has taught you about loving, trusting and obeying Him in the past three months. _____

_____

Pray also that you and your FAITH Team will not become apathetic in your walk with God or the calling of God in your life.

Day Two:
Read 2 Timothy 2:1-7
Pass it On
As you have walked through this FAITH commitment, you have grown spiritually. Your spiritual muscles have been exercised and developed. Now you are at a place where real ministry to others can be seen. You are also at a time in your spiritual life when you can pass Truth on to others.

Paul challenged Timothy to teach faithful men the things he learned and experienced, so that they could teach others. It's absolutely essential for God's work that we get serious about being multipliers and that we pass on the things of God. One disciple should teach another, who teaches another, and so on. Are you willing to be used by God to impact another group for Christ?

Write what you think is the biggest distraction in your life to continuing to disciple and share Christ with others:_____

_____

Now, read 2 Timothy 2:1-7 again.

Pray for yourself and the members of your FAITH team. Ask God to help you raise up an army of committed believers who will impact others for Christ and His kingdom.

Day Three:
Read Philippians 2:12-16
Lifelong Commitment
Many of us remember the days in grade school when kids would act like an angel when the teacher was in the room, but go crazy the minute she left the room. Paul challenged the Philippians to avoid "for your appearance sake" Christianity, when he said, "Just as you have always obeyed, not as in my presence only, but now much more in my absence."

The idea Paul was conveying to this early church was that continuance, commitment, love, discipline, and service should continue long after he left. The true test of the integrity of their faith could be seen when Paul was no longer in the picture.

Will your commitment survive months after FAITH is over? Is this a lifelong commitment or a semester fad? The lost world around us is desperately looking for those believers who faithfully run the race and hold on to the truth on a day by day basis.

Do you see this FAITH journey as an event, or a lifelong process? Will you be successful in your devotion to Christ, even when others aren't watching? Who will help you be accountable for your walk with Christ, once FAITH is over?_____

Pray specifically that you and your FAITH Team will be "finishers" and not simply well-meaning starters.

Day Four:
Read Colossians 2:1-10
Falling Away

Can strong believers be seduced by the world? Do students grounded in the Word and encouraged by other believers still face threats to their faith? The answer is a resounding *yes*!

Paul reminded the Colossian believers that they were to "walk in Him" firmly rooted and established in their faith. This was not a bunch of milk-fed baby believers easily swept away by the enemy. These were people committed to Christ. Yet Paul's next words bring them back to sobering reality:"See to it that no one takes you captive through hollow and deceptive philosophy." Paul knew these new Christians were susceptible to falling away because of the enemy's deceptive schemes. We are susceptible also. Unless we remain consistent in our walk with Christ and open to the Spirit's leadership in our daily lives, we, too, will fall into sin.

Are you watching for things, people, or teachings that can cause you to be distracted from your faithful walk with God? Is there any attitude, action, or relationship in your life right now that could one day grow into a major problem unless you deal with it honestly with God now?

Pray for steadfastness in your faith and an awareness of false teachings and influences around you and your FAITH Team.

Day Five:
Read 1 Timothy 6:17-21
Much Has Been Given to You

Since, as a Christian, you have been given much, much is expected of you. This is a good philosophy by which to live our lives. Paul wrote, "Command them to do good, to be rich in good deeds." As trained believers walking with God, we are to effectively demonstrate Christ's work in our hearts as we live each day. Our actions should shout to the world that a change has taken place within us.

Show the world that your life has not changed because of your own passion or strength, but because of the Holy Spirit working in you and through you. Ask the Father to allow you to invest in the lives of other students as you give away your faith and minister to others. Through Student FAITH, you have been equipped in the basics of the gospel more thoroughly than most of your peers. Since you have been given much, much is required of you!

Do you see the importance of good works in your walk with Christ? In your world, what are *good works*? What is God leading you to be involved in that might bring honor and glory to His name?

Pray that you and your FAITH Team will keep the priority of sharing your faith and your lives with other people. Pray that just because a semester of FAITH is ending, you will not stop sharing the FAITH outline with other students.

Day Six:
Read 1 Peter 2:1-12
Aliens at School

Do you ever feel like an alien—a round peg in a square hole? We are—by God's design—aliens to the world. As believers, we will seem out of the ordinary; unusual, maybe even a little weird. Paul described us as fools for Christ's sake. In 1 Peter, we are described as "a chosen people, a royal priesthood, a holy nation." We are different and we're set apart for God's use. But our witness for Christ depends on our choice to be aliens to the world.

In verse 12, we are told that in the midst of personal attack and misunderstanding, the world will see our good deeds and our commitment, and give glory to God. Are you willing to remain a stranger to the world?

If you are going to remain a stranger to the world, what will that mean about the choices you will make in your life? _____

_____

How are you going to stay consistent in your daily walk after the FAITH semester has ended?_____

Pray that you and your FAITH Team will continue to live committed lives after the FAITH semester ends.

Day Seven:
Read Acts 13:44-49
The Open Door for Ministry

God is always at work around us! His plans sometimes do not fit ours, but He is always moving to draw people to Himself. Paul and Barnabas had a heart to reach the Jews, but the feelings were not mutual. The Jews were offended at the message Paul was preaching. It seemed to these two men as if God was shutting a door, so they decided to open up another—if the Jews would not listen, maybe the Gentiles would!

In verse 48 we learn that the Gentiles, "were glad and honored the word of the Lord" when the Gospel was shared with them. Although one group rejected Paul's message, he kept on preaching boldly. As he did, God drew many people to Christ. Do you ever get discouraged when students don't respond the way you want them to respond? Are you ready to quit because results are not anywhere in sight? Where do you think God is leading you next?

Pray that you and your FAITH Team will have the wisdom to see where God is at work all around you. Ask God for a sensitive heart to respond to His leading today and in the future.

The Weekly Sunday School Leadership Team Meeting

Use this space to record ways your FAITH Team impacts the work of your Sunday School department or class. Use the information to report during weekly Sunday School leadership team meetings. Identify actions that need to be taken through Sunday School as a result of prayer concerns, needs identified, visits made by the Team, and decisions made by the persons being visited.

Highlight needs and reports affecting your class, department, or age group.

_____

_____

Pray now for this important meeting.

With what issues does the class need to deal because new and reclaimed members are participating in the class due to the fact that someone visited them during the past several months?

_____

_____

How does preparation for Sunday need to help persons consider participating in the FAITH Sunday School Evangelism Strategy®?

_____

_____

What are some changes FAITH/Sunday School leaders might want to make in future training courses? How has participation in this semester of FAITH or Student FAITH strategy met or exceeded expectations by Sunday School leadership?

_____

_____

For the Team Leader

This weekly feature suggests actions the Team Leader can take to support Team members, prepare for Team Time, and consider ways to improve visits. This work becomes part of the Team Leader's Home Study Assignments. Add any actions suggested by your church's FAITH strategy.

SUPPORT TEAM MEMBERS
❑ Contact Team members during the week. Remind them you are praying for them. Discuss prayer concerns and answers to prayer.
❑ Record specific needs and concerns of Team members in the space provided.
❑ Find specific ways to encourage Team members as they prepare for their written and verbal reviews.

TEAM TIME
❑ Review Home Study Assignments of Team members.
❑ Review instructions for Session 16.
❑ Be prepared to take your final verbal and written reviews.

PREPARE TO LEAD VISITS
❑ Review the FAITH Visit Outline.
❑ Make sure a Team member is ready to take the lead during the visits.

CONNECTING TO SUNDAY SCHOOL
❑ Share about FAITH during this week's Sunday School leadership meeting.

Celebrating Student FAITH

TEAM TIME

The Team Leader leads this time. Learners are primarily responsible for reciting the assigned portion of the FAITH visit outline and for discussing other Home Study Assignments.

Keep in mind how Learners also look to Leaders as role models, motivators, mentors, and friends. Team Time activities can continue in the car, as the Team travels to and from visits.

Check It

FAITH Visit Outline
- ❑ Listen while each Learner recites any designated portion of the FAITH Visit Outline. It may be best to ask Learners to recite the segment they seem to have the most difficulty in sharing during a visit.

Practice
- ❑ A brief time of practice can help Team members confidently approach the verbal review.

Session 15 Debriefing/FAITH testimony due
- ❑ Emphasize the importance of each Team member's being available to serve as an Assistant Team Leader during future semesters. Review the potential results of choosing not to continue participating in FAITH training.
- ❑ Ask for the Home Study Assignment "What FAITH Has Meant to Me" testimonies. Turn them in to the FAITH director.

Help for Strengthening A Visit
- ❑ Discuss some of the things that have been learned by making evangelistic prospect, ministry, and Opinion Poll visits. Make sure Team members know who will be responsible for taking the lead in making the visits after the written and oral reviews.

Notes
_____
_____

Actions I Need to Take with Learners During the Week

- • Write thank-you notes. Include a note of congratulations for Learners' accomplishments. Indicate your continued support.

_____
_____

A Quick Review

As a Team Leader, you are concerned about enlisting two people for your own future Team. You are also involved in helping your present Team members identify persons who would be on their team, particularly if they will be Team Leaders. It is significant for you to model reenlistment and help Team members identify persons they could enlist for the next semester of training.

The Person God Uses

The person God uses continues to grow as a Great Commission Christian.
What have you learned about faith during the past several months? The word *faith* describes the trust a person has in God; it identifies confidence in God even when we cannot tell what will happen next.

People of faith take God at His word and, like Abraham, are led by God to places they have never been and to people they have never seen (Gen. 12:8-9). People of faith believe God's promises and are filled with a growing awareness of His promises. People of faith make themselves available to God and allow themselves to be used in extraordinary ways.

Faith is no longer merely a word we use in church. Faith is no longer just a religious term that refers to our belief. Neither is faith merely an acronym that reminds us of a simple, yet powerful, gospel presentation.

You have experienced ways to grow in faith. You have seen what personal Bible study, prayer, witnessing, and ministry does for you as a believer. You have experienced benefits of God's direct impact on your life as you seek His leadership. You have learned to depend on Him in ways you perhaps have never done before. You have realized that ". . . without faith, it is impossible to please God, for he who comes to him must believe that he exists, and that He rewards those who earnestly seek Him" (Heb. 11:6, NIV).

Congratulations! You have accomplished another 16 weeks of faithful participation in FAITH Sunday School evangelism training. Hopefully, you continue to see results in your life and in the life of your church.

Student FAITH Advanced Written Review

My Score: _____
(Highest Possible Score: 60)
The only way you can fail this test is not to take it!

(Sessions 1-15; point value: 8)

1. *Match the following list of words or phrases with the most appropriate definition.*

_____ Divine appointment

_____ Baptism testimony

_____ Follow-up visits

_____ Assimilation

_____ Sunday School leadership meetings

_____ The Daily Journey

_____ *Student Baptism* tract

_____ Enroll students in Sunday School

a. Taking the actions needed to help a new member fit into and become part of the class and church

b. Resource used when helping a person consider understanding/making a commitment to believer's baptism

c. Evidence that God has been at work preparing a person to hear/respond to the gospel

d. Scheduled time when Faith Team Leader shares reports with other age-group workers of persons being cultivated and reached

e. Shared during a visit to help explain your experience after accepting Christ as Savior.

f. Visit by Team to deal with baptism, enrollment, or assimilation

g. Quiet time study

h. Can be attempted any time: during initial visit, follow-up visit, or Opinion Poll visit, and in daily life

(Course content esp.
Sessions 2-4;
point value: 8)

2. *Place in correct sequence the following eight actions that might occur in a visit:*

____ Use *A Step of Faith (Student Edition)*
____ Return baptism commitment card to the pastor
____ Conduct a follow-up visit
____ Ask the Key Question
____ Share baptism testimony
____ Explain *Student Baptism* tract
____ Share the gospel presentation
____ After visit, complete information on FAITH Visit Assignment Card

(Session 1 content,
Session 2 quiz;
point value: 1)

____ **3.** *Choose the best response: Student FAITH Advanced is designed to help make connections between the FAITH team and which of the following persons or groups?*

a. the unchurched
b. Sunday School members
c. persons who make a commitment during a visit
d. all of the above.

(Session 2 content,
Session 3 quiz;
point value: 1)

____ **4.** *True or False: A FAITH visit is completed once a person makes a profession of faith.*

(Session 2 content,
Session 3 quiz;
point value: 1)

____ **5.** *True or False: Part of the FAITH Team's responsibility in follow-up is to engage other Sunday School class members in assimilation.*

(Session 3 content,
Session 4 quiz;
point value: 1)

____ **6.** *Indicate the correct response: Use the* **Student Baptism** *tract when—*

a. making a follow-up visit for a student who enrolled in Sunday School during a FAITH visit;
b. making a follow-up visit for a student who has a ministry need as discovered during a FAITH visit;
c. making a follow-up visit for a student who accepted Christ;
d. a Student FAITH Team member has completed sharing the FAITH gospel presentation.

(Session 3 content,   ___ **7.** *Three words—After, Next, Although—*
Session 4 quiz;   *help you remember an appropriate*
point value: 1)   *format for—*

a. elaboration of your evangelism testimony;
b. baptism testimony;
c. details of your Sunday School testimony.

(Session 3 content,   **8.** *List three requirements for a person to be*
tract, Session 4 quiz;   *baptized, as identified in the* Student
point value: 3)   Baptism *tract.*

_____

_____

_____

(Session 4 content;   ___ **9.** *True or False: A different FAITH*
Session 5 quiz;   *Team makes the follow-up visit on a*
point value: 1)   *prospect who makes a profession of faith.*

(Session 4 content,   ___ **10.** *Choose the best response(s):*
Session 5 quiz;   *Which of the following are opportunities*
point value: 4)   *to take when making follow-up visits?*

a. to answer questions about the decision
b. uncover needs in the home
c. discuss making the profession of faith public
d. describe opportunities for growth through Bible study/worship.

(Session 5 content,   ___ **11.** *Which of the following statements is*
Session 6 quiz;   *false about the use of the Opinion Poll?*
point value: 1)
a. Use the Opinion Poll when your Student FAITH ministry is needing more
    prospects to visit.
b. Ask the Opinion Poll questions if you discover a person is already a Christian
    or church member.
c. A Team can ask Opinion Poll questions while standing at the door, rather than
    entering the house.
d. Even if a student chooses not to answer the questions, try to get basic
    information to help (begin) building a relationship between him (or her) and
    the FAITH Team and the Sunday School class or department.

(Session 5 content,
Session 6 quiz;
point value: 1)

12. *What is the purpose for using the Opinion Poll you would share with the person being visited?*

_____

_____

_____

(Session 5 content,
Session 6 quiz;
point value: 2)

_____ **13.** *Choose the best response(s): What should you do if a student answers the last question on the Opinion Poll with a* faith *answer?*

a. Celebrate/affirm the student's response, ask that they briefly share what Jesus means to them, and ask them to pray for the ministry of your church.
b. Try to enroll him or her in the appropriate Sunday School class or department if not participating in any ongoing Bible study group.
c. Respond with a loud Amen and jump up and down in celebration.

(Session 5 content,
Session 6 quiz;
point value: 1)

_____ **14.** *Choose the best response: What should you do if a person answers the last question on the Opinion Poll with a* works *answer?*

a. Record the response, thank him, and move on to the next house.
b. Tell him he is going to hell without Jesus, invite him to Sunday School, and leave.
c. Ask for permission to share what the Bible says about answering that question, then share the FAITH gospel presentation and use *A Step of Faith (Student Edition)* to ask the person if he is willing to accept God's forgiveness.

(Session 6 content,
Session 7 quiz;
point value: 2)

_____ **15.** *Choose the best response: To understand forgiveness it is important to understand the meaning of redemption. The word* redemption *refers to—*

a. providing trading stamps at a store;
b. buying back something;
c. becoming perfect.

(Session 6 content,
Session 7 quiz;
point value: 1)

16. *What does universalism mean?*

_____

_____

_____

(Session 7 content,
Session 8 quiz;
point value: 1)

____ **17.** *Choose the best response: Why is it important to understand that God cannot allow sin into heaven because He is holy?*

a. God's holiness and justice are seen as synonymous in many ways.
b. When a person realizes God is holy he responds with anguish over his sins: " . . . I am ruined! For I am a man of unclean lips" (Isa. 6:5, NIV).
c. When a person realizes God is holy he responds with commitment: "Here I am. Send me!" (Isa. 6:8, NIV).
d. Sin is totally foreign and against the nature of God, and God will not tolerate anything in His presence not made holy.
e. All of the above.

(Session 7 content,
Session 8 quiz;
point value: 1)

____ **18.** *True or False: God is not merciful.*

(Session 7 content
Session 8 quiz;
point value: 1)

____ **19.** *True or False: God's judgment against sin is merciful.*

(Session 7 content
Session 8 quiz;
point value: 1)

____ **20.** *The best way of understanding the meaning of* repent *is to—*

a. change directions in a car;
b. change your attitude and actions, from sin to God;
c. change your clothes;
d. turn or burn.

(Session 8 content;
Session 9 quiz;
point value: 1)

____ **21.** HEAVEN HERE is important to share because—

a. it is a good *H* phrase;
b. it reminds us of the abundant life Jesus provides now;
c. it reminds us of that real Christians do not sin any more;
d. all of the above.

(Session 8 content;   **22.** *HEAVEN HEREAFTER is important*
Session 9 quiz;   *to share because—*
point value: 1)

a. it is a good *H* phrase;
b. it gives opportunity during the gospel presentation to dispel misconceptions people have about heaven;
c. it gives opportunity to emphasize the fact that believers will spend eternity in God's presence;
d. all of the above.

(Session 9 content,   **23.** *True or False: When making a*
Session 10 quiz;   *ministry (or Sunday School) visit to*
point value: 1)   *members, use a different visit outline than*
    when making an evangelistic visit.

(Session 9 content,   **24.** *Which of the following are valid ways a*
Session 10 quiz;   *Team will know to make a ministry visit?*
point value: 2)

a. The Visit Assignment Form will indicate a ministry visit.
b. The Opinion Poll will indicate ministry visitation assignments to be made that week.
c. A FAITH Team might learn of the need of a member at the last minute and determine to visit.
d. Door-to-door visitation will reveal persons who need a Sunday School/ministry visit.

(Session 9 content,   **25.** *Why would a Team want to share the*
Session 10 quiz;   *FAITH gospel presentation to a class*
point value: 2)   *member during a ministry visit?*

_____

_____

(Session 10 content,   **26.** *Choose the best response(s):*
Session 11 quiz;   *Which of the following actions can a FAITH*
point value: 4)   *Team do with family members in the home?*

a. Ask to enroll the person if he or she is not participating in a Sunday School.
b. Engage the person in conversation and include the person in the ministry or evangelism visit as appropriate to their age or situation.
c. Have a Team member work with the person one on one—particularly if the person is young while the other Team members focus on the older member(s) of the family.
d. Gather information on the person(s) and be prepared to share it through the FAITH Visit Assignment Form for the appropriate Sunday School class/department.

(Session 11 content, Session 13 quiz; point value: 1)	____ **27.** *True or False: Divine appointments always result in the gospel being shared and accepted.*

(Session 11 content, Session 13 quiz; point value: 1)	____ **28.** *True or False: Planned, assigned visits hold as much potential for divine encounters as do spontaneous, daily-life visits.*

(Session 11 content, Session 13 quiz; point value: 1)	____ **29.** *Choose the best response: If a student you visit does not respond the way you have learned the FAITH Visit Outline, your best response is to—*

a. pull out your Journal and show the person how he is to respond;
b. realize that you may be experiencing a difficulty; stop the visit to pray;
c. realize that you may be experiencing a difficulty; look for ways to make connections so the person will remain open to responding to the gospel or ministry.

(Session 11 content, Session 13 quiz; point value: 1)	____ **30.** *True or False: No matter what happens, you have not had a successful visit unless you share the FAITH gospel presentation and the student makes a commitment.*

(Session 14 content, Session 15 quiz; point value: 1)	____ **31.** *Choose the best response: If a student asks a question while you are sharing the gospel presentation, it is generally best to—*

a. tell the person his question is not appropriate at this time;
b. postpone answering the question unless it is to clarify your response or briefly supplement the presentation with information about the message of the gospel;
c. show him an example of a FAITH Tip;
d. have a Team member distract him while the others figure out what to say.

(Session 15 content; point value: 1)

32. *Describe the impact made if only one Team Leader chooses to drop out of active participation in FAITH training.*

_____

_____

_____

(Session 15 content; point value: 1)

33. *If you fail to ask a person to prayerfully consider God's leadership in participating in FAITH training, then in effect you have said ____ for him or her.*

(Session 15 content; point value: 1)

34. *Fill in the blank with the correct words: Although you can pre-enlist a potential Team member any time, it is best to officially enroll a person on a FAITH Team _____ _____ before the first session of the next semester.*

a. three days
b. three weeks
c. three months

Verbal Review

My Score: _____
(Highest Possible Score: 67)

FAITH VISIT OUTLINE

____ PREPARATION

____ **INTRODUCTION**
____ **INTERESTS**
____ **INVOLVEMENT**
  ____ Church Experience/Background
    ____ Ask about the student's church background.
    ____ Listen for clues about the student's spiritual involvement.
  ____ Sunday School Testimony
    ____ Tell general benefits of Sunday School.
    ____ Tell a current personal experience.
  ____ Evangelistic Testimony
    ____ Tell a little of your pre-conversion experience.
    ____ Say: "I had a life-changing experience."
    ____ Tell recent benefits of your conversion.
____ **INQUIRY**
____ Key Question: In your personal opinion, what do you understand it takes for a person to go to heaven?
    ____ Possible answers: Faith, works, unclear, no opinion
____ Transition Statement: I'd like to share with you how the Bible answers this question, if it is all right. There is a word that can be used to answer this question: FAITH (spell out on fingers).

____ PRESENTATION

____ **F is for Forgiveness.**
____ We cannot have eternal life and heaven without God's forgiveness.
  ____ "In Him [meaning Jesus] we have redemption through His blood, the forgiveness of sins"—Ephesians 1:7a, NKJV.
____ **A is for AVAILABLE.**
____ Forgiveness is available. It is—
____ AVAILABLE FOR ALL
  ____ "For God so loved the world that He gave His only begotten Son, that whoever believes in Him should not perish but have everlasting life"—John 3:16, NKJV.
____ BUT NOT AUTOMATIC
  ____ "Not everyone who says to Me, 'Lord, Lord,' shall enter the kingdom of heaven"—Matthew 7:21a, NKJV.

____ **I is for IMPOSSIBLE.**
____ It is impossible for God to allow sin into heaven.
____ GOD IS—
    ____ • LOVE
       ____ John 3:16, NKJV.
    ____ • JUST
       ____ "For judgment is without mercy"—James 2:13a, NKJV.
____ MAN IS SINFUL
       ____ "For all have sinned and fall short of the glory of God"—Romans 3:23, NKJV.
____ Question: But how can a sinful person enter heaven, where God allows no sin?
____ **T is for TURN.**
____ Question: If you were driving down the road and someone asked you to turn, what would he or she be asking you to do? (change direction)
____ Turn means repent.
____ TURN from something—sin and self
       ____ "But unless you repent you will all likewise perish"— Luke 13:3b, NKJV.
____ TURN to Someone; trust Christ only
       ____ (The Bible tells us that) "Christ died for our sins according to the Scriptures, and that He was buried, and that he rose again the third day according to the Scriptures"— 1 Corinthians 15:3b-4, NKJV.
       ____ "If you confess with your mouth the Lord Jesus and believe in your heart that God has raised Him from the dead, you will be saved"— Romans 10:9, NKJV.
____ **H is for HEAVEN.**
____ Heaven is eternal life.
____ HERE
       ____ "I have come that they may have life, and that they may have it more abundantly"—John 10:10b, NKJV.
____ HEREAFTER
       ____ "And if I go and prepare a place for you, I will come again and receive you to Myself; that where I am, there you may be also"— John 14:3, NKJV.
____ HOW
       ____ How can a person have God's forgiveness, heaven and eternal life, and Jesus as personal Savior and Lord?
       ____ Explain based on leaflet picture, F.A.I.T.H. (Forsaking All I Trust Him), Romans 10:9.

____ **INVITATION**

____ **INQUIRE**
____ Understanding what we have shared, would you like to receive this forgiveness by trusting in Christ as your personal Savior and Lord?
____ **INVITE**
       ____ Pray to accept Christ.
       ____ Pray for commitment/recommitment.
       ____ Invite to join Sunday School.

____ INSURE
____ Use A Step of Faith to insure decision.
     ____ Personal Acceptance
     ____ Sunday School Enrollment
     ____ Public Confession

Visitation Time

DO IT

As you go . . .

Your visitation schedule may be adjusted somewhat tonight. Allow for the schedule changes, but encourage Teams to return for Celebration Time. This sharing time should be a special time of closure and reports.

Celebration Time

SHARE IT

As you return to share . . .

- Other reports and testimonies
- Session 16 Evaluation Card
- Participation Card
- Visitation forms updated with results of visits

The Weekly Sunday School Leadership Team Meeting

Use this space to record ways your FAITH Team impacts the work of your Sunday School department or class. Use the information to report during weekly Sunday School leadership team meetings. Identify actions that need to be taken through Sunday School as a result of prayer concerns, needs identified, visits made by the Team, and decisions made by the persons being visited.

Highlight needs and reports affecting your class, department, or age group.

_____

_____

Pray now for this important meeting.

What are ways the department or class can celebrate the work of the Holy Spirit through members who have participated in FAITH training?

_____

What actions can be taken to encourage members and leaders to prepare for the next semester of FAITH training?

_____

_____

How does preparation for Sunday need to consider persons who might attend because they received a witness by members during the week?

_____

_____

Answers to
Student FAITH Advanced
Written Review

My Score: _____
(Highest Possible Score: 60)
The only way you can fail this test is not to take it!

(Sessions 1-15;
point value: 8)

1. *Match the following list of words or phrases with the most appropriate definition.*

(*C*) Divine appointment

a. Taking the actions needed to help a new member fit into and become part of the class and church

(*E*) Baptism testimony

b. Resource used when helping a person consider understanding/making a commitment to believer's baptism

(*F*) Follow-up visits

c. Evidence that God has been at work preparing a person to hear/respond to the gospel

(*A*) Assimilation

d. Scheduled time when Faith Team Leader shares reports with other age-group workers of persons being cultivated and reached

(*D*) Sunday School leadership meetings

e. Shared during a visit to help explain your experience after accepting Christ as Savior.

f. Visit by Team to deal with baptism, enrollment, or assimilation

(*G*) The Daily Journey

g. Quiet time study

(*B*) *Student Baptism* tract

h. Can be attempted any time: during initial visit, follow-up visit, or Opinion Poll visit, and in daily life

(*H*) Enroll students in Sunday School

Course content esp.
Sessions 2-4;
point value: 8)

2. *Place in correct sequence the following eight actions that might occur in a visit:*

(3) Use *A Step of Faith (Student Edition)*
(8) Return baptism commitment card to the pastor
(5) Conduct a follow-up visit
(1) Ask the Key Question
(6) Share baptism testimony
(7) Explain *Student Baptism* tract
(2) Share the gospel presentation
(4) After visit, complete information on FAITH Visit Assignment Card

(Session 1 content,
Session 2 quiz;
point value: 1)

(D) **3.** *Choose the best response: Student FAITH Advanced is designed to help make connections between the FAITH team and which of the following persons or groups?*

a. the unchurched
b. Sunday School members
c. persons who make a commitment during a visit
d. all of the above.

(Session 2 content,
Session 3 quiz;
point value: 1)

(F) **4.** *True or False: A FAITH visit is completed once a person makes a profession of faith.*

(Session 2 content,
Session 3 quiz;
point value: 1)

(T) **5.** *True or False: Part of the FAITH Team's responsibility in follow-up is to engage other Sunday School class members in assimilation.*

(Session 3 content,
Session 4 quiz;
point value: 1)

(C) **6.** *Indicate the correct response: Use the Student Baptism tract when—*

a. making a follow-up visit for a student who enrolled in Sunday School during a FAITH visit;
b. making a follow-up visit for a student who has a ministry need as discovered during a FAITH visit;
c. making a follow-up visit for a student who accepted Christ;
d. a Student FAITH Team member has completed sharing the FAITH gospel presentation.

(Session 3 content, **(B)** ***7.*** *Three words—After, Next, Although—*
Session 4 quiz;   *help you remember an appropriate*
point value: 1)   *format for—*

a. elaboration of your evangelism testimony;
b. baptism testimony;
c. details of your Sunday School testimony.

(Session 3 content,   ***8.*** *List three requirements for a person to be*
tract, Session 4 quiz;   *baptized, as identified in the* Student Baptism
point value: 3)   tract.
<u>(1) already has trusted Christ; understands that baptism does not bring</u>
<u>about salvation but is a symbol of what Jesus has done and an expression</u>
<u>of obedience; (3) is not ashamed to follow Christ's example and command</u>

(Session 4 content; **(F)** ***9.*** *True or False: A different FAITH Team*
Session 5 quiz;   *makes the follow-up visit on a prospect*
point value: 1)   *who makes a profession of faith.*

(Session 4 content, **(A, B, C, D)** ***10.*** *Choose the best response(s):*
Session 5 quiz;   *Which of the following are opportunities*
point value: 4)   *to take when making follow-up visits?*

a. to answer questions about the decision
b. uncover needs in the home
c. discuss making the profession of faith public
d. describe opportunities for growth through Bible study/worship.

(Session 5 content, **(B)** ***11.*** *Which of the following statements is*
Session 6 quiz;   *false about use of the Opinion Poll?*
point value: 1)

a. Use the Opinion Poll when your FAITH ministry is needing more prospects to visit.
b. Ask the Opinion Poll questions if you discover a person is already a Christian or church member.
c. A Team can ask Opinion Poll questions while standing at the door, rather than entering the house.
d. Even if a person chooses not to answer the questions, try to get basic information about the person to help (begin) making connections between him (or her) and the Team and the Sunday School class or department.

(Session 5 content, **12.** *What is the purpose for using the Opinion*
Session 6 quiz; *Poll you would share with the person being*
point value: 1) *visited?*
(<u>We</u> <u>are</u> <u>trying</u> <u>to</u> <u>develop</u> <u>a</u> <u>more</u> <u>responsive</u> <u>ministry</u> <u>to</u> <u>our</u> <u>area.</u> <u>Would</u> <u>you</u>
<u>please</u> <u>help</u> <u>us</u> <u>by</u> <u>giving</u> <u>your</u> <u>opinion</u> <u>on</u> <u>a</u> <u>few</u> <u>questions?</u>)

(Session 5 content, (<u>A, B</u>) **13.** *Choose the best response(s): What*
Session 6 quiz; *should you do if a student answers the last*
point value: 2) *question on the Opinion Poll with a* faith
answer?

a. Celebrate/affirm the student's response, ask that they briefly share what Jesus
   means to them, and ask them to pray for the ministry of your church.
b. Try to enroll him or her in the appropriate Sunday School class or department
   if not participating in any ongoing Bible study group.
c. Respond with a loud Amen and jump up and down in celebration.

(Session 5 content, (<u>C</u>) **14.** *Choose the best response: What should*
Session 6 quiz; *you do if a person answers the last question*
point value: 1) *on the Opinion Poll with a* works *answer?*

a. Record the response, thank him, and move on to the next house.
b. Tell him he is going to hell without Jesus, invite him to Sunday School, and
   leave.
c. Ask for permission to share what the Bible says about answering that question,
   then share the FAITH gospel presentation and use *A Step of Faith (Student
   Edition)* to ask the person if he is willing to accept God's forgiveness.

(Session 6 content, (<u>B</u>) **15.** *Choose the best response: To understand*
Session 7 quiz; *forgiveness it is important to understand the*
point value: 2) *meaning of redemption. The word* redemption
refers to—

a. providing trading stamps at a store;
b. buying back something;
c. becoming perfect.

(Session 6 content, **16.** *What does universalism mean?*
Session 7 quiz;
point value: 1)

(<u>This</u> <u>belief</u> <u>system</u> <u>teaches</u> <u>that</u> <u>ultimately</u> <u>all</u> <u>people</u> <u>will</u> <u>be</u> <u>allowed</u> <u>into</u> <u>heaven.</u>
<u>Universalism</u> <u>is</u> <u>"inclusive"</u> <u>in</u> <u>that</u> <u>it</u> <u>accepts</u> <u>all</u> <u>beliefs</u> <u>that</u> <u>are</u> <u>sincere.</u>)

(Session 7 content, Session 8 quiz; point value: 1)

(E) **17.** *Choose the best response: Why is it important to understand that God cannot allow sin into heaven because He is holy?*

a. God's holiness and justice are seen as synonymous in many ways.
b. When a person realizes God is holy he responds with anguish over his sins: " . . . I am ruined! For I am a man of unclean lips" (Isa. 6:5, NIV).
c. When a person realizes God is holy he responds with commitment: "Here I am. Send me!" (Isa. 6:8, NIV).
d. Sin is totally foreign and against the nature of God, and God will not tolerate anything in His presence not made holy.
e. All of the above.

(Session 7 content, Session 8 quiz; point value: 1)

(F) **18.** *True or False: God is not merciful.*

(Session 7 content Session 8 quiz; point value: 1)

(F) **19.** *True or False: God's judgment against sin is merciful.*

(Session 7 content Session 8 quiz; point value: 1)

(B) **20.** *The best way of understanding the meaning of* repent *is to—*

a. change directions in a car;
b. change your attitude and actions, from sin to God;
c. change your clothes;
d. turn or burn.

(Session 8 content; Session 9 quiz; point value: 1)

(B) **21.** *HEAVEN HERE is important to share because—*

a. it is a good *H* phrase;
b. it reminds us of the abundant life Jesus provides now;
c. it reminds us of that real Christians do not sin any more;
d. all of the above.

(Session 8 content;   *(C)* **22.** HEAVEN HEREAFTER *is important*
Session 9 quiz;   *to share because—*
point value: 1)

  a. it is a good *H* phrase;
  b. it gives opportunity during the gospel presentation to dispel misconceptions people have about heaven;
  c. it gives opportunity to emphasize the fact that believers will spend eternity in God's presence;
  d. all of the above.

(Session 9 content,   *(F)* **23.** *True or False: When making a*
Session 10 quiz;   *ministry (or Sunday School) visit to*
point value: 1)   *members, use a different visit outline than*
                                 when making an evangelistic visit.

(Session 9 content,   *(A, C)* **24.** *Which of the following are valid ways a*
Session 10 quiz;   *Team will know to make a ministry visit?*
point value: 2)

  a. The Visit Assignment Form will indicate a ministry visit.
  b. The Opinion Poll will indicate ministry visitation assignments to be made that week.
  c. A FAITH Team might learn of the need of a member at the last minute and determine to visit.
  d. Door-to-door visitation will reveal persons who need a Sunday School/ministry visit.

(Session 9 content,   **25.** *Why would a Team want to share the*
Session 10 quiz;   *FAITH gospel presentation to a class*
point value: 2)   *member during a ministry visit?*
(If a person answers the Key Question with a works answer;
for practice with a believer)

(Session 10 content, *(A, B, C, D)* **26.** *Choose the best response(s):*
Session 11 quiz;   *Which of the following actions can a FAITH*
point value: 4)   *Team do with family members in the home?*

  a. Ask to enroll the person if he or she is not participating in a Sunday School.
  b. Engage the person in conversation and include the person in the ministry or evangelism visit as appropriate to their age or situation.
  c. Have a Team member work with the person one on one—particularly if the person is young while the other Team members focus on the older member(s) of the family.
  d. Gather information on the person(s) and be prepared to share it through the FAITH Visit Assignment Form for the appropriate Sunday School class or department.

Session 11 content,   __F__ **27.** *True or False: Divine appointments*
Session 13 quiz;   *always result in the gospel being shared and*
point value: 1)   *accepted.*

(Session 11 content,   __T__ **28.** *True or False: Planned, assigned visits*
Session 13 quiz;   *hold as much potential for divine encounters*
point value: 1)   *as do spontaneous, daily-life visits.*

(Session 11 content,   __C__ **29.** *Choose the best response: If a student*
Session 13 quiz;   *you visit does not respond the way you have*
point value: 1)   *learned the FAITH Visit Outline, your best*
                             response is to—

a. pull out your Journal and show the person how he is to respond;
b. realize that you may be experiencing a difficulty; stop the visit to pray;
c. realize that you may be experiencing a difficulty; look for ways to make connections so the person will remain open to responding to the gospel or ministry.

(Session 11 content,   __F__ **30.** *True or False: No matter what*
Session 13 quiz;   *happens, you have not had a successful visit*
point value: 1)   *unless you share the FAITH gospel*
                             presentation and the student makes a
                             commitment.

(Session 14 content,   __B__ **31.** *Choose the best response: If a student*
Session 15 quiz;   *asks a question while you are sharing the*
point value: 1)   *gospel presentation, it is generally best to—*

a. tell the person his question is not appropriate at this time;
b. postpone answering the question unless it is to clarify your response or briefly supplement the presentation with information about the message of the gospel;
c. show him an example of a FAITH Tip;
d. have a Team member distract him while the others figure out what to say.

Session 15 content;
point value: 1)

32. *Describe the impact made if only one Team Leader chooses to drop out of active participation in FAITH training.*
(*Answer should reflect a personal response.*)

(Session 15 content;
point value: 1)

33. *If you fail to ask a person to prayerfully consider God's leadership in participating in FAITH training, then in effect you have said (NO) for him or her.*

(Session 15 content;
point value: 1)

34. *Fill in the blank with the correct words: Although you can pre-enlist a potential Team member any time, it is best to officially enroll a person on a FAITH Team (three weeks) before the first session of the next semester.*

a. three days
b. three weeks
c. three months

CHRISTIAN GROWTH STUDY PLAN

Preparing Christians to Serve

In the **Christian Growth Study Plan (formerly Church Study Course),** this book **A Jouney in FAITH: Student Journal** is a resource for course credit in the subject area Evangelism: Youth of the Christian Growth category of diploma plans. To receive credit, read the book, complete the learning activities, show your work to your pastor, a staff member or church leader, then complete the information on the next page. The form may be duplicated. Send the completed page to:

Christian Growth Study Plan
127 Ninth Avenue, North, MSN 117
Nashville, TN 37234-0117
FAX: (615)251-5067

For information about the Christian Growth Study Plan, refer to the current Christian Growth Study Plan Catalog. Your church office may have a copy. If not, request a free copy from the Christian Growth Study Plan office (615/251-2525).

A Journey in FAITH: Student Journal
COURSE NUMBER: CG-0489

PARTICIPANT INFORMATION

Social Security Number (USA Only) | Personal CGSP Number* | Home Phone | Date of Birth (Mo., Day, Yr.)

Name (First, MI, Last)
☐ Mr.   ☐ Miss
☐ Mrs. ☐

Address (Street, Route, or P.O. Box) | City, State, or Province | Zip/Postal Code

CHURCH INFORMATION

Church Name

Address (Street, Route, or P.O. Box) | City, State, or Province | Zip/Postal Code

CHANGE REQUEST ONLY

☐ Former Name | City, State, or Province | Zip/Postal Code

☐ Former Address | City, State, or Province | Zip/Postal Code

☐ Former Church

Signature of Pastor, Conference Leader, or Other Church Leader | Date

*New participants are requested but not required to give SS# and date of birth. Existing participants, please give CGSP# when using SS# for the first time.
Thereafter, only one ID# is required. *Mail To:* Christian Growth Study Plan, 127 Ninth Ave., North, MSN 117, Nashville, TN 37234-0117. Fax: (615)251-5067